Praise for
Outcasts United

"Textured [and] uplifting . . . celebrate[s] the most old-fashioned of virtues: diligence, self-discipline, regard for others."
—*The Washington Post*

"The story has a suspenseful season-on-the-brink feel as St. John lovingly depicts youngsters from Liberia, Sudan, Iraq and Afghanistan struggling not only to form a team but also to fit in while maintaining their own identities." —*Chicago Tribune*

"Meet the Fugees, a Clarkston, Georgia, soccer team made up of refugee boys from such war-torn nations as Sudan, Kosovo, and Iraq. In a rich and touching narrative *New York Times* reporter Warren St. John relates the boys' stories. The book is also a striking portrait of a uniquely American place: Clarkston, a once-traditional Southern town turned 21st-century immigrant haven." —*Sports Illustrated*

"Not merely about soccer, St. John's book teaches readers about the social and economic difficulties of adapting to a new culture and the challenges facing a town with a new and disparate population. . . . This wonderful, poignant book is highly recommended."
—*Library Journal* (starred review)

"Remarkable . . . a marvellous story, all the more moving for being written straight by a talented reporter." —*The Times* (London)

"[A] richly detailed, uplifting account of a young Jordanian immigrant who created a soccer program in Georgia for young refugees from war-torn nations . . . educational and enriching."

—*Kirkus Reviews*

"St. John hits a trifecta . . . a fascinating and fast-moving account of big-picture politics, small-town sports, and some very memorable people."

—*Booklist*

"Inspiring . . . deeply satisfying . . . [a] bighearted book."

—Shelf Awareness

"A brilliant and empathetic depiction of our common quest for meaning and happiness. Warren St. John invites us into the lives of a community of refugees, their bewildered neighbors in a small town, and a Jordanian woman who not only coaches but also mentors, mothers, and inspires some remarkable boys, to create a heartwarming tale about the transformations that occur when our disparate lives connect."

—ISHMAEL BEAH, author of *A Long Way Gone*

"Truly unforgettable, *Outcasts United* offers a stirring lesson in the power of a single person to transform the lives of many. It's an incisive window into the world ahead for all of us, where cultural diversity won't be an ideal or a course requirement or a corporate initiative but a fact of life that has to be wrestled with and reconciled, if never quite resolved."

—REZA ASLAN, author of *No god but God*

OUTCASTS UNITED

Also by Warren St. John

Rammer Jammer Yellow Hammer:
A Road Trip into the Heart of Fan Mania

Left to right, standing: Idwar Dikori *(Sudan)*, Luma Mufleh *(coach)*, Grace Balegamire *(Congo)*, Qendrim Bushi *(Kosovo)*, Mafoday Jawneh *(Gambia)*, Bienvenue Ntwari *(Burundi)*, Shahir Ariwar *(Afghanistan)*, Josiah Saydee *(Liberia)*, Eldin Subasic *(Bosnia)*, Tracy Ediger *(team manager)*, Tareg Kabsoun *(Sudan)*. *Left to right, kneeling:* Santino Jerke *(Sudan)*, Robin Dikori *(Sudan)*, Prince Tarlue *(Liberia)*, Mohammed Mohammed *(Iraq)*, Jeremiah Ziaty *(Liberia)*.

OUTCASTS UNITED

*An American Town, A Refugee
Team, and One Woman's Quest
to Make a Difference*

WARREN ST. JOHN

Spiegel & Grau Trade Paperbacks
New York
2009

2009 Spiegel & Grau Trade Paperback Edition

Published in the United States by Spiegel & Grau, an imprint of
The Random House Publishing Group, a division of
Random House, Inc., New York.

SPIEGEL & GRAU is a trademark of Random House, Inc.

RANDOM HOUSE READER'S CIRCLE and colophon is a
trademark of Random House, Inc.

Originally published in hardcover in the United States by Spiegel &
Grau, an imprint of The Random House Publishing Group, a division
of Random House, Inc., in 2009.

Library of Congress Cataloging-in-Publication Data
St. John, Warren.
Outcasts united : a refugee team, an American town / Warren St. John.
p.   cm.
ISBN 978-0-385-52204-5
eBook ISBN 978-0-385-52959-4
1. Mufleh, Luma. 2. Soccer coaches—Georgia—Clarkson—Biography.
3. Refugee children—Georgia—Clarkson. 4. Refugees—Africa.
I. Title.
GV942.7.L86 2008
796.334092—dc22
[B]
2008040697

PRINTED IN THE UNITED STATES OF AMERICA

www.randomhousereaderscircle.com

12 14 16 18 19 17 15 13 11

For Nicole

OUTCASTS UNITED

Introduction

On a cool spring afternoon at a soccer field in northern Georgia, two teams of teenage boys were going through their pregame warm-ups when the heavens began to shake. The field had been quiet save the sounds of soccer balls thumping against forefeet and the rustling of the balls against the nylon nets that hung from the goals. But as the rumble grew louder, all motion stopped as boys from both teams looked quizzically skyward. Soon a cluster of darts appeared in the gap of sky between the pine trees on the horizon and the cottony clumps of cloud vapor overhead. It was a precision flying squadron of fighter jets, performing at an air show miles away in Atlanta. The aircraft banked in close formation in the direction of the field and came closer, so that the boys could now make out the markings on the wings and the white helmets of the pilots in the cockpits. Then with an earthshaking roar deep enough to rattle the change in your pocket, the jets split in different directions like an exploding firework, their contrails carving the sky into giant wedges.

On the field below, the two groups of boys watched the spectacle with craned necks, and from different perspectives. The players of the home team—a group of thirteen- and fourteen-year-old boys from the nearby Atlanta suburbs playing with the North Atlanta Soccer Association—gestured to the sky and wore expressions of awe.

The boys at the other end of the field were members of an all-refugee soccer team called the Fugees. Many had actually seen the machinery of war in action, and all had felt its awful consequences firsthand. There were Sudanese players on the team whose villages had been bombed by old Russian-made Antonov bombers flown by the Sudanese Air Force, and Liberians who'd lived through barrages of mortar fire that pierced the roofs of their neighbors' homes, taking out whole families. As the jets flew by the field, several members of the Fugees flinched.

"YOU GUYS NEED to wake up!" a voice interrupted as the jets streaked into the distance. "Concentrate!"

The voice belonged to Luma Mufleh, the thirty-one-year-old founder and volunteer coach of the Fugees. Her players resumed their practice shots, but they now seemed distracted. Their shots flew hopelessly over the goal.

"If you shoot like that, you're going to lose," Coach Luma said.

She was speaking to a young Liberian forward named Christian Jackson. Most of the Fugees had experienced suffering of some kind or another, but Christian's was rawer than most. A month before, he had lost three siblings and a young cousin in a fire at his family's apartment in Clarkston, east of Atlanta. Christian escaped by jumping through an open window. The smallest of the dead children was found under a charred mattress, an odd detail to investigators. But the Reverend William B. J. K. Harris, a Liberian minister in Atlanta who reached out to the family after the fire, explained that during Liberia's fourteen years of civil war, children were taught to take cover under their beds during the fighting, as a precaution against bullets and mortar shrapnel. For the typical American child, "under the bed" was the realm of ghosts and monsters. For a child from a war zone, it was supposed to be the safest place of all.

Not long before the fire, Luma had kicked Christian Jackson off the Fugees for swearing at practice. Swearing was against her rules. She had warned him once, and then when he swore again, she told him to leave and not to come back. That was how Luma ran her team. Not long after the fire, Christian showed up at the Clarkston Community Center field where the Fugees practiced, and watched quietly from behind a chain-link fence around the playing area. Under normal circumstances, Luma might have ignored him—she gave second chances, but rarely third. But Luma summoned Christian over and told him he could rejoin the team so long as he understood that he was on probation. If he swore again at practice or during a game, he was gone for good. No exceptions. Christian said he understood. This was his first game back.

Luma shouted to her players to gather around her and gave them their position assignments—Christian was told to play striker, on offense—and they took the field. Forty or so parents had gathered on the home team's sideline to cheer on their boys, and they clapped as their sons walked onto the pitch. There was no one on the Fugees' sideline. Most of the players came from single-parent families, and their mothers or fathers—usually mothers—stayed home on weekends to look after their other children, or else worked, because weekend shifts paid more. Few had cars to allow them to travel to soccer games anyway. Even at their home games, the Fugees rarely had anyone to cheer them on.

The referee summoned the Fugees to the line to go over their roster and to check their cleats and numbers. Luma handed him the roster, and the referee wrinkled his brow.

"If I mispronounce your name, I apologize," he said. He ticked through the names awkwardly but respectfully. When he got hung up on a syllable, the boys would politely announce their own names, then step forward to declare their jersey numbers.

A few minutes later, a whistle sounded and the game began.

The head coach of the North Atlanta team was a screamer. From the outset, he ran back and forth on his sideline, barking commands to his players in a hoarse bellow: "Man on! Man on!" "Drop it! Drop it!" "Turn! Turn! Turn!" His words echoed over the quiet field like a voice from a public address system. Luma paced silently on her side of the field and occasionally glanced over at the opposite sideline with a perturbed look on her face. She was all for instruction, but her method was to teach during practice and during the breaks. Once the whistle blew, she allowed her players to be themselves: to screw up, to take chances, and to create. All the shouting was wearing on her nerves.

When North Atlanta scored first, on a free kick, the team's coach jumped up and down on the sidelines, while across the field parents leaped from their folding lawn chairs in celebration: more grating noise. Luma pursed her lips in a tiny sign of disgust and kept pacing, quietly. She made a substitution on defense but otherwise remained silent.

A few moments later, Christian Jackson shook himself free on the right side, dribbled downfield, and fired a line drive into the top right corner of the net: goal. Luma betrayed no reaction other than to adjust her tattered white Smith College baseball cap and to continue pacing. The Fugees soon regained possession; they controlled the ball with crisp passes and moved into range of the goal. A Fugees forward struggled free of traffic to take a shot that flew a good twenty feet over the crossbar and into the parking lot behind the field, and soon after, let loose another that was wide by a similar margin. Luma paced. Meanwhile, with each of his team's shots the North Atlanta coach shouted more instructions to his players, ever more adamantly. He was getting frustrated. If his players had followed his instructions to the word, they could've scored on Manchester United. But as it was, they ended the first half trailing the Fugees 3–1.

A 3–1 lead at halftime would have pleased most soccer coaches. But Luma was seething. Her head down, she marched angrily to a corner of the field, the Fugees following behind sullenly. They could tell she was unhappy. They braced themselves for what they knew was coming. Luma ordered them to sit down.

"Our team has taken nine shots and made three—they've taken two shots and made one," she told them, her voice sharp and strident. "You're outrunning them, outhustling them, outplaying them—why are you *only winning three to one*?

"Christian," she said, looking at the boy who sat on the grass with his arms around his knees, his eyes downcast. "This is one of your worst games. I want it to be one of your best games. I want to sit back and watch good soccer—do you *understand*?"

At that moment, the voice of the North Atlanta coach—still scream-ing at his players—drifted down the field to the Fugees' huddle. Luma pulled up and turned her narrowed gaze toward the source of the of-fending noise.

"See that coach?" Luma said, tilting her head in the direction of the screamer. "I want him to sit down and be quiet. That's when you know we've won—when he sits down and shuts up. Got it?"

"Yes, Coach," her players replied.

When the Fugees took the field for the second half, they were trans-formed. They quickly scored three goals—an elegant cross, chested in with highlight-reel grace by a Sudanese forward named Attak, followed by a cannon shot from Christian from ten yards out. Mo-ments later Christian dribbled into the box and faked to his left, a move that left the North Atlanta goalie tangled in his own limbs, before shooting right: another score. The opposing coach was still yelling—"Man on! Man on!"—so the Fugees kept shooting. Another goal. And another. When the frustrated North Atlanta players started hacking away at their shins and ankles, the Fugees brushed them off and scored yet again.

At 8–2, the North Atlanta coach, hoarse now nearly to muteness, wiped the sweat from his forehead with the back of his hand, quietly wandered over to his bench, and sat down, flaccid and defeated. The Fugees tried to stifle their smiles. If Luma felt any sense of satisfaction, it was difficult to discern. She remained perfectly stone-faced. The referee blew his whistle three times to signal the end of the game. The final score was 9–2 Fugees. Christian Jackson had scored five goals.

The teams shook hands and the Fugees quickly ran to the bench for water and oranges, which awaited them in two white plastic gro-cery bags. A few moments later, the referee approached. He looked to be in his late fifties, white, with a graying mustache. He asked Luma if he could address her players. Luma hesitated. She was uncomfort-able handing over her team's attention to anyone, especially a stranger. A little warily, she summoned her team, who gathered in front of the referee some ten yards from their bench.

"Gentlemen," he said, "I'd like to thank you. You played the ball the entire game, and you didn't take any cheap shots. They got frustrated and started hacking, and you didn't retaliate. So I'd like to commend you on your sportsmanship." The referee paused for a moment and swallowed hard. "And that was one of the most beautiful games of soccer I've ever seen," he said.

THIS WAS THE first time I'd ever seen the Fugees play. I'd shown up knowing little about the team other than that the players were refugees and the coach a woman, and that the team was based in a town called Clarkston. In a little more than a decade, the process of refugee resettlement had transformed Clarkston from a simple southern town into one of the most diverse communities in America. And yet few in Atlanta, let alone in the world beyond, had taken notice. Mention the "refugees of Clarkston" and even many Atlantans will ask first if you're referring to those who had arrived in town from New Orleans after Hurricane Katrina. Next, they'll likely ask, "Where's Clarkston?"

I came away from that first game intrigued. I had just seen a group of boys from a dozen war-ravaged countries come together as a team and create improbable beauty on the soccer pitch. How? Their coach, an intense and quiet presence who hid beneath the brim of her Smith College baseball cap and emerged only to dole out ferocious bits of inspiration or wisdom, presented another mystery. There was a palpable sense of trust and camaraderie between the players and their coach, and an equally powerful sense of fragility in all the tension and long silences. In fact, things with the Fugees were more fragile than I could have realized that day. The team had no home field, owing to the myopia of local politicians who felt threatened by the presence of these newcomers. The players' private lives were an intense daily struggle to stay afloat. They and their families had fled violence and chaos and found themselves in a society with a completely different set of values and expectations. Luma herself was struggling to hold her team—and herself—together. She had volunteered—naively, as she would admit—to help these boys on the field and off, unaware of the scope and intractability of their difficulties: post-traumatic stress, poverty, parental neglect in some cases, grief, shattered confidence, and, in more than one instance, simple anger at having to live the way they did. Luma, I would learn, had no particular background in social or human-rights work. She was just a normal woman who wanted, in her own way, to make the world a better place, and who, it turned out, was willing to go to extraordinary lengths to see that mission through. Luma had vowed to come through for her players and their families or to come apart trying, and on several occasions it seemed the latter outcome was more likely.

But more than anything that day, it was the surprising kinship of these kids from different cultures, religions, and backgrounds that drew me into the story and made me want to understand and tell it. One moment in the game underscored this for me more than any other.

THERE WAS A player on the Fugees who was plainly less gifted at soccer than his teammates—a tiny defender from Afghanistan named Zubaid. In retrospect, it seems he might have been farsighted. When the soccer ball rolled his way, he would draw his foot back, swing his leg with all his might, and as often as not, miss the ball entirely, with all the awkward, unalloyed zeal of a batter swinging for the fences and whiffing. After this happened a third or fourth time, I asked Luma what the boy's story was; his presence on the field was so awkward that it required some sort of explanation. Luma didn't seem the least bit offended. In fact, she seemed especially proud that Zubaid was on the field. He had never missed a practice or one of the afternoon tutoring sessions Luma required of her players, she explained. He was on the field simply because by the standards she'd established for the Fugees, he deserved to be.

That was the background, but the specific image that stuck in my mind that day was this: every time the ball rolled Zubaid's way, his teammates, faster and more agile than he was to a player, never interfered or snuck in to take it away from him. Instead, two or three members of the Fugees would drop in five or so yards behind him, just far enough out of the way so as not to seem conspicuous, to form a protective cordon between Zubaid and the goal. When he missed the ball with an ungainly swing of the leg, they were there to cover for him, but always subtly, and never in a way that demeaned him or his effort.

Eventually, late in the game, one of the North Atlanta forwards got loose with the ball on Zubaid's side of the pitch, and he rushed upfield to defend. He extended his leg, and the ball locked between the tops of the two players' forefeet with a loud *thwump*. The ball stopped, and the North Atlanta player tumbled forward onto the turf: a perfect tackle. Much to his surprise, it seemed, Zubaid found himself alone, still standing and with possession of the ball, which he quickly passed toward a teammate at midfield. At the next lull, when the ball went out of bounds, Zubaid was set upon by his teammates as though he'd scored the winning goal.

SOON AFTER THAT first game, I resolved to pull up stakes in New York and to move to Atlanta to tell the story of the Fugees. I saw a great deal of soccer over the next few months, but the most moving moments for me—and the most instructive and insightful—came not on the sidelines but over hot cups of sugary tea, over meals of stewed cassava or beans and rice, or platters of steaming Afghan mantu, on the sofas and floors of the apartments of refugees in Clarkston. And yet I also found that the game of soccer itself provided a useful framework for trying to understand how this unlikely group of people had come together. Unlike basketball, baseball, or football, games that reset after each play, soccer unfolds fluidly and continuously. To understand how a goal was scored, you have to work back through the action—the sequences of passes and decisions, the movement of the players away from the action who reappear unexpectedly in empty space to create or waste opportunities—all the way back to the first touch. If that goal was scored by a young refugee from Liberia, off an assist from a boy from southern Sudan, who was set up by a player from Burundi or a Kurd from Iraq—on a field in Georgia, U.S.A., no less—understanding its origins would mean following the thread of causation back in time to events that long preceded the first whistle.

Relatively quickly, it became clear that the story of the Fugees was also the story of a place, and that place offered as many intriguing mysteries as the boys and their coach. Until relatively recently, Clarkston had been a homogenous, white southern town, situated on 1.1 square miles of Georgia clay about thirteen miles east of downtown Atlanta. The town's motto spoke to its humble origins: "Small Town . . . Big Heart." But the resettlement process, which had the effect of cramming perhaps a century's worth of normal migration patterns into roughly a decade, had tested the sentiment behind Clarkston's motto.

Adding to the complication: the newcomers in Clarkston were not a homogenous linguistic or cultural group of, say, Somalis, whose appearance had transformed some small American towns like Lewiston, Maine, but a sampling of the world's citizens from dozens of countries and ethnic groups. The local high school in Clarkston, once all white, now had students from more than fifty different countries. Cultures were colliding in Clarkston, and the result was a raw and exceptionally charged experiment in getting along.

When I first decided to write about the Fugees, I wasn't sure how, or even if, the story of the remaking of Clarkston and the story of a refugee soccer team there would explicitly overlap. But about a month before I planned to leave New York to head to Clarkston to follow the Fugees, I got a clue that the stories were more intertwined than I could have realized. A dispute erupted between the mayor of Clarkston, a retired heating and plumbing contractor named Lee Swaney, and a group of young Sudanese refugees who were playing casual games of soccer on the only general-use field in the town park. The local paper, the *Atlanta Journal-Constitution,* got wind of the dispute and asked the mayor to explain his stance.

"There will be nothing but baseball down there as long as I'm mayor," he told the paper. "Those fields weren't made for soccer."

The mayor's proclamation had a direct impact on the Fugees, who had recently lost their home field after a dispute with their hosts at the local community center. Luma had hoped to relocate the Fugees to the town park—the very park from which Mayor Swaney had banned soccer. And so with only a few weeks to go before tryouts, she found herself scrambling to find her team a home.

The mayor's decree hinted at tensions that went well beyond issues of turf management. In Clarkston, soccer, it seemed, meant something different from what it meant in most places. It was the international game in a town that had had its fill of international influences. The experiment in getting along, it seemed to me, was apparently very much ongoing, and the results would have relevance well beyond Clarkston. The question of how to cope with cultural, ethnic, and religious diversity—that loaded concept—is a pressing one. As the author Mary Pipher wrote about refugees who had been resettled in Nebraska in her book *The Middle of Everywhere,* "The refugee experience of dislocation, cultural bereavement, confusion and constant change will soon be all of our experience. As the world becomes globalized, we'll all be searching for home."

WHEN I THINK about Clarkston, I sometimes visualize the town as a lifeboat being lowered from a vast, multilevel passenger ship. No one aboard chose this particular vessel. Rather, they were assigned to it—the refugees by resettlement officials they never met, the townspeople by a faraway bureaucratic apparatus that decided, almost haphazardly, to put a sampling of people from all over the world in the modest little boat locals thought they had claimed for themselves. In an instant, the boat was set upon a roiling sea, its passengers left to fend for themselves. Everyone on the boat wanted the same thing: safety. But to get there, they would first have to figure out how to communicate with each other, how to organize themselves, how to allocate their resources, and which direction they should row. I imagine their heads bobbing in and out of view between the troughs and crests of the wind-whipped sea as they begin their journey. And I wonder: What will they do? What would *I* do in that same situation? And: Will they make it?

IT'S HARD TO know exactly where to begin the story of the Fugees. The violence that led young Grace Balegamire from Congo to Clarkston in the early twenty-first century had its origins in the 1870s, when King Leopold II of Belgium established the Free State of Congo, a corporate state that pillaged the region around the Congo River of its natural resources, terrorized the population, and gave way over time to a collection of politically unstable nations divided by ethnic tension. The tribal violence that drove Beatrice Ziaty, a Liberian refugee whose sons Jeremiah and Mandela played on the Fugees, from Monrovia to Clarkston grew ultimately from the decision of a group of Americans in the mid-nineteenth century to relocate freed slaves from the United States after emancipation, a process that created a favored and much-resented ruling tribe with little or no organic connection to the nation it ruled. The story might begin in 1998, when Slobodan Milosević decided to unleash the Yugoslav army on the people of Kosovo and gave his soldiers the go-ahead to rampage through villages in Kosovo such as Kacanik, where Qendrim Bushi's family had a small grocery store that Serb soldiers torched—though that conflict too had beginnings in age-old political and ethnic tensions in that region. Or one might start near Clemson, South Carolina, where Lee Swaney—the future mayor of Clarkston, Georgia—was born in 1939, well before integration changed the South.

For now, though, let's begin the story amid the nineteen hills of the ancient city of Amman, Jordan, where Luma Mufleh grew up and where she learned to love a game that would create so much joy and cause so much trouble years later in a little town in Georgia, half a world away.

Part One

CHANGES

Chapter One

Luma

The name Luma means "dark lips," though Hassan and Sawsan al-Mufleh chose it for their first child less because of the shade of her lips than because they liked the sound of the name—short, endearing, and cheerful—in the context of both Arabic and English. The al-Muflehs were a wealthy, Westernized family in Amman, Jordan, a teeming city of two million, set among nineteen hills and cooled by a swirl of dry desert breezes. The family made its fortune primarily from making rebar—the metal rods used to strengthen concrete—which it sold across Jordan. Hassan had attended a Quaker school in Lebanon, and then college in the United States at the State University of New York in Oswego—"the same college as Jerry Seinfeld," he liked to tell people.

Luma's mother, Sawsan, was emotional and direct, and there was never any doubt about her mood or feelings. Luma, though, took after her father, Hassan, a man who mixed unassailable toughness with a capacity to detach, a combination that seemed designed to keep his emotions hidden for fear of revealing weakness.

"My sister and my dad don't like people going into them and knowing who they are," said Inam al-Mufleh, Luma's younger sister by eleven years and now a researcher for the Jordanian army in Amman. "Luma's very sensitive but she never shows it. She doesn't want anyone to know where her soft spot is."

As a child, Luma was doted on by her family, sometimes to an extraordinary degree. At the age of three, Luma idly mentioned to her grandmother that she thought her grandparents' new Mercedes 450 SL was "beautiful." The next day, the grandparents' driver showed up at Hassan and Sawsan al-Mufleh's home with a gift: a set of keys to the Mercedes, which, they were told, now belonged to their three-year-old daughter.

Hassan too doted on his eldest child. He had high expectations for her, and imagined her growing up to fulfill the prescribed role of a woman in a prominent Jordanian family. He expected her to marry, to stay close to home, and to honor her family.

From the time Luma was just a young girl, adults around her began to note her quiet confidence, which was so pronounced that her parents occasionally found themselves at a loss.

"When we would go to the PTA meetings," Hassan recalled, "they'd ask me, 'Why are you asking about Luma? She doesn't need your help.'"

Sometimes, Luma's parents found themselves striving to please their confident daughter, rather than the other way around. Hassan recalled that on a family vacation to Spain when Luma was ten or eleven years old, he had ordered a glass of sangria over dinner, in violation of the Muslim prohibition against drinking alcohol. When the drink arrived, Luma began to sob uncontrollably.

"She said, 'I love my father too much—I don't want him to go to hell,'" Hassan recalled. He asked the waitress to take the sangria away.

"I didn't drink after that," he said.

Luma encouraged—or perhaps demanded—that her younger sister, Inam, cultivate self-sufficiency, often against Inam's own instincts or wishes.

"She was a tough older sister—very tough love," Inam said. "She would make me do things that I didn't want to do. She never wanted me to take the easy way out. And she wouldn't accept me crying."

Inam said that she has a particularly vivid memory of her older sister's tough love in action. The al-Muflehs had gathered with their cousins, as they often did on weekends, at the family farm in a rural area called Mahes, half an hour from Amman. Inam, who was just seven or eight at the time, said that Luma took her and a group of young cousins out to a dirt road to get some exercise. The kids set off jogging, with Luma trailing them in the family Range Rover. It was hot and dry and hilly, and one by one, the kids began to complain. But Luma wouldn't have any of it. She insisted that they keep running.

"She was in the car, and we were running like crazy," Inam recalled. "Everyone was crying. And if I would cry, she would just look at me."

That withering look, which Luma would perfect over the years, had the stinging effect of a riding crop. Despite the pain, little Inam kept running.

Luma's drill-sergeant routine at Mahes became a kind of family legend, recalled to rib Hassan and Sawsan's firstborn for her tough exterior. The family knew another side of Luma—one that others rarely encountered—that of a sensitive, even sentimental young woman with a deep concern for those she perceived to be weak or defenseless. Luma laughed along with everyone else. She enjoyed a good joke and a well-earned teasing, even at her own expense. But jokes aside, Luma's tough love had its intended effect.

"I wanted to prove to my sister that I could do anything," she said. "I always remember that my sister pushed me and I found out I was able to do it."

THE AL-MUFLEHS WERE intent on raising their children with their same cosmopolitan values. They sent Luma to the American Community School in Amman, a school for the children of American expatriates, mostly diplomats and businessmen, and elite Jordanians, including the children of King Hussein and Queen Noor. Luma learned to speak English without an accent—she now speaks like a midwesterner—and met kids from the United States and Europe, as well as the children of diplomats from all over the world.

Luma's childhood was idyllic by most measures, and certainly by comparison to those of most in Jordan. She went to the best school in Amman and lived at a comfortable distance from the problems of that city, including poverty and the tensions brought on by the influx of Palestinian and later Iraqi refugees. But her maternal grandmother, Munawar, made a point of acknowledging and aiding the poor whenever she could. Beggars regularly knocked on her door because they knew that on principle she would always give them alms. And when relatives would tell her she was being taken advantage of because of her generosity, Munawar would brush them off.

"She would say we had an obligation because we were so privileged," Luma recalled. "And she would say, 'God judges them, not us.'"

Munawar's home abutted a lot in Amman where young men played soccer in the afternoons. As a kid, Luma would climb a grapevine on the concrete wall behind the house and watch the men play. She eventually got the nerve to join in, and she would play until her grandmother saw her and ordered her inside on the grounds that it was improper for a young woman to be around strange men.

"She would have a fit if she saw me playing soccer with men," Luma said. "And then she'd say, 'We are not going to tell your father about this.'"

At the American Community School, Luma was free from the strictures of a conservative Muslim society and at liberty to play sports as boys did. She played basketball, volleyball, soccer, and baseball with the same intensity, and stood out to her coaches, particularly an African American woman named Rhonda Brown.

"She was keen to learn," Brown said. "And no matter what you asked her to do, she did it without questioning why."

Brown, the wife of an American diplomat at the U.S. embassy in Amman, coached volleyball. She had played volleyball in college at Miami University in Ohio and, when she found herself bored in the role of a diplomat's wife, had volunteered to coach the women's varsity volleyball team at the ACS. When she showed up to coach, Brown said, she was disappointed at what she found.

"These girls were lazy—incredibly lazy," she said.

Luma was the notable exception. Though Brown didn't know much about the Jordanian girl, she noticed her dedication right away and felt she was the kind of player a team could be built around.

Coach Brown asked a lot of her players, and especially of Luma. She expected them to be on time to practice, to work hard, to focus, and to improve. She believed in running—lots of running—and drilling to the point of exhaustion. Brown challenged her players by setting an example herself. She was always on time. She was organized. When she asked her players to run five kilometers, she joined them, but with a challenge: "Because you're younger I expect you to do it better than me," she told them. "If I beat you, you can expect the worst practices ever."

"They ran," Brown said.

Brown's coaching philosophy was built on the belief that young people craved leadership and structure and at the same time were capable of taking on a tremendous amount of responsibility. She didn't believe in coddling.

"My feeling is that kids have to have rules," Brown explained. "They have to know what the boundaries are. And kids want to know what their limits are. It's important for them to know that people have expectations of them."

Brown was resigned to the fact that her players might not like her at first. But she took a long view toward their development and their trust in her. She was willing to wait out the hostility until her players broke through.

"I'm stubborn," Brown said. "I don't give in a lot. You can come across as mean, and until they see what kind of person you are they might not like you."

In fact, Luma didn't like Brown at all. She felt singled out for extra work and didn't appreciate all the extra running. But she kept her mouth shut and didn't complain, partly, she said, out of a suspicion that she and her teammates would benefit from the harsh treatment.

"I knew my teammates were lazy—talented but lazy," Luma said. "And part of me was like, *Maybe I want the challenge. Maybe these very harsh, very tough practices will work.*"

Over time, the practices began to have an effect. The team improved. They were motivated, and even the slackers on the team began working hard. Along the way, Luma started to pick up on a seeming contradiction. Though she told herself she disliked Coach Brown, she wanted desperately to play well for her. "For the majority of the time she coached me, I hated her," Luma said. "But she had our respect. She didn't ask us to do anything she wouldn't do. Until then I'd always played for me. I'd never played for a coach."

When Luma was in high school and still playing for Coach Brown, the junior varsity girls' soccer team at the American Community School found itself in need of a coach. Luma volunteered. She emulated Brown—putting the team through five days a week of running drills and pushing the young women to work harder and to get better. Luma loved it. She liked the way the daily problems of the world seemed to recede once she took the field, the subtle psychological strategies one had to employ to get the best out of each player, and most of all the sense of satisfaction that came from forging something new out of disparate elements: an entity with its distinct identity, not a collection of individuals, but a new being, a team. And she wasn't afraid to admit she also liked being in charge.

But as she got older and accustomed to the liberty she had as a woman at ACS—where she could coach and play sports as she pleased—she began to feel at odds with the Jordanian society in which she had grown up. She wanted to be able to play pickup games of soccer with whoever was around, without regard to gender. She wanted the liberty to be as assertive in her daily life as Coach Brown had taught her to be on the court. Her family's social status created additional pressure for her to follow a more traditional path. There were obligations, as well as the looming threat that she might be pressured into marrying someone she didn't love.

"When you come from a family that's prominent, there are expectations of you," she said. "And I hated that. It's a very patriarchal society, and as modern as it is, women are still second-class citizens. I didn't want to be treated that way."

Coach Brown picked up on Luma's yearning. At a team sleepover, the players and coach went around the room predicting where everyone would be in ten years. Coach Brown joked that Luma would be "living illegally in the United States." Everyone laughed, including Luma. But she disagreed.

"In ten years, I'll be there legally," she said.

"I knew from even our brief time together that she wanted something else for her life," Brown recalled.

Toward the end of Luma's junior year, she and her parents decided she would attend college in the United States. Hassan and Sawsan wanted their daughter to continue her Western education, a rite of sorts for well-to-do Jordanians. But Luma was more interested in life in the United States than she was in what an education there might do for her in Jordan. "America was the land of opportunity," she said. "It was a very appealing dream of what you want your life to be like." Within the family, Luma's grandmother alone seemed to understand the implications of her going to college in the United States.

"If she moves to America," Munawar told the family, "there's a chance she won't come back."

Luma's first trip to the United States came when she enrolled at Hobart and William Smith College, a coed school in the Finger Lakes region of New York, not too far from where her father had gone to college. She played soccer her first fall there, but midway through the season injured a knee, sidelining her for the rest of the year. Luma liked the school well enough, but winter there was colder than anything she had experienced in Amman, and the campus was remote. She wondered if she had made the right choice in going so far from home. Luma decided to look at other schools, and soon visited Smith College, the women's school in Northampton, Massachusetts. The campus seemed to perfectly embody the setting Luma had envisioned for herself when she left Jordan for America. It was set in a picturesque New England town with a strong sense of community and security. And as a women's college, Smith was focused on imbuing its students with the very sort of self-reliance and self-confidence Luma felt she had been deprived of at home. Luma fell in love with the place and transferred for her sophomore year.

At Smith, Luma had what she described as a kind of awakening. She was taken by the presence of so many self-confident, achieving women, and also by the social mobility she saw evident in the student body. Her housemate, for example, was the first in her family to go to college, and there she was at one of the preeminent private colleges in the United States. *That would never happen in Jordan,* Luma remembered thinking to herself at the time.

Luma's friends at Smith remember her as outgoing and involved—in intramural soccer and in social events sponsored by the college's house system. Few understood her background; she spoke English so well that other students she met assumed she was American.

"One day we were hanging out talking about our childhoods and she said, 'I'm from Jordan,'" recalled Misty Wyman, a student from Maine who would become Luma's best friend. "I thought she'd been born to American parents overseas. It had never occurred to me that she was Jordanian."

On a trip home to Jordan after her junior year at Smith, Luma realized that she could never feel comfortable living there. Jordan, while a modern Middle Eastern state, was not an easy place for a woman used to Western freedoms. Professional opportunities for women were limited. Under Sharia law, which applied to domestic and inheritance matters, the testimony of two women carried the weight of that from a single man. A wife had to obtain permission from her husband simply to apply for a passport. And so-called honor killings were still viewed leniently in Sharia courts. As a member of a well-known family, Luma felt monitored and pressured to follow a prescribed path. A future in Jordan felt limited, lacking suspense, whereas the United States seemed alluringly full of both uncertainty and possibility.

Before she left to return to Smith for her senior year, Luma sought out friends one by one, and paid a visit to her grandmother. She didn't tell them that she was saying goodbye exactly, but privately, Luma knew that to be the case.

"When I said goodbye I knew I was saying goodbye to some people I'd never see again," she said. "I wanted to do it on my own. I wanted to prove to my parents that I didn't need their help."

Luma did let on to some of her friends. Rhonda Brown recalled a softball game she and Luma played with a group of American diplomats and expatriates. When the game had finished, Brown went to pick up the leather softball glove she'd brought with her from the United States, but it was gone—stolen, apparently. Brown was furious. She'd had the glove for years, and it was all but impossible to get a softball glove in Jordan at the time. Luma had a glove that she too had had for years. She took it off her hand and gave it to her coach.

"She said, 'You take this glove,'" Brown recalled. "'I won't need it. I don't think I'm coming back.'"

Brown—who soon moved to Damascus, and later to Israel with her husband and family—lost touch over the years with her star player, but she kept Luma's glove from one move to the next, as a memento of the mysteriously self-possessed young woman she had once coached. Fifteen years later, she still has it. "The webbing has rotted and come out," Brown told me from Israel, where I tracked her down by phone. "That glove was very special to me."

IN JUNE 1997, a few weeks after graduating from Smith, Luma gave her parents the news by telephone: She was staying in the United States—not for a little while, but forever. She had no intention of returning home to Jordan.

Hassan al-Mufleh was devastated.

"I felt as if the earth swallowed me," he said.

Hassan's devastation soon gave way to outrage. He believed he had given every opportunity to his daughter. He had sent her to the best schools and had encouraged her to go to college in the United States. He took her decision to make a home in the States as a slap in the face. Luma tried to explain that she felt it was important for her to see if she could support herself without the social and financial safety net her parents provided at home. Hassan would have none of it. If Luma wanted to see how independent she could be, he told her, he was content to help her find out. He let her know that she would be disinherited absolutely if she didn't return home. Luma didn't budge. She didn't feel that she could be herself there, and she was willing to endure a split with her family to live in a place where she could live the life she pleased. Hassan followed through on his word, by cutting Luma off completely—no more money, no more phone calls. He was finished with his daughter.

For Luma, the change in lifestyle was abrupt. In an instant, she was on her own. "I went from being able to walk into any restaurant and store in the United States and buy whatever I wanted to having nothing," she said.

Luma's friends remember that period well. They had watched her painful deliberations over when and how to give her parents the news that she wasn't coming home. And now that she was cut off, they saw their once outgoing friend grow sullen and seem suddenly lost.

"It was very traumatic," said Misty Wyman, Luma's friend from Smith. "She was very stressed and sick a lot because of the stress."

"There was a mourning process," Wyman added. "She was very close to her grandmother, and her grandmother was getting older. She was close to her sister and wasn't sure that her parents would ever let her sister come to visit her here. And I kind of had the impression from Luma that she had been her father's pet. Even though he was hard on her, he expected a lot from her. She was giving up a lot by not going home."

So Luma made do. After graduation, she went to stay with her friend Misty in Highlands, North Carolina, a small resort town in the mountains where Misty had found work. Luma didn't yet have a permit to work legally in the United States, so she found herself looking for the sorts of jobs available to illegal immigrants, eventually settling on a position washing dishes and cleaning toilets at a local restaurant called the Mountaineer. Luma enjoyed the relative calm and quiet of the mountains, but there were moments during her stint in Appalachia that only served to reinforce her sense of isolation. Concerned that her foreign-sounding name might draw unwelcome attention from locals, Luma's colleagues at the Mountaineer gave her an innocuous nickname: Liz. The locals remained oblivious of "Liz's" real background as a Jordanian Muslim, even as they got to know her. A handyman who was a regular at the Mountaineer even sent Liz flowers, and later, sought to impress her by showing off a prized family heirloom: a robe and hood once worn by his grandfather, a former grand dragon of the Ku Klux Klan.

"I was so shaken up," Luma said.

After a summer in Highlands, Luma kicked around aimlessly, moving to Boston then back to North Carolina, with little sense of direction. Her news from home came mostly through her grandmother, who would pass along family gossip, and who encouraged Luma to be strong and patient with her parents. Someday, Munawar said, they would come to forgive her.

But for now, Luma was on her own. In 1999, she decided to move to Atlanta for no other reason than that she liked the weather—eternal-seeming springs and easy autumns, with mercifully short and mild winters—not unlike the weather in Amman. When Luma told her friends of her plan, they were uniformly against it, worried that a Muslim woman from Jordan wouldn't fit in down in Dixie.

"I said, 'Are you crazy?'" Misty recalled.

Luma didn't have much of a retort. She knew next to no one in Atlanta. She had little appreciation for how unusual a Muslim woman with the name Luma Hassan Mufleh would seem to most southerners, and certainly no inkling of how much more complicated attitudes toward Muslims would become a couple of years into the future, after the attacks on September 11. Luma arrived in Atlanta with little mission or calling. She found a tiny apartment near Decatur, a picturesque and progressive suburb east of Atlanta anchored by an old granite courthouse with grand Corinthian columns. She knew nothing yet about Clarkston, the town just down the road that had been transformed by refugees, people not unlike herself, who had fled certain discontent in one world for uncertain lives in another. But like them, Luma was determined to survive and to make it on her own. Going home wasn't an option.

Chapter Two

Beatrice and Her Boys

In 1997, at about the same time Luma was graduating from Smith College in Massachusetts, a woman named Beatrice Ziaty was struggling with her husband and sons—Jeremiah, Mandela, Darlington, and Erich—to survive in the middle of a civil war in Monrovia, the capital of Liberia. Rival rebel factions had laid siege to the city, and soldiers roamed about, some decked in women's wigs and costumes—partly because of a superstitious belief that such costumes would fend off harm and partly because of the sheer terror such surreal getups induced in others. Bullets from the fighting cut down civilians with regularity, and mortars pierced the rooftops of family dwellings without warning. Then one night, the Ziatys were startled by a knock at the door.

Beatrice's husband was a paymaster, a midlevel bureaucrat whose job entailed handing out wages to employees of the former government, and the men at the door wanted whatever cash he could access. Yelling, with machine guns, and in disguises, the men seemed like emissaries from hell. Beatrice couldn't make out what faction they belonged to, or if they were simply common thugs.

"You got all the government money—we got to get rid of you," one of the men said to Ziaty.

"Why? I'm only paymaster," he protested. "I want to take care of the people. I only want to work to give the people a check! I got no government money."

"You have to give the government money. If not, we will kill you."

"I don't have!" he pleaded.

THE ZIATYS' STORY, as well as any, shows the extent to which modern refugees can trace their displacement to the mistakes, greed, fears, crimes, and foibles of men who long preceded them, sometimes by decades—or longer. Liberia had been founded in 1821 by a group of Americans as a colony for freed slaves who lived there first under white American rule and then, in 1847, under their own authority, as Africa's first self-governing republic. For the next 130 years, the Americo-Liberian minority—just 3 percent of the population—backed by the U.S. government, ruled the nation of around 2.5 million as a kind of feudal oligarchy.

Americo-Liberian rule came to a brutal end on April 12, 1980, when Samuel Doe, an army sergeant who had been trained by American Green Berets, stormed the presidential compound with soldiers, disemboweled President William Tolbert, and proclaimed himself Liberia's new leader. Doe was a member of the Krahn tribe, a tiny ethnic group that composed just 4 percent of the population, far less than the larger tribes in Liberia, the Gio and Mano. With the Krahn essentially replacing the Americo-Liberians as an American-backed oppressive ruling elite, it was only a matter of time before other ethnic groups felt aggrieved enough to revolt as well.

The man who consolidated their rage was a former Doe associate named Charles Taylor, a Liberian who had gone to college in Boston and New Hampshire and, after being convicted in an embezzling scheme, escaped an American jail through a window, using a hacksaw and a rope of knotted bedsheets.

Taylor began with a band of just 150 soldiers in a Gio section of the country. Their motto: "Kill the Krahn." His incitement to ethnic vio-

lence worked and his force grew, in no small part because of boys—
some of them orphans whose parents had been killed by Doe, some
of them kidnapped from their families by Taylor's own militias—that
he armed and drugged into a killing frenzy. By 1990 he had laid siege
to Monrovia. Water was cut off. There was no food or medicine. Soldiers terrorized citizens and looted at will. More than 100,000 Krahn
refugees flooded into Ivory Coast, even as Doe's Krahn soldiers committed atrocities of their own. Over one hundred and fifty thousand
Liberians died.

In 1996, Taylor made another attack on Monrovia and the Krahn
who lived there. "Fighters on both sides engaged in cannibalism, rip-
ping out hearts and eating them," wrote Martin Meredith in his book
The Fate of Africa. "One group known as the 'Butt Naked Brigade'
fought naked in the belief that this would protect them against bullets." Even soldiers from ECOMOG—a regional peacekeeping force
deployed to separate the warring factions—joined in the looting.
"Monrovia," Meredith wrote, "was reduced to a wrecked city."

MONROVIA, OF COURSE, was where Beatrice Ziaty lived. She and
her husband were Krahn and remained in the sector of the city under Krahn control. During the siege of 1996, they hid in their house
as battles raged outside. When her youngest son, Jeremiah, fell sick,
Beatrice could do nothing but pray. It was too dangerous to go outside for help.

"There was no food, no medicine, nothing," she said. "I saw my
child sick for five days. When that child doesn't die, then you tell
God, 'Thank you.'"

Eventually, though, even the Ziatys' home failed to provide refuge.
The men who came in the night for Beatrice's husband began to beat
him when he said he didn't have access to any stash of government
money. Beatrice panicked. She grabbed Jeremiah and Mandela, her
next oldest, and ran for the back door, which let out onto an alley full
of shadows. The last words she heard her husband speak echo in her
mind today as clearly as when they were spoken that night.

"Oh, what do you do!" he cried. "They are killing me! Oh—they
are killing me!"

WITH JEREMIAH AND Mandela, Beatrice trekked through the darkened streets of Monrovia, past checkpoints manned by menacing teenage boys and young men burdened by the weight of guns and bandoliers absurdly oversize for their small frames. The soldiers were content to let the Krahn leave Monrovia. Beatrice and her sons made it out of town and began walking east, toward the border with Ivory Coast. She scavenged for food and hitched rides when she could. But mostly she lumbered through the bush until, after ten days of travel, she arrived at an overflowing refugee camp across the border. She had left behind Darlington, who was staying with his grandparents in the Liberian countryside. Eventually Darlington got word of his mother's whereabouts and made his own harrowing two-day trek on foot to the camp to reunite with his mother and younger brothers.

Together and with the help of other refugees, Beatrice and her sons built a mud hut for shelter. Then they waited—for what, they weren't exactly sure. The end of the war—if it ever occurred—wouldn't be enough to lure them back to Monrovia. Beatrice's husband was gone. The city was in shambles. Taylor, whose forces laid waste to Monrovia, would come to power in an election in 1997—famously employing the campaign slogan "He killed my ma, he killed my pa. But I will vote for him."—winning largely because people feared he would restart a civil war if he lost. He used the power of his post to continue the killing until he eventually became the rare example of a Liberian leader who fell out of favor with Washington. He went into exile in Nigeria, was indicted for war crimes by the UN, and was eventually captured in an SUV stashed with cash and heroin on the Nigeria-Cameroon border.

Beatrice passed the time in the camp by standing in lines to apply for resettlement by the United Nations, an act she undertook out of equal parts desperation and stubbornness. She knew the odds that she would be selected were minuscule—but what else was there to do? The camp, home to more than twenty thousand refugees from the war in Liberia, was squalid, with frequent food shortages and a quiet threat in the form of soldiers who worked in the camp to recruit young men back into the war. In such conditions, education for her boys was next to impossible. Beatrice focused her energies on surviving, protecting her sons from recruitment, and getting out.

Beatrice and her sons spent five years in that camp. Against all odds and after countless interviews with UN personnel, Beatrice learned that she and her boys had been accepted by the United Nations High Commissioner for Refugees (UNHCR) for resettlement. They would be sent first to Abidjan, the largest city in Ivory Coast, and from there they'd fly to New York and then to Atlanta, Georgia, and their new home in Clarkston, a place they had never heard of.

THE ZIATYS' RESETTLEMENT followed a typical path. They were granted a $3,016 loan by the U.S. Office of Refugee Resettlement for four one-way plane tickets to the United States. (Beatrice repaid the money in three years.) The family was assigned to an International Rescue Committee caseworker, who would oversee their resettlement in the United States. On September 28, 2003, the Ziatys made the two-day journey from Abidjan to Atlanta. Bleary-eyed and disoriented, they met the IRC caseworker at the airport. The woman drove them past downtown Atlanta, with its gaudy skyscrapers and gleaming gold-domed capitol building, to their new home, a two-bedroom dwelling in Clarkston's Wyncrest apartments. The cupboards had been stocked with canned goods. The walls were dingy and bare. There were some old sofas to sit on, and mattresses on the floor. The Ziatys stretched out on them and went to sleep.

At the encouragement of the IRC, Beatrice Ziaty began her job search almost immediately. Like all refugees accepted into the United States for resettlement, she would have only three months of government assistance to help her get on her feet, to say nothing of the debt she owed on her plane tickets. With the IRC's help, she landed a job as a maid at the Ritz-Carlton Hotel in the Buckhead section of Atlanta—one of the most exquisite hotels in the South, and in Atlanta's most exclusive neighborhood. It was an hour's commute by bus from Clarkston.

Beatrice wasn't worried about the work. She was sturdy and self-sufficient—that's how she'd gotten to Atlanta, after all—but she didn't like the idea of leaving her boys behind. They were going to school during the day, but she wouldn't get home from work until well after dark. She encouraged them to stay inside until she returned in the evening. Beatrice didn't know how to use the bus system in Atlanta, but a fellow Liberian offered to show her the way from Wyncrest to the bus stop on her first day of work. At five-thirty a.m. she set out for the Ritz.

The work there was hard. Maids were expected to clean fifteen to sixteen rooms a day by themselves, and though the shifts were technically eight hours long, in reality it took much longer to clean so many rooms, extra work that occurred, Beatrice said, off the clock. Beatrice's back ached when she made it back to the bus stop at around ten o'clock. Without her friend to guide her this time, she was on her own. As she rode the bus back through the strange glimmering landscape of Atlanta, she tried to put the fear of the last few years out of her mind. She allowed herself the uncharacteristically optimistic thought that maybe she and her family were finally safe.

The bus heaved to a stop in Clarkston. Beatrice got off, hopeful she had chosen the right stop. She looked around and tried to recall the way back to her apartment. It was easy to get turned around in Clarkston—there were no tall buildings to help her orient herself—and it would take Beatrice the better part of a month to feel confident about the way back to Wyncrest. She set out haltingly along the sidewalk. It was a cool October night filled with the sounds of chirping crickets and the intermittent whoosh of passing cars. Beatrice heard a noise and looked over her shoulder. A man was following her. She sped up and clutched her bag. It contained her new driver's license, social security card, work permit, and all the cash she possessed. She felt the man's hand on her arm.

"Halt," he said. "Give me the purse."

Beatrice let go of the bag and braced for a blow that never came. The man ran, and she took off running herself in the opposite direction. Eventually she stopped, out of breath, and began to sob between gasps for air. She didn't know where she was, or how to call the police. She was tired, and tired of running. A stranger, another man, found her and asked what had happened. He was friendly, and called the police. The officers took Beatrice home and offered to help find the mugger. But she didn't get a good look at him. She only knew his accent was African.

The incident robbed Beatrice of the hope that her new home would provide her and her family with a sense of security. She became obsessed with her boys' safety. In Liberia, a neighbor would always look after her kids if she needed to leave them to run an errand or to visit a friend. But Beatrice didn't know anyone in Clarkston. Many of her new neighbors didn't speak English, and some of the ones who did frightened her. There was plenty of gang activity in and around Wyncrest. Gunshots frequently pierced the quiet at night. For all Beatrice knew, the man who mugged her lived in the next building over. She didn't particularly trust the police either. She'd been told by Liberians she'd met that the police would take your children away if you left them alone. So she told the boys and told them again: When you come home from school, go into the apartment, lock the door, and stay inside.

ONE EVENING NOT long after the mugging, Jeremiah disobeyed Beatrice. He was playing outside alone at dusk when a policeman on patrol stopped and asked him where his parents were. He had to think fast.

"She's inside sleeping," he told the cop.

"Well, then go inside," the officer said.

Later that evening, Jeremiah told his mother what had happened. She went into a rage, fueled by the anxiety that had been building up for months.

"When you come home from school, go inside and you lock yourself in the house," Beatrice shouted at him. "When you come from school you will lock yourself up!"

Chapter Three

"Small Town . . . Big Heart"

Before refugees like Beatrice Ziaty started arriving, Mayor Swaney liked to say, Clarkston, Georgia, was "just a sleepy little town by the railroad tracks."

Those tracks suture a grassy rise that bisects Clarkston and still carry a dozen or so freight trains a day, which rattle windows and stop traffic. Few, though, in Clarkston complain about the trains with much conviction. Amid the strip malls, office complexes, fast food joints, and sprawling parking lots of modern-day Atlanta, the sight of lumbering freight cars contributes to a comforting sense that Clarkston has not been entirely swallowed by the creeping sameness of urban sprawl. Indeed, while many small towns around Atlanta have been absorbed into the city or big county governments, Clarkston has retained its independence. Clarkston residents elect their own mayor and city council and have their own police department. A pastoral island of around 7,200 amid an exurb of some five million people, Clarkston is still, improbably enough, a town.

Clarkston was settled originally by yeoman farmers and railroad men in the years after the Civil War. They built the town's first Baptist church on land near a creek that was a popular site for baptisms, ground the church still occupies. Back then, Clarkston was sometimes called Goatsville, perhaps because goats were used to keep grass low by the tracks, perhaps as a pejorative by city folks—no one seems quite sure. But the name lives on, by allusion at least, in the mascot of Clarkston High School: the Angoras.

For the better part of the next hundred years, little of consequence happened in Clarkston. It was a typical small southern town, conservative and white, and not too far removed in temperament from the next town over, Stone Mountain, a longtime headquarters of sorts for the Ku Klux Klan and the site of cross burnings as recently as the late 1980s. Folks in Clarkston sent their kids to Clarkston High School, went to services at one of the churches on Church Street, and bought their groceries at a local independent grocery store called Thriftown, which was located in the town shopping center, across the tracks from the churches and City Hall. Life in Clarkston was simple, and few from the outside world paid the town much note, which suited the residents of Clarkston just fine.

That began to change in the 1970s, when the Atlanta airport expanded to become the Southeast's first international hub and, eventually, one of the world's busiest airports. The airport brought jobs, and the people working those new jobs needed places to live. A few enterprising developers bought up tracts of cheap land in Clarkston because of the town's location, just outside the Atlanta Perimeter—a beltway that encircles the city and offers easy access to the airport and downtown. They built a series of apartment complexes—mostly two-story affairs with multiple buildings arranged around big, commuter-friendly parking lots. Developers got a boost when MARTA, the Atlanta public transit system, built its easternmost rail station outside Clarkston. More complexes went up, with idyllic-sounding names only real estate developers could concoct: Kristopher Woods, Brannon Hill, Willow Branch, and Olde Plantation.

Middle-class whites moved in, and over time the population of Clarkston more than doubled. No one paid much attention at the time, but the addition of the apartment complexes had another effect, creating in a sense two Clarkstons. Older Clarkston residents lived on one side of town in roughly 450 old houses, simple gabled structures with front porches and small front yards. Working-class newcomers lived in the apartment complexes. They were separate worlds—economically, socially, and otherwise—but since they were packed together on about one square mile, there wasn't much space between them.

In the 1980s whites began to leave the apartments in Clarkston. The migration paralleled the white flight from other old residential neighborhoods close to downtown Atlanta. Crime was rising, and newer suburbs farther from town were roomier and more ethnically homogenous. Middle-class whites in Clarkston, flush from Atlanta's economic boom following the opening of the airport, could afford to move. Vacancies rose and rents fell. Crime surged. Landlords filled the apartment complexes through government housing programs, which brought in African American tenants, and simultaneously cut back on upkeep, allowing the complexes to fall into disrepair. Pretty soon, Clarkston, or at least the part of Clarkston consisting of apartment complexes, found itself caught in a familiar cycle of urban decay.

In the late 1980s, another group of outsiders took note of Clarkston: the nonprofit agencies that resettle the tens of thousands of refugees accepted into the United States each year. The agencies—which include the International Rescue Committee, the organization founded in 1933 by Albert Einstein to help bring Jewish refugees from Europe to the United States, as well as World Relief, Lutheran Family Services, and others—are contracted by the government to help refugee families settle in to their new lives. They help find the families schools, jobs, and access to social services. But first they have to find a place for them to live.

From the perspective of the resettlement agencies, Clarkston, Georgia, was a textbook example of a community ripe for refugee resettlement. It was not quite thirteen miles from downtown Atlanta, a city with a growing economy and a bottomless need for low-skilled workers to labor in construction, at distribution centers and packaging plants, and in the city's hotels and restaurants. Atlanta had public transportation in the form of bus and rail, which made getting to those jobs relatively easy even for those too poor to own cars, and Clarkston had its own rail stop—at the end of the line. With all those decaying apartment complexes in town, Clarkston had a surplus of cheap housing. And though the town was cut through by two busy thoroughfares, Ponce de Leon Avenue and Indian Creek Drive, as well as a set of active railroad tracks, it had enough navigable sidewalks to qualify as pedestrian-friendly—important for a large group of people who couldn't afford automobiles. The apartment complexes were within walking distance of the main shopping center, which was now drooping and tired, with a porn shop across the parking lot from a day-care center, but its proximity to the complexes meant that residents could get their food without hitching a ride or taking a train or bus.

The first refugees arrived in Clarkston in the late 1980s and early 1990s from Southeast Asia—mostly Vietnamese and Cambodians fleeing Communist governments. Their resettlement went smoothly, and none of the older residents in town raised any objection, if they even noticed these newcomers. After all, the apartments were still a world away from the houses across town. So the agencies, encouraged by the success of that early round of resettlement, brought in other refugees—survivors of the conflicts in Bosnia and Kosovo, and oppressed minorities from the former Soviet Union. World Relief and the International Rescue Committee opened offices in Clarkston to better serve the newcomers, and resettled still more refugees—now from war-ravaged African countries including Liberia, Congo, Burundi, Sudan, Somalia, Ethiopia, and Eritrea. Between 1996 and 2001, more than nineteen thousand refugees were resettled in Georgia, and many of those ended up in or around Clarkston. The 2000 census revealed that fully one-third of Clarkston's population was foreign-born, though almost everyone suspected the number was higher because census estimates did not account for large numbers of refugees and immigrants living together in Clarkston's apartments. In a relatively short amount of time, Clarkston had completely changed.

NEARLY ALL OF Clarkston's longtime residents had a story about the moment they noticed this change. For Emanuel Ransom, an African American who had moved to Clarkston from Pennsylvania in the 1960s and who served on the city council, it was when he picked up on a sudden spike in the amount of garbage the town was producing each year. When he investigated, he found that the singles and nuclear families that had inhabited the town's apartment complexes were being displaced by families of refugees living eight or ten to an apartment—and producing a proportionate amount of garbage, which the town had to haul away.

"The city didn't realize that we were being inundated with people coming in, because it was a gradual thing," Ransom said. "Nobody understood."

For Karen Feltz, a chain-smoking anthropologist and city council member, it was when she noticed a Liberian woman in her neighborhood walking up and down the street with a jug on her head, cursing at the devil. After seeing the woman talking to herself on several occasions, Feltz began to fear she might be suffering a psychiatric breakdown. She approached the woman's husband, a minister, who shrugged off her concerns.

"He said, 'She can talk to the devil if she wants to,'" Feltz recalled, with a laugh. "I thought, *Oh my God—I'm living in the twilight zone!*"

To many Clarkston residents, it felt as if their town had transformed overnight.

"You wake up one morning," said Rita Thomas, a longtime homeowner in Clarkston, "and there it is."

THE CHANGE IN Clarkston was an accelerated version of demographic changes taking place all across America because of immigration and refugee resettlement. But in at least one way it was unique. While some towns such as Lewiston, Maine, and Merced, California, have attracted large numbers of a single ethnic group or nationality—in Lewiston's case, Somalis, in Merced's case, Hmong, and in countless cities in the Southwest and West, Latinos—Clarkston was seeing new residents who were from everywhere. If a group of people had come to the United States legally in the last fifteen years, chances are they were represented in Clarkston in perfect proportion to the numbers in which they were accepted into the country at large. The town became a microcosm of the world itself, or at least of the parts plagued with society-shattering violence. And in the process, in less than a decade, little Clarkston, Georgia, became one of the most diverse communities in the country.

———

INDEED, WHILE THE freight trains continued to rumble through town a dozen times a day, little in Clarkston looked familiar to the people who'd spent their lives there. Women walked down the street in hijabs and even in full burkas, or *jalabib*. The shopping center transformed: while Thriftown, the grocery store, remained, restaurants such as Hungry Harry's pizza joint were replaced by Vietnamese and Eritrean restaurants, a Halal butcher, and a "global pharmacy" that catered to the refugee community by selling, among other things, international phone cards. A mosque opened up on Indian Creek Drive, just across the street from the elementary and high schools, and began to draw hundreds. (Longtime Clarkston residents now know to avoid Indian Creek Drive on Friday afternoons because of the traffic jam caused by Friday prayers.) As newcomers arrived, many older white residents simply left, and the demographic change was reflected in nearly all of Clarkston's institutions. Clarkston High School became home to students from more than fifty countries. Fully a third of the local elementary school skips lunch during Ramadan. Attendance at the old Clarkston Baptist Church dwindled from around seven hundred to fewer than a hundred as many white residents left town.

While many of the changes in Clarkston were incremental and hard to notice at first, other events occurred that called attention to the changes and caused the locals to wonder what exactly was happening to their town. A group of Bosnian refugees who had come from the town of Bosanski Samac came face-to-face in Clarkston with a Serbian soldier named Nikola Vukovic, who they said had tortured them during the war, beating them bloody in the town police station for days. (They eventually sued Vukovic, who was living just outside of Clarkston in the town of Stone Mountain and laboring at a compressor factory for eight dollars an hour, and won a $140 million judgment, but not before Vukovic fled the United States.)

A mentally disturbed Sudanese man who was left at home with his five-year-old nephew went into a rage for reasons unknown and beheaded the boy with a butcher knife. He was found by a policeman walking by the railroad tracks in a daze, his clothing drenched in blood. "I've done something real bad," he told police, before leading them back to the apartment. Family members blamed the act on the post-traumatic stress the young man suffered after being tortured in a refugee camp, an explanation that hardly soothed the anxieties of older Clarkston residents, given the number of people in their town from just such camps.

A young member of the Lost Boys of Sudan, the 3,800 refugees who resettled in the United States after a twelve-year flight through the desert and scrub of war-ravaged Sudan, died after getting bludgeoned by another Sudanese refugee in a fight over ten dollars. An Ethiopian man was arrested and later convicted for conducting the brutal practice of female circumcision on his young daughter. And so on. Each of these events fed the perception that the refugees were bringing violent pasts with them to Clarkston, and caused even empathetic locals to worry for their own safety.

THE CITIZENS OF many communities might have organized, or protested, or somehow pushed back, but Clarkston wasn't a protesting kind of place. The old town's quiet, conservative southern character didn't go in for rallies and bullhorns. And the troubles of the 1980s had destabilized the community and imbued longtime residents with a sense of futility when it came to resisting change. Rather than making noise, during the first decade of resettlement the older residents of Clarkston simply retreated into their homes.

Karen Feltz remembers that when she moved to Clarkston from the nearby Atlanta neighborhood of Five Points—a community with a vibrant nightlife and where neighbors say hello and look after one another—she was struck by the strange wariness of her neighbors. Few people talked. A sense of community was missing. It took a while, but Feltz said she came to realize that the sudden changes brought on by resettlement had simply made people afraid.

"You're talking about one-point-one square miles of encapsulated southern ideologies," Feltz said of her town. "People living their safe quiet lives in their white-bread houses, and all of a sudden every other person on the street is black, or Asian, or something they don't even recognize, and 'Oh my God, let's just shut down and stay in our houses!'"

For all the unique circumstances of Clarkston's transformation, there was something altogether normal about the townsfolk's withdrawal from the public sphere. In 2007, a group of researchers led by the Harvard political scientist Robert Putnam published a study detailing the results of surveys they had done with some thirty thousand residents of forty-one ethnically diverse communities in the United States. Their findings underscored the cost of diversity: when people have little in common, they tend to avoid each other and to keep to themselves.

"Inhabitants of diverse communities tend to withdraw from collective life," the authors wrote, "to distrust their neighbors, regardless of the color of their skin, to withdraw even from close friends, to expect the worst from their community and its leaders, to volunteer less, give less to charity and work on community projects less often, to register to vote less, to agitate for social reform more, but have less faith that they can actually make a difference, and to huddle unhappily in front of the television."

In Clarkston, the withdrawal from collective life was matched by growing resentment at the forces and people that had caused the town to change in the first place: the resettlement agencies and the refugees. For a surprisingly long time—the better part of a decade—townsfolk kept their anger to themselves. But as resentment built, it would begin to find its expression.

"Nobody knew what to do about it, so they just sort of ignored it," Karen Feltz said of the influx of refugees. "And that's how we got in trouble."

THE FIRST SIGNS of trouble surfaced in interactions between the refugees and the Clarkston Police Department in the late 1990s. The police chief at the time was a man named Charlie—or Chollie, to people in Clarkston—Nelson, an old-school presence whose office wall was adorned with a poster of Barney Fife, the goofball deputy on *The Andy Griffith Show,* captioned with the phrase, "Hell no, this ain't Mayberry."

The refugees were a constant problem, in Nelson's eyes. They didn't understand English. Many were poor drivers. Some, when pulled over, gesticulated and cried out, and even reached out to touch his officers—a sign of disrespect if not outright aggression to most

American police officers. Nelson looked askance at diversity training and opposed offering any "special treatment" for refugees, particularly in the arena of traffic violations. Writing traffic tickets to
refugees became one of Clarkston's more reliable sources of revenue.
A study by the *Atlanta Journal-Constitution* found that the average
Georgia town of Clarkston's size raised about 9 percent of its budget
from traffic tickets. In Clarkston, by contrast, the number was 30
percent. Nelson argued that he was simply enforcing the law. It wasn't
his fault, he said, if some refugees hadn't learned the rules of the road
in the United States. But the refugees felt singled out.

"A lot of our community members felt harassed, discriminated
against," said Salahadin Wazir, the imam of the Clarkston mosque,
whose congregation was often ticketed for parking improperly around
the mosque at Friday prayers. "They were all just pulled over for anything."

Eventually, some members of the refugee community became so
fed up with what they saw as harassment from Nelson's force that
they decided to act. For many, doing so meant making a leap of faith.
Most had come from war-ravaged regions where the police and other
authority figures were not only untrustworthy but frequently active
agents of oppression. To stand up to the police in America was to take
the nation's promise of justice for all at face value. In one incident, a
Somali cabdriver, after getting pulled over by a Clarkston police officer for reasons he thought bogus, summoned other cabbies from the
Somali community on his CB radio. His colleagues quickly drove to
the site of the police stop. The officer feared a riot might occur and let
the driver off with a warning.

In 2001, Lee Swaney—a longtime city council member and a self-
described champion of "old Clarkston," that is, Clarkston before the
refugees—ran for mayor. As an advocate of life as it was in a simple
southern town, Swaney fit the part. The owner of a heating and air-
conditioning business, he had a big walrus-y mustache and sleepy eyes
that made him look older than his sixty-eight years. He drove a big
white pickup truck of the sort you might expect to see on a ranch,
wore cowboy boots and an American flag lapel pin, and spoke with a
thick, low-country accent that betrayed his South Carolina upbringing. Swaney's platform reflected his old-school values: he promised

the citizens of Clarkston that if elected, he'd work hard to lure a good old-fashioned American hamburger joint to open up within the city limits.

A year and a half after Swaney took office, something happened that pushed the tensions in Clarkston over the edge: refugee agency officials announced that they planned to relocate some seven hundred Somali Bantu to Georgia, many of them to Clarkston.

The Somali Bantu presented an extraordinary challenge for resettlement officials. An assemblage of agricultural tribes from the area of East Africa now comprising Tanzania, Malawi, and Mozambique, the Somali Bantu had undergone more than three hundred years of almost uninterrupted persecution. They were kidnapped and sold into slavery with impunity in the eighteenth and nineteenth centuries by Arab slave traders. Later, under the sultanate of Zanzibar and subsequent rule by the Italian colonial government, the Somali Bantu were enslaved to work on plantations, a condition that persisted until as recently as the 1930s. When the British granted Somalia its independence in 1960, the Bantu were hounded, abused, and brutalized by ethnic Somalis. When the Somali civil war began in 1991, the persecution accelerated dramatically as warring factions forced the Somali Bantu off their land in the fertile Juba River valley. Amid the lawlessness and the systematic campaigns of rape, torture, and killing, the Somali Bantu fled en masse with other persecuted Somalis to the empty and dangerous open spaces of northeast Kenya and into four main refugee camps established there by the United Nations. By the late 1990s, the population of those camps exceeded 150,000.

This history of persecution and wandering had torn at the social fabric of the Somali Bantu and left them, on the whole, poor, deeply traumatized, and far removed from the trappings of the modern world. They had little in the way of education. Many lived their lives in primitive conditions, with no running water or electricity. Their cultural isolation was acute as well. The Somali Bantu were sometimes referred to by Somalis as the "ooji"—from the Italian word *oggi,* meaning "today"—for their perceived inability to think beyond the moment, a misunderstanding rooted in the different way the agrarian Somali Bantu conceived of time.

Somali Bantu slated for resettlement in the United States, it was clear, would need a great deal of help. They would need to learn English and how to fill out job applications, and they would have to acclimate themselves to the mores and expectations of the American workplace. They would have to accomplish their assimilation while somehow coping with the psychological aftermath of extreme trauma. Many Somali Bantu women had been raped, and not a few of the refugees had seen family members and fellow villagers slaughtered before their eyes. One Somali Bantu I met told me with good humor about his initial puzzlement over window blinds. Having never seen them in his time living in a windowless dwelling in Somalia or his makeshift shelter at a Kenyan refugee camp, he had no idea how they worked or what they did.

FEW IN CLARKSTON knew anything about the history of Somali Bantu when they learned through media reports that another wave of refugees was coming to their town. But some, like Karen Feltz, the anthropologist councilwoman, began to do some research. What she found alarmed her. She understood that the Bantu would need a great deal of help, but she was unclear about who exactly was going to provide it. The resettlement agencies were underfunded and overwhelmed as it was. Feltz wondered if the agencies were even aware of the magnitude of the challenge that awaited them. She began to ask questions. Feltz wanted first to know where exactly in Clarkston the agencies planned to house the newly arrived Bantu refugees. The agencies said they planned to scatter the Bantu around the various apartment complexes in town, wherever they could find vacancies. The Bantu, Feltz learned, would be living in the same complexes as many of the ethnic groups that historically had persecuted them.

When Feltz heard this, she said, she "had a fit."

"These people are afraid of the police to begin with," Feltz said. "If something happened, they would never come forward and say anything. Who are they going to tell? They think everybody's out to get them. The people they're living with—who raped their women, stole their children, and murdered their men? Do you think they're going to say anything? These people would be living lives of terror!"

To Feltz and many others in Clarkston, the housing plan encapsulated everything that was wrong with the way refugee resettlement was being handled in their town. The federal government didn't provide the agencies with enough money to do the job required of them, and the agencies—in addition to lacking a basic understanding of the plights of the people they were resettling—weren't willing to admit that they were too overwhelmed to do the job. So the refugees kept coming.

Ultimately, Feltz believed, two groups of people would pay the price for this collective failure: the refugees themselves, and the residents of Clarkston, a small town with few resources and no expertise in handling the cultural assimilation of a group of traumatized and impoverished East African farmers into the American South.

Anger over the Bantu resettlement plan prompted Mayor Swaney to act. He reached out to the heads of the agencies to see if they might be willing to answer questions from locals at a town hall meeting. The provost of Georgia Perimeter College, a community college just outside the city limits of Clarkston, agreed to provide an auditorium and to act as a moderator. And representatives from the agencies, sensing a rare opportunity to speak directly to the locals, agreed to make themselves available as well. The day before the meeting, Mayor Swaney struck a hopeful tone in an interview with the *Atlanta Journal-Constitution*.

"Maybe we can find a way for everybody to work together, live together, and play together," he said.

ON THE EVENING of March 31, 2003, about a hundred and twenty Clarkston residents filed into an auditorium at Georgia Perimeter College and began to fill out index cards with questions. Agency representatives and immigration experts took their seats behind a table on stage. The provost stood to begin the question-and-answer session. He looked down at the index cards submitted from the audience. The first question was "What can we do to keep refugees from coming to Clarkston?"

The tone of the meeting scarcely improved. Residents finally gave voice to years of frustration over the resettlement process. The agency officials, taken aback by the show of hostility, became defensive. When one resident asked why the town had not been consulted in advance about the relocation of the Somali Bantu, an aid agency representative calmly reminded the crowd that this was America and the law didn't require people to ask City Hall for permission before they rented an apartment. In truth, the agencies might have been even harsher had they not had the politics of the moment in mind. Most strongly felt that without resettlement, Clarkston would've been much worse off. The agencies bargained with the landlords of those big apartment complexes, demanding that they clean up and maintain their buildings and that they cut refugee families slack on deposits and first month's rent in exchange for a steady flow of new tenants. There were already gangs, addicts, and a rougher element living in those apartments when the agencies began sending refugees to the landlords; without the refugees and the upkeep on which the agencies insisted, most in the resettlement community felt, Clarkston might have deteriorated into a slum.

Eventually, the patience of the resettlement officials and refugee advocates at the meeting wore down. Some refugee advocates in the crowd began to attack the residents as callous, and even as racist.

"Aren't you happy you saved a life?" one refugee supporter growled at Rita Thomas, a longtime resident and civic booster of Clarkston who had spoken out against the resettlement process.

"I certainly am," Thomas snapped. "But I would have liked for it to have been my choice."

At the end of the evening, most in attendance felt that rather than soothing the hostility over resettlement, the meeting had congealed it. Jasmine Majid, a Georgia state official who coordinated refugee resettlement and who had been on the stage, told an Atlanta newspaper afterward that some of the questions asked at the forum "reflect a very sad and negative aspect of Clarkston."

Locals left the meeting just as discouraged.

"It was terrible," Karen Feltz said. "We were really trying to sort things out, and make things better. But it didn't turn out that way."

Chapter Four

Alone Down South

Luma Mufleh knew nothing of Clarkston or the refugees there when she moved to the nearby town of Decatur, only a few miles west of Clarkston down Ponce de Leon Avenue. Decatur was coming into its own as a liberal enclave in mostly conservative Atlanta. There was a groovy café, the Java Monkey, a bar specializing in European beer called the Brick Store Pub, and an old-school bohemian music venue called Eddie's Attic. Luma found a job waiting tables. She made a few friends and, as if by reflex, began looking around for opportunities to coach soccer. As it happened, the Decatur-DeKalb YMCA, just down the road from the old courthouse and the home of one of the oldest youth soccer programs in the state, was looking for a coach for their fourteen-and-under girls' team. Luma applied and got the job.

Luma coached the only way she knew how—by following the example set for her by Coach Brown. She was more demanding than any of the girls or their parents expected—she made her players run for thirty-five minutes and do sets of sit-ups, push-ups, and leg lifts before each practice. And she refused to coddle them. Luma explained to her girls that they would be responsible for their actions and for meeting their obligations to the team. Players who couldn't make practice were expected to call Luma themselves; there would be no passing off the excuse-making to Mom or Dad. Likewise, if a player had problems with the way Luma ran the team—complaints about playing time, favoritism, or the like—she would be expected to raise those concerns directly with the coach.

Luma's approach did not sit well with all of her players' parents. Some were mystified as to why their daughters had to run themselves to exhaustion, while others couldn't understand why Luma punished the girls—with extra laps or time on the bench—when their parents dropped them off late for practice.

Luma's rule-making wasn't entirely about establishing her authority over the team—though that was part of it. She also believed that the team would benefit once individual players started to take responsibility for themselves. Luma herself had been coddled by her parents in an atmosphere of privilege and entitlement, and believed that she had paid for these comforts by sacrificing her self-reliance and independence. If Luma was going to coach, she was going to do so with this basic lesson as a backdrop, whether her players' parents understood it right away or not. Time would tell whether her approach produced results.

"Parents would get upset about certain things she did," said Kim Miller, a researcher at the Centers for Disease Control in Atlanta, whose daughter Maritza played on Luma's team for three years. "They'd say, 'Oh—can you believe she made them run barefoot?' or 'Oh—can you believe she made them run laps because we were stuck in traffic?' Luma was really tough. They had to take responsibility for what they did. If you were angry with the coach, it wasn't 'Go home and tell your mom.' She didn't want to hear from the mommies. She wanted the girls to be responsible."

When confronted by unhappy parents, Luma displayed a confidence incongruous with her status as a newcomer, an attitude that put off some parents and intrigued others. Once when Luma ordered her players to practice barefoot to get a better feel for the soccer ball, a team mother objected on the grounds that her daughter might injure her toes.

"This is how I run my practice," Luma told her. "If she's not going to do it, she's not going to play."

During Luma's first season as coach, her team lost every game. But over time, her methods began to pay off. Dedicated players returned, and those who didn't buy in left. The players worked hard and improved. They stopped questioning Luma's methods and began to absorb and intuit them. In her third season, Luma's twelve-and-under girls' team went undefeated and won their year-end tournament.

The players and parents who went through that experience speak about it now in near mystical terms.

"I don't usually use this word," said Kim Miller, Maritza's mother. "But it was magical. She helped cultivate them and truly gave them more skills than soccer. She helped them thrive."

Now fifteen and an active soccer player, Maritza Miller describes her time on Luma's team as life changing. "She realized from the start that it's not something just on the field," Maritza said. "It's about trust. None of my other coaches thought that way."

LUMA MADE THE team the focus of her energies in those early days in Georgia. But however fulfilling, coaching soccer couldn't distract Luma from frequent bouts of homesickness for her friends and family. She still wasn't speaking to her parents, who would hang up the phone on her if she ever called home, and she missed her younger sister Inam, who was now a teenager and no longer the little girl Luma remembered. Then in 2002, Luma's grandmother Munawar, her lifeline to her family, died in Jordan.

When Luma was grieving, her preferred therapy was to get into her daffodil yellow Volkswagen Beetle, put on some music—something fast and peppy—and simply drive. She didn't particularly know her way around Atlanta, but the unfamiliar surroundings—the strange mixture of gleaming glass office buildings, columned houses, stucco McMansions, and long, desolate stretches of worn-out row houses—distracted her with a sense of discovery. In Atlanta, one could traverse gaping boundaries of race and class by simply crossing a street.

On one of those trips, Luma found herself lost in what seemed to be a run-down area beyond the eastern side of the Perimeter, only a few miles east of Decatur. What she saw confused her. Amid the decrepit apartment complexes, the soulless strip malls, the gas stations, and the used-car dealerships, there were women walking the streets in chadors and hijabs and others in colorful African robes and head-dresses. Luma came upon a small grocery store with a sign indicating that it was a Middle Eastern market called Talars. She pulled into the parking lot, went in, and took a deep breath, filling her lungs with the old familiar smells of cardamom, turmeric, and cumin. Luma could hardly believe it. She stocked up on groceries—pita bread, hummus, and halloumi, a salty sheep and goat's milk cheese that was one of Luma's favorites—then went home to make herself a meal like her grandmother might've made.

Luma became a regular customer at Talars, and each time she visited she again confronted the strange sight of African and Middle Eastern dress on the streets. She had discovered Clarkston the way most Atlantans did—by accident—and like most of the people who drove through Clarkston, Luma was too preoccupied with her own worries to give much thought to the unusual tableau around her.

LUMA ALSO HAD to make a living, and waiting tables wasn't bringing in the sort of income she needed to survive in Atlanta. Neither did it suit her nature. Luma was better at giving instructions than taking them. She looked into the possibility of opening a franchise of an ice cream parlor chain, and when that didn't pan out, decided to start her own business, a café that sold ice cream and sandwiches, a place where people could spend the day and relax without being hassled. She found an available storefront in downtown Decatur midway between her apartment and the YMCA, and cobbled together a group of investors from the friends and contacts she'd made around Atlanta, including some of the parents of her players at the Y. In 2003 Luma opened her own café—Ashton's, named after a friend's dog—in an out-of-the-way building in Decatur alongside the still busy Atlanta-to-Athens railroad line.

Running Ashton's was tough. Luma found herself putting in sixteen-hour days, preparing food early in the morning and cleaning up late after the close. It was lonely work, but Luma had taken on the challenge of succeeding, for herself and for her investors. She still wasn't speaking with her parents in Jordan, and her desire to prove her independence to her family back home drove her to work even harder. But the plan wasn't working out. Ashton's was too far off the beaten path in Decatur to lure in enough customers to make money, and Luma found herself working longer and longer hours to keep the place afloat. She was still coaching her girls' team in the evenings, and she was exhausted.

One afternoon Luma decided to drive to Talars to pick up some of her favorite foods from back home. Distracted by her anxiety over losses at Ashton's, she inadvertently drove past the store, and had to make a U-turn in the parking lot of a dreary old apartment complex called the Lakes. While turning around, she came across a group of boys playing soccer on the asphalt. From behind her windshield she could see the boys playing the game with the sweaty mixture of passion, joy, and camaraderie she recognized from the games played in the empty lot on the other side of the fence from her grandmother's house in Amman. But unlike in Amman, the boys playing in Clarkston seemed to come from a confusion of backgrounds—they were white, black, and brown. Luma parked her car and watched.

"I stayed there for over an hour," she recalled. "They were barefoot but they were having such a good time."

The sight of boys of so many ethnicities in one place began to open Luma's eyes to what was happening in Clarkston, just down the road from her own home. She asked friends about Clarkston, including a woman she'd met in Decatur who worked with refugees at one of the resettlement agencies. Luma began to learn the particulars of the difficulties refugees faced upon arriving in the United States. At the time, thousands of refugees had already been resettled in and around Clarkston, and more were coming every month.

"I'd never questioned why they had a Middle Eastern grocery store in Clarkston," she said. "I knew there were refugees, but I had no clue about the numbers."

On another trip to the grocery store in Clarkston, Luma pulled into the same parking lot. A game was under way. Luma reached into the backseat and retrieved a soccer ball, then got out of her car, approached the boys, and asked if she could join in. The boys were wary. She was a stranger—a grown-up and a woman to boot. There were all manner of crazies in the apartment complexes in Clarkston—maybe she was one of those. But Luma also had a new ball, and the one the boys were playing with was scuffed and ragged. They reluctantly allowed her to join in. Once the game started, the boys saw that Luma could play. She set them up with quick passes and broke up attacks on her team's goal. Soon, Luma was running herself sweaty, pleasantly lost in a game with strangers. It was a rare moment of connection in a world that for Luma still seemed impenetrable and socially separate.

"It reminded me what I missed about my community at home," she said. "And at the time I felt like such an outsider."

OVER THE NEXT few weeks and months, Luma continued to stop in at the Lakes on her trips to Talars. She was getting to know the boys, learning bits about their pasts and their families' struggles. Some had just arrived and spoke little English. Her Arabic and functional French helped her communicate with kids from the Middle East and Sudan, as well as the Congo and Burundi. They began to open up, gradually, about their lives. Luma learned that the boys lived in all kinds of improvised family arrangements, often not with parents but with uncles, aunts, and cousins. In snatches of conversation she got a glimpse of the boys' isolation from the new world around them and their desire to connect. The loneliness that resulted from being uprooted was something that Luma intuitively understood. Luma also learned that pickup soccer on the town's parking lots was the only kind of soccer the refugee kids could afford; even the modest fees required to play soccer at the local public schools were prohibitively high for most of the boys' families.

Luma couldn't help but notice how much more passionate these boys were for the game compared to the girls she coached at the YMCA. They played whenever they could, as opposed to when they had to, and they didn't need the trappings of a soccer complex or the structure of a formal practice to get inspired. Luma decided that the kids really needed a free soccer program of their own. She didn't have the foggiest idea of how to start or run such a program. She certainly couldn't fund it, and with a restaurant to run and a team of her own to coach, she hardly had time to spare. But the more she played soccer in the parking lots around Clarkston and the more she learned about the kids there, the more she felt a nagging urge to engage, and to do something.

Eventually, Luma floated the idea of starting a small, low-key soccer program for the refugees to the mother of one of her players, who was on the board at the YMCA. To her surprise, the Y offered to commit enough money to rent the field at the community center in Clarkston and to buy equipment. Luma figured she could devote a few hours a week to a soccer program and still keep Ashton's running. She decided to give it a try. With the help of some friends, Luma crafted a flyer announcing soccer tryouts at the Clarkston Community Center, in English, Vietnamese, Arabic, and French. She made copies and on a warm early summer day drove around Clarkston in her Volkswagen and posted the flyers in the apartment complexes. She wasn't sure that anyone would show up.

Chapter Five

The Fugees Are Born

Perhaps no one in Clarkston was as excited to hear about the prospect of a free soccer program as eight-year-old Jeremiah Ziaty. Jeremiah loved soccer. Since arriving in the United States with his mother, Beatrice, and older brothers, Mandela and Darlington, Jeremiah had been cooped up in his family's Clarkston apartment on strict orders from his mother. She was protective to begin with, but after she was mugged on her very first commute home from her job at the Ritz-Carlton Hotel, Beatrice had taken a hard line. She wanted the boys inside when they got home from school. When Jeremiah asked his mother if he could try out for the new soccer team in town, she was unyielding.

"Certainly I say, Jeremiah," Beatrice told him, "you won't play soccer every day."

But soccer was one of the few things that could tempt Jeremiah into defying his mother.

TRYOUTS WERE TO be held on the field of the Clarkston Community Center, a dilapidated brick and cream-colored clapboard building on Indian Creek Drive that had once served as the old Clarkston High School before being abandoned by the county in 1982. The building and property were refurbished in 1994, complete with a spiffy playing field in the back, by a group of Clarkston boosters who wanted a community center for the town. At the time, the center was run by an energetic African American named Chris Holliday, who early on found that though the community center was governed by a board of trustees made up mostly of longtime Clarkston residents, it was the refugee community that seemed to embrace the center with special zeal. Cooped up in small apartments around town, they were desperate for any place to go, eager to meet neighbors—or even better, real American locals—and they signed up for English and computer classes in large numbers. As Holliday was running these programs inside the community center building, the field out back was going largely unused. When it came to figuring out what sort of activities should take place on the field, Holliday said, the refugees were nearly unanimous.

"Overwhelmingly," he said, "the refugee community kept saying 'We need soccer.'"

When the community center offered a soccer program for young kids, Holliday said, there was no question about which group— Americans or refugees—was more intent on playing.

"Refugee parents ran to get their kids enrolled," he said, laughing at the memory. "I mean, we had moms *signing people up*."

Along the way, though, some longtime residents on the board of the community center began to question Holliday's focus on programs for refugees. Like so much in Clarkston, the community center was becoming a chit in the battle over the town's identity. Art Hansen, a professor of migration studies at nearby Clark Atlanta University and a volunteer on the community center board in those days, said that he and other advocates for the refugees had begun to think of the community center as a kind of "refugee town hall." But at a dedication ceremony for the soccer field out back, Hansen said, he learned that not everyone in Clarkston felt the same way. When Hansen mentioned his delight at seeing a group of refugee children take the field to play soccer, he was rebuked by a couple of Clarkston residents who served on the center's board and the city council.

"They very clearly said they didn't like all these newcomers here," Hansen recalled. "There was this clear other sentiment saying, 'This is the old Clarkston High School. This is a Clarkston building. This belongs to the old Clarkston—the real Clarkston. Not these newcomers.'"

Emanuel Ransom, the black Pennsylvanian who had moved to Clarkston in the 1960s, had worked hard to turn the old Clarkston High School into a community center and served on its board. He felt strongly that the newcomers didn't do their part to chip in to keep the center running, and resented that the place he'd worked hard to create was becoming so closely identified with refugees.

"I've never been a refugee," Ransom explained to me over a coffee at the local Waffle House one morning, in a version of a complaint I would hear many times in Clarkston. "But I know when I was in a foreign country, I almost had to learn their culture to survive, to eat. I didn't have to become a citizen or anything—speak the language fluently—but I had to do things to get by. And I wasn't asking for anything. Anything I wanted, I had to learn it or earn it."

With the refugees at the community center, Ransom said, "Nobody wants to help—it's just give me, give me, give me."

But there was one reason that even the most xenophobic community center supporters grudgingly accepted the idea of a refugee soccer program on the new field out back: it was great PR to the world outside of Clarkston. The community center depended largely on foundation grants for funds, and grant applications featuring support of refugee programs had proven successful in securing donations for the center's budget. The fact that Luma's program was funded by the Decatur-DeKalb YMCA, which paid the community center for use of its field, didn't prevent the community center from billing itself as a home to a refugee soccer program, even if many of the center's board members would have preferred the facility to focus on programs for what Emanuel Ransom called "real Americans."

LUMA HAD LITTLE appreciation for the degree to which the community center—the home of her new soccer program—had become embroiled in the battle over Clarkston's identity when she pulled her Volkswagen Beetle into the center's parking lot on a sunny June afternoon in 2004, before her team's first tryouts. She was uncertain too about what kind of response her flyers would generate among the boys in the complexes around Clarkston. They were naturally wary. A church in town offered a free youth basketball program that doubled as a Christian outreach operation, a fact that offended Muslim families who had dropped in unawares. Luma didn't know what to expect.

But on the other side of town, Jeremiah Ziaty left no doubt about his enthusiasm for the new team. His mother was still at work when he set out from the family's apartment, a small backpack on his shoulder, ready to play.

When Jeremiah arrived, he joined twenty-two other boys on the small field out back of the community center. On the sideline, he unzipped his backpack carefully, as though it contained a fragile and precious artifact, which in a way it did: a single black oversized sneaker. Jeremiah took off his flip-flops and slipped the shoe on his right foot, leaving his left foot bare, and took the field.

Before tryouts began, a sense of puzzlement seemed to settle on the boys: Where, they wondered, was the coach? Luma was right in front of them, but a woman soccer coach was a strange sight to young Africans, and especially to the young Muslim boys from Afghanistan and Iraq. During a shooting drill at an early practice, Luma was instructing the boys on how to strike the ball with the tops of their feet when she overheard a lanky Sudanese boy talking to the others.

"She's a girl," he said. "She doesn't know what she's talking about."

Luma ordered him to stand in goal. She took off her shoes as the boy waited beneath the crossbar, rocking back and forth and growing more anxious by the moment. She asked for a ball, which she placed on the grass. Then, barefoot, as the team looked on, she blasted a shot directly at the boy, who dove out of the way as the ball rocketed into the net.

Luma turned toward her team.

"Anybody else?" she asked.

ON THAT FIRST day of tryouts, Jeremiah, in particular, played with all of the joyful abandon you might expect of an eight-year-old who had been stuck inside for months in a dark two-bedroom apartment. Soon the other boys had given him a nickname—One Shoe—which Jeremiah didn't seem to mind in the least. At the end of the practice, he took his shoe off, carefully wiped it down, and placed it in his backpack before slipping on his flip-flops and starting the two-mile walk back home.

"See you later, Coach," he said to Luma as he left the field.

"See you later, One Shoe," she said.

WHEN BEATRICE ZIATY found out her son was sneaking off to play soccer with strangers after school, all hell broke loose.

"You're too small," Beatrice scolded him. "Don't go out of the house!"

Jeremiah started to cry. And he cried. He begged his mother to let him play, but Beatrice held her ground. She wasn't going to let anything bad happen to her son. And she certainly wasn't going to be defied—after all she'd done to get the family here. Inside, though, Beatrice was torn. She knew an eight-year-old boy needed to run, to get outside. She knew it wasn't fair to keep him confined to a small apartment all the time.

"You say you have a coach," she finally said to Jeremiah. "Why you can't bring the coach to me to see?"

"Momma," he said, "I will bring her."

The conversation took place outside, in front of the Ziatys' apartment. Luma came in her Beetle and parked out front. Beatrice walked outside with Jeremiah and explained her concerns to Coach Luma: She wanted to know that her son would be safe and with an adult. She wanted to know how to get in touch with Luma if something went wrong. And she wanted to make sure that Jeremiah wasn't walking alone through Clarkston.

"She did the bulk of the talking," Luma recalled. "She said that Jeremiah was her baby and she wanted to know where he was going."

Luma promised to pick Jeremiah up before practice and to drop him off afterward. He wouldn't have to walk alone. She gave Beatrice her cell number and promised to be reachable.

"I'll treat him like he's my own kid," Luma told her. "He's going to be my responsibility."

Beatrice agreed to give the situation a try. Jeremiah climbed into Luma's Volkswagen and sat among the soccer balls and bright orange plastic cones strewn about—she used the car as a mobile equipment locker—and together they were off to practice. One Shoe had no intention of letting his mother down.

IN THOSE EARLY practices, Luma made a point not to ask her players about their pasts. The soccer field, she felt, should be a place where they could leave all that behind. But occasionally, as the kids became more comfortable with her, they would reveal specifics about their experiences in ways that underscored the lingering effects of those traumas. Luma learned that Jeremiah, for example, had been at home the night that his father was killed. Once, in an early practice, Luma expressed frustration that a young Liberian player seemed to suddenly zone out during play. Another Liberian who knew the boy told her she didn't understand: the boy had been forced by soldiers to shoot a close friend. Luma wasn't a social worker, and she had no background in dealing with profound psychological trauma. In such moments, she felt perilously in over her head.

"How do you react when someone tells you he saw his father get killed?" she said. "I didn't know."

Luma picked up on another problem facing her young players. Many had come from societies that had been fractured by war, and as a consequence they never had access to any kind of formal education. It wasn't uncommon for some refugee children to be both illiterate in their native languages and innumerate—they had never learned the simplest math skills. Without this basic education in their own languages, they were playing catch-up in schools where classes were taught in a new language many of the boys could barely understand, if at all. While the public school system around Clarkston offered English-as-a-second-language programs, the schools were overwhelmed with newcomers. To move students through the system, many refugees were placed in standard classes that, while appropriate for their ages, did not take into account their lack of schooling or their deficiencies in English. The clock was ticking on these young students; if they didn't get help and find a way to succeed in school, they would fail out or simply get too old for high school, at which point they would be on their own. Given the enthusiasm for soccer in the refugee community, Luma wondered if perhaps the game and her team could be an enticement for after-school tutoring that might give young refugees a better chance to succeed. She resolved to get help from volunteers and educators for tutoring before practices, and to require her players to attend or else lose their spots on her team.

Somewhere along the way, the team got a name: the Fugees. Luma was unsure of who exactly came up with the name, which many opposing teams assumed was a reference to the hip-hop band. But in fact it was simply short for "refugees." The name stuck, and over time began to take on its own meaning among the kids in Clarkston, one separate from its etymology. In Clarkston, the Fugees meant soccer.

That first season, the Fugees played in a recreational, or "rec," league, an informal division teams were required to play in before they could be admitted to more formal competition in the "select" grouping. There wasn't much of an equipment budget, so Luma relied on donations, which didn't always work out. A batch of jerseys given to the Fugees turned out to be absurdly large, like nightshirts. Someone donated a box of old cleats, which Luma distributed to her players. When one of those players went to kick the ball, the sole of his shoe went flying into the air to hysterical laughter from his teammates; the shoes were so old that the glue holding them together had rotted. Luma stoically refused to acknowledge the equipment problems, at least to her players. She didn't want them to get discouraged by what they didn't have. She even made a point of wearing the same clothes to practices and games—soccer shorts, a ratty green T-shirt, and her dingy Smith baseball cap—because she noticed her players almost always wore the same clothes themselves.

Luma began the work of trying to make a competitive team out of her young recruits. She had to teach them the basics of organized play—how to execute throw-ins, how to stay onside. But soon enough, a far bigger challenge began to reveal itself. Luma noticed that when she would tell the boys to divide into groups for drills, they would instinctively divide themselves according to their ethnic backgrounds or common languages. In scrimmages, boys would overlook open teammates to pass to their own kind. And each group, she learned, had its own prejudices toward others.

"The Afghan and Iraqi kids would look down at the African kids," Luma said. "And kids from northern Africa would look down at kids from other parts of Africa. There was a lot of underlying racism and a lot of baggage they brought with them."

Somehow, Luma would have to find a way to get kids from so many cultures and backgrounds to play as a unit.

"It was about trying to figure out what they have in common," she said.

WHILE LUMA WAS trying to find a way to get the kids to play together, she was also getting to know their parents, mostly single mothers. She found they needed help—in understanding immigration documents, bills, school registration, and the like. With her Arabic and French, she was able to translate documents and find help through the network of people she was getting to know in the resettlement community. She arranged appointments with doctors and social workers. Luma gave her cell phone number out to her players and their families, and soon they were calling with requests for help negotiating their new lives. Teachers learned to call Luma during crises when her players' parents couldn't be found or were at work. All the while, Luma began to marvel at the impact of even the simplest of gestures on her part. The families were extraordinarily grateful, which they showed by offering Luma tea and inviting her to dinners. Luma found herself both appreciated and needed, and couldn't help but notice how much more fulfilling this kind of work was than running Ashton's. In fact, Ashton's was losing money—and fast. Luma faced the possibility of having to close and even of declaring bankruptcy. The stress, she said, was overwhelming. She didn't want to disappoint her investors, and she had wanted more than anything to prove to her parents back home that she was capable of succeeding on her own.

"I had never failed like that before," she said. "There was a lot of shame. It was my friends who had invested in the business. Filing for bankruptcy at the age of twenty-eight was not something I had aspired to do. I was as low as when I had gotten cut off from my family. Nothing was going right."

One afternoon Luma was driving Jeremiah home when he let slip that he was hungry. Luma told him he should eat when he got home, but Jeremiah said there wasn't any food there—that it was, in his words, "that time of the month." It was a curious phrase for a nine-year-old boy. Luma probed, and Jeremiah explained that at a certain time each month, food stamps ran out. The family had to go hungry until another batch arrived. Luma was floored. She had understood that her players' families were poor, but she hadn't realized that they might actually be going hungry. She drove straight to the store and bought groceries for Jeremiah's family, but the episode stayed with her. Each night at the café, she tossed away leftover food without a thought. The idea that her players were going hungry cast her work at Ashton's in a new light.

"You're worrying if you're going to have enough people coming in to buy three-dollar lattes when just down the road there are people who can't afford to eat," she said.

The incident settled Luma's mind on the question of Ashton's. It was time for her to admit her failure and to walk away. She closed the café and filed for personal bankruptcy. But while the failure of Ashton's was a blow to Luma's ego, it also represented an opportunity to focus her life on things that she felt were more meaningful. She wanted to start a business that could employ women like Beatrice, providing them a living wage without requiring them to commute halfway across Atlanta by bus or train. With little capital, Luma didn't have many options. But she had an idea. She envisioned a simple cleaning business for homes and offices that would employ refugee mothers. She could drum up the clients through her local contacts, and work side by side with her players' mothers, who could work in the daytime while their children were at school and get home to their families in the evenings.

But mostly, Luma wanted to coach the Fugees. She let her girls' team know that she wouldn't be coaching them anymore. She was going to focus all of her energy on her new program and on trying to better the lives of the newcomers whose struggles she felt she understood. But doing so meant taking on far more responsibility than running a café. Luma felt she was ready for the challenge.

"When I got to know the families and their struggles, I knew I couldn't fail," she said. "I couldn't quit when things didn't go right. I was on the hook to succeed."

INDEED, WITH LITTLE idea of how it would all turn out and no inkling of the coming political storm around refugee resettlement in Clarkston, Luma was directing her life wholeheartedly toward the refugee community there. In the process, she slowly began to see the outlines of a larger purpose to her life in America, and she felt the warmth of a new family forming around her.

"I thought I would coach twice a week and on weekends—like coaching other kids," Luma said. "It's forty or sixty hours a week—coaching, finding jobs, taking people to the hospital. You start off on your own, and you suddenly have a family of a hundred and twenty."

The family would continue to grow, because whether Clarkston was ready or not, the refugees kept coming.

Chapter Six

Paula

Many of the refugees in Clarkston had been displaced by events far removed from their immediate lives—the decision of some despot hundreds of miles away to clear a region of a particular ethnic or political group in order to seize its resources, or the sudden appearance of soldiers in a village, fighting for a remote cause with no concern for collateral damage. For these refugees, the events that sent them running for their lives had a mysterious and unknowable quality, like a life-altering natural disaster. For others, though, there was no mistaking the reasons for their flight, the specific people who had driven them to flee, or even how their seemingly circumscribed personal stories fit into the broader political narratives of their countries and ethnic groups.

Paula Balegamire fell into the latter category. A refugee from the Democratic Republic of Congo, she had arrived in Clarkston with her six children in 2004 after escaping Africa's deadliest conflict in modern times: the second civil war in Congo—formerly Zaire—which raged from 1998 to 2002 and claimed an estimated 5.4 million lives. To get to safety in a new country, Paula had been forced to make a terrible choice: to remain near her husband, Joseph, who had been thrown into one of Congo's most notorious prisons in a political purge, and to live under constant threat of violence or death herself; or to leave her husband behind and take her children to a life in an unknown town in another hemisphere.

The long chain of dominoes that led to that aching choice first began to fall more than a hundred years before, in 1884 in Berlin, and tumbled through the twentieth century until ultimately bursting through the doorway of a small house at 19 rue Lweme in Brazzaville, the capital of the Republic of Congo, in the middle of the night on January 28, 2001.

The Democratic Republic of Congo, Paula's homeland, occupies territory deep in the heart of Africa that remained mostly beyond the reach of Western powers until the 1870s, when the Welsh-born explorer Henry Morton Stanley became the first Westerner to successfully traverse Central Africa and returned to a hero's welcome in Europe. Stanley was soon courted by King Leopold II of Belgium, a weak monarch who believed that Belgium should emulate other European powers by establishing its own colonies in Central Africa. In 1884 at a conference of European leaders in Berlin, Leopold held himself out as a kind of protector of the Congo's people and proposed the formation of a political entity there called the Congo Free State.

Leopold formed a corporation with himself as the lone shareholder and funded Stanley to return to the Congo region to build a railway deep into the jungle that would allow for the systematic looting of its natural resources, primarily rubber and ivory. Extraordinary brutality followed. Leopold's men enslaved natives and literally worked them to death. Families were separated, noncompliant villages burned, and those who disobeyed the brutal security apparatus, the Force Publique, had their right hands chopped off, or worse.

The savagery went unchallenged until a report written by a British consul named Roger Casement detailed the horrors that had befallen the people of the Congo—he estimated that three million had died, while current scholars put the number at between five and ten million—causing an uproar in Europe that gave birth to the modern human rights movement and that eventually, in 1908, forced Leopold to cede control of the Congo Free State to the Belgian parliament.

The Belgian government oversaw the Congo for another fifty-two years, during which it gradually lost control to ethnic and regional leaders. The emergence of African nationalism further weakened Belgian control of its colony, and in 1960, the Republic of Congo was granted independence. A parliament of regional leaders in Congo elected a nationalist named Patrice Lumumba as prime minister.

The new nation was really an arbitrary assemblage of ethnic groups and tribes with little in common save their location within an imposed and haphazardly drawn border, so ethnic and tribal tensions immediately set in. Lumumba, after turning to the Soviet Union for backing, was tortured and killed by a commander named Joseph Desire Mobutu, an act done with the blessing, if not the outright aid, of the CIA.

Mobutu renamed the country Zaire and appointed himself president, a post he held for thirty-two years with the support of the United States, which was eager to have a Cold War ally in the heart of Africa. Mobutu soon became the caricature of a violent, dictatorial kleptocrat. Recognizable to Westerners for his leopard-skin pillbox hat and gaudy large-frame glasses, Mobutu bought villas and yachts in Europe, flew around on the Concorde, and stashed billions of dollars in Swiss banks, including one he bought for himself. To distract the public from his misrule, he fomented ethnic rivalries and supported guerrilla movements in neighboring countries that killed countless civilians. Nevertheless, President Ronald Reagan praised Mobutu as "a voice of good sense and good will."

But when the Cold War ended, financial and political support from Washington waned. To continue funding his extravagance, Mobutu simply appropriated the national treasury, printing money whenever he needed it, which led to staggering inflation that further weakened his failing country.

An aging Mobutu supported Hutu militias in the eastern districts of his country and in Rwanda, militias that ultimately contributed to the Rwandan genocide. He then found his country destabilized when hundreds of thousands of Hutu refugees fled into refugee camps in the eastern provinces of North and South Kivu, fearing retribution from Tutsis in Rwanda. Mobutu's own army allied with Hutus in those camps, a move that led a broad coalition of Tutsis and other ethnic groups in eastern Zaire to form their own militia and join forces with the governments of Rwanda and Uganda against Mobutu. The leader of this coalition was a man named Laurent-Désiré Kabila, a former Marxist rebel who had been educated in France and was, until his rapid ascension to power, a relative unknown in Congo. Kabila's coalition defeated Mobutu's entrenched regime with surprising ease, and in May 1997, Kabila entered Kinshasa and declared himself president of a country he renamed the Democratic Republic of Congo. Mobutu fled the country for Morocco, where he died a few months later.

PAULA AND JOSEPH Balegamire were from Bukavu, the capital city of South Kivu on the border with Rwanda, which had been overrun with Hutu refugees in the wake of the Rwandan genocide. Paula taught dressmaking and her husband was an information officer at a local farmers' collective. They were Tutsis—and allied with a group in Laurent Kabila's coalition led by a military commander named Anselme Masasu Nindaga. When Kabila assumed the presidency in Kinshasa, he brought Masasu, as he was more commonly known, along with other generals to work in his new government, and the commanders in turn brought along people of their own ethnic groups and regions. The Balegamires joined up and moved from the east to Kinshasa. But Kabila soon revealed he had little interest in maintaining this broad coalition. He appointed close friends and family to government positions, began to jail political dissidents and human rights advocates, and prevented the United Nations from investigating the slaughter of thousands of refugees in eastern Rwanda, for which his own men were responsible. He soon fell out with his former ally Anselme Masasu Nindaga as well, whom he suspected of plotting a coup. In 1997 Kabila had Masasu arrested and sentenced to twenty years in prison.

During the next two years the Kabila government engaged in a relentless purge of anyone it thought might have been associated with the plots against him—especially Tutsis from eastern Congo, and anyone who had ever had anything to do with Masasu. As Tutsis from Kivu, the Balegamires were especially vulnerable. According to a report by Amnesty International, "Anyone from the Kivu region, or with links to the region, appears to have been at risk of arrest and incommunicado detention without any judicial authorization or supervision." Some were tortured, others "disappeared." Congo was descending once again into an all-out ethnic war.

Paula and Joseph began to fear for their lives. Paula took her children out of Kinshasa and headed east, traveling by bus to Rwanda and eventually traversing Lake Tanganyika to Tanzania and, later, Zambia. Eventually, Paula concluded that conditions were safe enough to return to Kinshasa, after a month on the move, but soon after she arrived with her children, violence against those from the east resumed.

In January, a group of twenty-nine men—most of them former associates of Masasu, including Joseph Balegamire—left Kinshasa in small dug-out canoes and paddled across five kilometers of the muddy Congo River to Brazzaville, the capital city of the former French colony the Republic of Congo, in an effort to escape the violence. The men took refuge in a small house on Franceville Street that had been rented by a fellow refugee from across the river. When the house became too crowded, nineteen of the men, including Joseph, moved to another small house at 373 rue Lweme, in the Plateau des 15 Ans section of Brazzaville. The men received letters from the United Nations, noting that they had been in touch with the organization—important protection should they encounter deportation threats from the local government. They sought out representatives of Amnesty International to inform them about the torture, disappearances, and killings of people from Kivu that were being carried out by the Kabila government across the river.

Eventually, Paula Balegamire and her children joined her husband in Brazzaville. The house on the rue Lweme was overcrowded with the men who had fled Kinshasa, so their wives and children stayed with other refugees around Brazzaville so as not to draw the attention of local security forces who were hostile to the refugees pouring into the city. The plan was to lie low until the UN's High Commissioner for Refugees (UNHCR) could place the families in a safe refugee camp, or even better, in a country far from the violence.

On January 16, 2001, a few weeks after the men had fled Kinshasa, a bodyguard approached Laurent Kabila at the presidential palace there and fired at least two shots into his back. The assassin, a man named Rachidi Minzele, was immediately shot and killed, taking with him the only definitive knowledge about the motives behind his deed, which spawned a confounding web of conspiracy theories. Kabila's son Joseph assumed control of the country ten days later, when Laurent-Désiré Kabila died of his wounds.

Back in Brazzaville, news of Kabila's death sent a shudder through the men who had fled Kinshasa weeks before. As they feared, the younger Kabila immediately began a crackdown against his father's political enemies—especially those associated with Anselme Masasu Nindaga. Nindaga himself was executed. Scores of others were rounded up, thrown into prison, and tortured into implicating friends, neighbors, and associates. Countless more were killed or vanished.

The crackdown didn't stop at the banks of the Congo River. Kabila's security forces had been cooperating with the government in Brazzaville to patrol the riverbanks for refugees and fleeing political rivals who could be detained as suspects in the quickly growing conspiracy. In the middle of the night of January 28, police descended on the house on the rue Lweme and arrested the men inside, including Paula's husband, Joseph Balegamire.

Paula was five months pregnant and had five children when her husband was arrested. She and the wives of the other men who had been arrested began a panicked search for their husbands. They besieged the local UNHCR office, demanding to know the whereabouts of men who had applied to the UN for safety. Pressed by the UN and Amnesty International for an explanation, the government in Brazzaville at first denied any knowledge of the men's whereabouts, then later said they had been moved to the interior of the country for their own safety. Days later, through a report on an African radio news service, the wives and families of the men learned the dreadful truth. The government in Brazzaville had handed the nineteen men over to Joseph Kabila, in obvious violation of international law, which forbids nations from sending asylum applicants back to countries where they may face harm. No one knows exactly why the men were handed over. A rumor circulated that they were given to Kabila as part of a prisoner exchange. Perhaps Kabila's government simply paid a bounty. But whatever the reason, there was little doubt about what awaited the men when they arrived into Kabila's hands.

The men were jailed in one of Central Africa's most notorious prisons: the Central Penitentiary and Re-education Center in Kinshasa, known to most locals by its old name, Makala. Makala was—and is—a place of extraordinary brutality. A 2003 U.S. State Department report on human rights in the Democratic Republic of Congo stated that at least sixty-nine people had died in the prison during the previous year, some from torture, others from malnutrition or disease. Inmates at Makala were regularly deprived of the most basic necessities. For several weeks in September 2002, the State Department reported, the prison provided inmates no food whatsoever.

The nineteen men from Brazzaville were stashed, along with other Kabila rivals and political dissidents, into a high-security section of Makala called Pavilion One. They were held incommunicado, and without formal charges. Eventually, they were lumped into a group of 135 people who were charged in the assassination of Laurent Kabila and the plotting of the supposed earlier coup attempt. In trials that were roundly denounced by human rights groups, the nineteen were eventually given life sentences. They were among the fortunate. Some thirty of the supposed Kabila plotters were sentenced to death.

The United Nations—embarrassed by the handover of men who had sought its protection to such obviously dire circumstances—responded by expediting resettlement proceedings for the wives and children of the men whose trust the institution had violated. But resettlement in Europe or the United States presented the women with a painful decision. Separated from each other and half a world away, they could not advocate for their jailed husbands as effectively as if they stayed together nearby. Further, inmates in Makala depended on family and friends to bribe guards to get them food and other basics. But Paula had her children to care for. She could not return safely to Kinshasa, and even Brazzaville was becoming risky. Congolese security forces from Kinshasa were now combing Brazzaville for Kabila's political enemies, and violence against Tutsis was becoming widespread. Paula lived in Brazzaville for nearly three more years, in a state of unrelenting fear. Her children couldn't attend school. She had no reliable income. But she held out hope that things would calm down and that her husband might be freed. At one point, it seemed possible. Kabila announced an amnesty for some of the men imprisoned at Makala, but in the end, Joseph was not among those released. The final straw came, Paula said, when she and another woman were nearly corralled by a mob intent on burning them alive. The two women escaped, and Paula resolved to get out of Brazzaville however she could. The UNHCR offered her resettlement in the United States, and in November 2004, Paula left Brazzaville with her five children, destined for Georgia.

Paula and her family—Josue, the oldest; Grace; daughter Christelle; twin boys Manace and Ephraim; and a newborn baby girl, Gloria—were placed in an apartment complex called Willow Ridge. Through the International Rescue Committee, Paula found a job as a seamstress at a factory that made sports jerseys. The work wasn't bad, but the commute was more than an hour each way, requiring Paula to leave home at five-thirty each morning. Through contacts in the refugee community, she eventually met Luma, who encouraged her sons Grace and Josue to come out to play soccer and eventually hired Paula to work at her cleaning company. Since arriving in the United States, Paula's only contact with her husband has come through telephone calls he was able to make on cell phones borrowed from the friends and family members of other inmates at Makala. Grace, who was just five when he last saw his father, said he can barely remember his face. If the family is to be reunited, Paula said, it would have to be in the United States.

"There's no point in thinking about where to go back to," she said, "because there's nowhere to go back to."

Chapter Seven

"Coach Says It's Not Good"

On September 26, 2005, a weary twelve-year-old boy named Bienvenue Ntwari slowly opened the door of his Clarkston apartment and, squinting against the sudden blinding light of the midday sun, took his first real look at America. Two days before, Bienvenue had set out with his mother, Generose, his older brother, Alex, and younger brother, Ive (pronounced EE-vay), from a refugee camp in Mozambique.

The family landed in Atlanta at night. They wandered off the airplane into a vertiginous swirl of strange images, sounds, and languages. They walked through the long corridors of the airport, past moving sidewalks, blinking murals, stands of strange-looking food, and a rush of people who all seemed to know exactly where in all that chaos they wanted to go. The family was met eventually by a caseworker from the International Rescue Committee, who helped them load their things into a car and drove them past the shimmering towers of downtown Atlanta, toward Clarkston. Along I-20, a vast and open superhighway that divides Atlanta into north and south, cars glided past with improbable speed. The streets in America were bizarrely smooth. From within this quick-flowing hallucination, it was impossible to make much sense of the images flowing by the windows. It was as if the family had been beamed magically from one world to another; they had little feeling for the miles traveled, the continents or oceans crossed, or the time elapsed. After a thirty-minute ride, the caseworker pulled into the Willow Ridge apartment complex, an assemblage of two-story buildings that sits atop a hill and abuts the roaring interstate highway they had just exited. The parking lot was quiet. Street lamps cast eerie pink-tinted orbs of light on the cracked asphalt. There was no one around. The family unloaded the car in a daze and followed the caseworker through a doorway hidden in a dark recess beneath a stairwell and into a bare-walled ground-floor apartment with mattresses on the floor. Generose, Alex, Bienvenue—"Bien" to friends and family—and Ive collapsed onto the mattresses and slept.

AS INTERMINABLE AS the journey was, it was really just the final leg of a wandering that began nearly five years before in Bujumbura, the bustling capital of Burundi, where Generose grew up and raised her boys. Bujumbura sits alongside the tranquil waters of Lake Tanganyika, at the foot of a fissured mountain range that rises sharply out of the flats and glows orange on clear days, when the sun sets over Congo to the west.

Burundi, the size of Connecticut and home to some 8.5 million, lies south of Rwanda, east of Congo, and north of Tanzania and is among the poorest countries in the world. In 2005, the annual per capita gross domestic product of the country was a mere four hundred dollars—which ranks it ahead of only the Democratic Republic of Congo and Zimbabwe among nations for which any data is available. As in Rwanda, a Tutsi minority had ruled over a Hutu majority in Burundi, with the blessing of the country's colonial stewards—first Germany and later Belgium—and continuing after independence in 1962.

In the early 1990s, though, hope for ethnic reconciliation began to emerge. In 1993, with the country's first free elections and the election of the country's first Hutu leader, a moderate intellectual named Melchior Ndadaye.

Four months later, in October 1993, he was assassinated by Tutsi hardliners. Soon after his death was announced by radio, enraged Hutus took their revenge on Tutsis, killing scores. Firmly in control of the military, Tutsi hardliners responded in kind, wiping out whole villages of Hutus. This tit-for-tat violence soon blossomed into all-out massacres. Within a year, 100,000 were dead. In the creeping ten-year civil war that followed, some 300,000 died, and countless tens of thousands fled into the mountains and into refugee camps in Tanzania and Mozambique.

In 2000, the killing was still going on. Hutu rebels fought for control of Bujumbura. Generose, fair skinned and with narrow facial features that identified her as a Tutsi, fled the city with her boys.

The family made it to Mozambique, where they lived for four years in two separate camps, hoping the whole time to hear from the United Nations office there that their application for asylum had been accepted. That day came in August 2005. The family learned they would be going to the United States, to a place called Atlanta, of which Generose was only faintly aware. She told her boys the news about two weeks before they were to depart, with strict instructions to tell no one.

"My mom told us not to go around the camp too much because she thought they might do something bad to us because they were jealous," Bien said.

Soon they were off. They flew through South Africa to New York before eventually arriving in Atlanta. It was the first time any of them had been on an airplane.

"All I remember," said Alex, now fifteen, "was that it was scary."

THAT FIRST MORNING in their apartment outside Clarkston, they awoke exhausted and disoriented. Generose groggily told her boys to gather their things and to get ready to leave again on the next stage of their journey. The boys laughed. Generose hadn't understood that they had reached their final destination, that the empty apartment where they had spent the night and where they were now gathered was where they would live. They were, in some confusing sense of the word, home.

Bienvenue wondered for a moment how much of what he remembered from the night before had been real and how much a dream. He decided to look outside. He opened the front door of the apartment and was blinded by a cascade of daylight. As his eyes adjusted, a few cars came into focus. He saw some other buildings, and some trees hovering in the distance. Bienvenue decided to venture outside. He walked up the concrete stairs to look around, and spied a boy, about his age, standing in the parking lot. Bien was nothing if not outgoing. He decided to try a few words of English out on his new neighbor.

"Hello, what your name?" he asked.

"Grace," the boy said, using the French pronunciation, *Grahss.* "Grace Balegamire."

"American?" Bien asked him.

"I'm from Congo," Grace said.

"Congo!" Bien said. *"Unasema Kiswahili?"* Do you speak Swahili? *"Ndiyo,"* said Grace. Yes.

The boys stood and talked. Bien explained that they had just arrived the night before, that he didn't know anyone or anything about America. He wanted to know what American kids were like. Were they nice? Were they different?

Grace laughed. Were they different! The boys at school, he told Bien, wore their pants low around their hips—almost to their knees, not like in Africa, where boys and men wore their pants around their waists, with belts and tucked-in shirts. American boys wore their hair long, in braids, like women. They weren't so nice either. Some had guns. They fought with each other. They made fun of people from Africa. Boys and girls got together and did things you weren't supposed to do.

It wasn't at all what Bien had expected to hear.

"He told me here in America," Bien recalled, "they got some *bad action.*"

Grace cut the conversation short. He was late, he said.

"For what?" Bien asked.

"Practice," Grace said.

"What practice?"

"Soccer practice," said Grace.

Bien loved soccer. In the camps in Mozambique, he'd played the game in bare feet with a ball made from plastic bags tied in a bundle, in friendly but fierce matches between boys from Burundi and from Congo. He fancied himself a natural, and wanted to know more. Grace explained: There was a soccer team for refugee kids like them, with lots of Africans and kids from places he'd never heard of. They played nearby. The coach was a woman. Grace offered to ask her if Bien could come to the next practice.

"I live over there," Bien said in Swahili, pointing toward the door beneath the stairwell behind them. "Come to my house and tell me what she says."

"Okay," Grace told him. "I will."

The boys went their separate ways, Grace to practice, and Bien to his new apartment to tell his brothers Alex and Ive of his discovery. *There were kids who spoke Swahili right outside, in the parking lot!* It was a big relief, and quickly transformed his view of what his life in America might be like.

"I thought we would be the only ones who spoke Swahili," Bien said. "We didn't think we'd have anybody to play with."

AT PRACTICE THAT afternoon, Grace asked Luma if he could bring a kid from Willow Ridge who had just arrived from Burundi. He didn't speak English, but he liked soccer. Maybe he was good. Grace wanted to know if he could join the team.

Luma was used to such requests. Caseworkers at the resettlement agencies often sent just-arrived kids to her, knowing that through the Fugees they might quickly make friends, that they'd be well looked after, get a chance to get exercise and, possibly, a release from some of the potentially overwhelming anxiety brought on by relocation. Her established players frequently brought along new arrivals as well. More than those flyers she posted around town at the beginning of each season, the players were her best recruiting tool.

Bien, like many of these newcomers, had arrived in the middle of a season, when the Fugees' roster was full. But Luma agreed to let him practice with the Fugees even if he wasn't eligible to play in games. He would be expected to follow the same rules as everyone else, and to show up on time or not to come at all.

That evening after practice, Grace came home to Willow Ridge to find Bien and his older brother, Alex, in the parking lot outside. Grace told Bien the news. The next practice would be the day after tomorrow, he said. They could go together. Alex could join Luma's older team with Grace's big brother Josue. The team was pretty good, Grace said, and the coach was strict. It was almost a warning. Bien wasn't intimidated, and he didn't care about rules.

"The only thing I wanted was to play soccer," Bien said later, recalling that day. "I didn't ask too many questions."

THE ARRIVAL OF new players like Bien and his brother Alex brought new talent to Luma's growing soccer program, along with new complications. Each addition potentially shifted the social balance of the team, as players connected over shared languages or cultures. Luma developed new rules on the fly to compensate. She forbade boys like Grace and Bien from speaking to each other in Swahili and required them instead to speak English—the team's lingua franca. She found she had to keep a constant lookout for emerging cliques, especially among players who were inclined to stick with their own kind.

"I'd say, 'Get in groups of four for a passing drill,'" Luma said, "and every single time people would group up with people from their own country. So I started saying to myself, 'I need a Liberian there, with a Congolese, an Afghan, and an Iraqi.'"

As the boys connected with Luma, another complicated dynamic began to take shape: they began to compete for her approval. It was perhaps true that any group of ten- to fifteen-year-old boys would jockey for the approval of an authority figure. But for the boys on the Fugees—newly arrived refugees trying to find comfort and security in a strange, often threatening environment—the craving for Luma's blessing was especially powerful. She was in many ways a surrogate parent, and like insecure siblings, the boys were on the lookout for any signs that others were favored. When Luma spoke casually in Arabic to an Iraqi or Sudanese player, other boys who didn't understand would feel left out and wounded. So Luma tried to make sure she didn't inadvertently speak Arabic, even when it was easier, and she disciplined herself not to play favorites. For her teams to work, Luma realized, everyone would have to feel they were treated fairly.

An early rivalry between two star players proved particularly instructive for Luma. Two of the most talented players on the oldest Fugees team—Jeremiah Ziaty's older brother Darlington and an Iraqi Kurd named Peshawa Hamad—spent months squabbling with each other, making cutting remarks about each other's religion and ethnicity as they battled for Luma's approval.

"They were both incredibly athletic and incredibly talented," Luma said. "And they couldn't figure out which one I liked more. Darlington didn't like that Peshawa and I spoke the same language. Peshawa didn't like that I was close with Darlington's family. He would make comments about Darlington being dark skinned. And they were both very selfish on the field."

As the team's biggest personalities, Peshawa and Darlington influenced other players, who felt pressured to take sides. So Luma set out to get the boys to work together. When she took groups of players out to movies, she made them sit next to each other. When she was invited to Darlington Ziaty's home for dinner, she brought Peshawa along. When Peshawa addressed her in Arabic, she responded in English. And in addition to subtle gestures, she laid down the law.

"She said we're all foreigners, and this is a team where everybody unites," recalled Yousph Woldeyesus, an Ethiopian player. "And she told them she was going to kick them off the team if they didn't."

The next season, Darlington and Peshawa became a dynamic scoring combination, and their team went undefeated.

BUT AS QUICKLY as the Fugees improved and came together, the teams could all fall apart from one season to the next. Players moved away and newcomers arrived, forcing Luma to start all over again with the lessons in team unity and organized soccer basics. Even from game to game, Luma had to work hard to keep her kids focused on what they had and not on the disparities with the competition in gear, uniforms, and support. The Fugees' outfits were often ragged compared to the shiny, new uniforms the competition wore. For a time they wore jerseys Luma had made out of T-shirts she bought in bulk at a local discount store. The Fugees' numbers had been written on the shirts in water-soluble ink, so as the game progressed, the numbers ran into blurry clouds on their sweat-soaked backs. The Fugees often played in mismatched socks, and they didn't have any of the fancy accessories—the matching, logoed equipment bags, which some teams had embroidered with players' names and numbers. And their sideline was always empty.

Luma noticed also that the Fugees seemed to provoke stronger reactions from the competition than had the girls' team she'd coached at the YMCA. It was as if they were some sort of Rorschach test for the people they encountered on the field. Sometimes the reactions were generous. After one game, Luma thought she was being chased by a parent from a rival team. When the man caught up with her, he said he and the other parents on his team had heard about the Fugees and wanted to know how they could help. They donated soccer balls and cleats.

But as often, the Fugees seemed to provoke hostility. Opponents sometimes mocked the Fugees' accents during play, or else asked the players why they had a "girl," as they always seemed to put it, for a coach. The father of the goalie of one of the Fugees' competitors filed a complaint with the league, accusing one of the younger members of the Fugees of threatening to slash his throat during a game, a charge the player vehemently denied. During a heated game outside Atlanta, players and even some parents directed a vulgar racial epithet at Fugees players from the sideline. Some of the trash talk was perhaps the sort that happens everywhere during the heat and frustration of competition. But much of the negativity directed at the Fugees also seemed born of resentment, from parents who had spent a small fortune on gear, soccer clinics, and team fees only to see their sons trounced by a haphazardly equipped group of kids with foreign accents. And occasionally, even the referees seemed to be piling on. They would grow frustrated at having to pronounce the names on the Fugees roster during the pregame roster check. Once, two line judges were reprimanded by a head referee for snickering when the name of a player named Mohammed Mohammed was called. Another time, a referee implied that Luma had been cheating on her team's age requirements when he saw that so many of the Fugees shared a birthday on January first. He was unaware that immigration officials often assign New

Year's Day as a birthday for refugees whose parents don't know their children's actual dates of birth. Luma was doubly offended by what the allegation said about her intelligence.

"I mean, come on," she said. "If I'm going to cheat I'm going to come up with something better than that."

THE HOSTILITY THE Fugees encountered, the deficiencies in their gear, their lack of support on the sidelines, seemed only to solidify the bonds among this otherwise disparate group of boys. They sensed they were underdogs and connected with each other over the prospect of evening the score once the whistle blew.

Luma grew closer with her players' families too. She identified with them. She too had left the familiarity of home for a new and sometimes alienating place. She understood what it was like to feel like an outsider, and she'd come especially to value friendships in this new place. Families in extreme poverty would ply Luma with dinners of rice, mantu, and freshly baked Afghan bread, leafy African stews, and foofoo, the doughy, elastic porridge made from ground cassava root. And over time they learned her preferences. Beatrice Ziaty, for example, liked to make especially fiery stews, but she cut back on the peppers whenever Luma was coming over because she knew the coach couldn't handle the hot food. And Luma's proclivities wore off on her impressionable young players as well, in sometimes unexpected ways. Once, she had taken Jeremiah to the grocery store when she agreed to babysit him for a night for Beatrice. In the supermarket, Jeremiah asked his coach to buy bacon, one of his favorite foods, so they could have it for breakfast. Luma explained that as a Muslim, even a secular one, she didn't eat pork, and suggested they pick turkey bacon instead.

A few weeks later, Beatrice herself was at the store, Jeremiah in tow, when she reached for a package of bacon at the meat counter.

"You can't eat that," Jeremiah told his mother. "Coach says it's not good."

Beatrice told her son that she liked pork—it was one of her favorite foods—and that as a Christian she was free to eat it as she pleased, which she intended to do. But Jeremiah wouldn't budge: he told his mother he wouldn't be getting near the stuff. Coach said it was no good. When I met the Ziatys, they had not had pork in their apartment in more than a year.

"Since Coach can't eat it, he will not eat it," Beatrice explained with a shrug.

So what do you do? I asked.

"I don't buy it!" Beatrice said.

But even as the Fugees congealed into a family, the world around them was still roiling.

Chapter Eight

"They're in America Now— Not Africa"

In January 2006, a Clarkston resident and Nigerian immigrant named Chike Chime was driving to a local pharmacy to buy some prescription eyedrops when he looked in his rearview mirror and saw a Clarkston police cruiser with its lights flashing. Chime (who pronounces his name CHEE-kay CHEE-may) puzzled over what he might have done wrong. He wasn't speeding—that he was sure of. He had just pulled out of the driveway of his apartment complex and hardly had a chance to accelerate when the cruiser's lights began to flash. Chime also wondered why he had been singled out. His vehicle had been hemmed in by a slow-moving car in front and another car behind; all three vehicles were moving along the narrow space on Montreal Road at a crawl. As he pulled his 2005 Honda Accord onto the shoulder and waited for the officer to approach, Chime held out hope that it had all been a misunderstanding and that he'd soon be on his way.

The officer behind the wheel of the cruiser was Timothy Jordan, a

Clarkston police officer hired by Chief Charlie—Chollie—Nelson and who had a troubled past. Jordan had been fired from another police force in the area for excessive use of force, and was found "unfit" to serve as a police officer in a psychological review, in part, the therapist wrote, because of his volatile temper. Jordan said he informed Chief Nelson about his past but was hired anyway. Another officer was assigned to work with Jordan for a time, to monitor his behavior. But by the time he pulled over Chike Chime in January 2006, Jordan was working the beat alone. Even so, there would be a witness to his interaction with Chime, in the form of a video camera mounted on the dashboard of his Clarkston Police Department cruiser.

AT FIRST GLANCE, Chike Chime appeared a typical, newly arrived Clarkston refugee. He had a dark complexion and spoke with a pronounced African accent. In fact, Chime had been in the United States for nearly fifteen years. He had come voluntarily as an immigrant, not as a refugee, for the same reason so many immigrants come to the United States—to make a better life for himself, to take advantage of economic opportunity not available to him in his home country of Nigeria. Chime lived for six years in Queens, New York, before moving to Atlanta, which he found more open and more accepting of a Nigerian immigrant than New York had been.

"It was more multiculturally advanced than New York," Chime said. "All races seem to be doing very well here. Discrimination wasn't as bad. I was impressed because you can get a job, you can live in a decent house, and you can start a small-scale business with not much money."

Chime was determined to do just that. He had sold insurance in New York and thought he could make a business of it in Atlanta, where the steady flow of immigrants and refugees provided a market for reliable, low-cost insurance policies for their cars and homes. For start-up capital, Chime pawned his car for $1,500, then hung a shingle in a modest strip mall just outside of Clarkston.

In the intervening eight years, Chime's business had grown steadily. His company was grossing some $120,000 a year, $50,000 of which Chime counted as profit. He had employees and had become well known in the community, where he supplemented his income by helping newcomers with their tax returns. He thought of himself as a walking embodiment of the American dream, and in fact, in Clarkston, Chime stood out for his success. He dressed well and every few years leased a new car. But his newly leased cars seemed to attract scrutiny and even hostility from local police officers who were used to seeing refugees riding around in beat-up vehicles with dented bumpers and sagging suspensions.

"I have a dark-skinned pigment and I lease new cars," Chime said. "You can't have dark skin and a new car in Clarkston without harassment."

It was after nine o'clock and dark when Jordan approached Chime's vehicle on the shoulder of Montreal Road. Jordan carried a large flashlight, not a standard-issue model, but a heavy light with a long metal casing like a baton. He had bought it himself. Jordan approached the car with his flashlight on and shone it in Chime's eyes. His tone was friendly; Jordan asked Chime how he was doing, and Chime, still in his car, asked the officer what he had done wrong. If Jordan assumed Chime was a recently arrived refugee, this inquiry might have startled him. Most refugees in Clarkston were terrified of police officers. Chime, though, had been in the United States long enough to know his rights and to understand the requirement of probable cause for traffic stops.

Officer Jordan seemed not to appreciate Chime's question. He ordered Chime to get out of the car and to produce his driver's license.

"I stopped you for speeding," Jordan said, his voice sharpening.

"I wasn't speeding. I just—" Chime responded.

Jordan snapped. He lashed out with his fists, grabbing Chime by his lapels and slamming him back against the car. Jordan then spun Chime around. Now Chime had his hands up and was leaning over the trunk, with Jordan, who on the video appears a full foot smaller than Chime, on his back. Chime protested that he was trying to get his driver's license from his wallet, as Jordan had ordered. But Jordan was now in full-on confrontation mode. He grabbed Chime around the head, which he pushed toward the ground, and twisted Chime's arms behind his back. Chime was now pleading for mercy, but with his arms behind his back and Jordan shoving his head down, Chime began to lose his balance, and to tip over toward his right. At this moment, Jordan, holding Chime's arms behind his back with one hand, took his metal flashlight and with a roundhouse motion bashed Chime on the back of the head.

Chime wasn't sure what had hit him. He was stunned, and fell toward the pavement with Jordan on top of him, pressing his face into the asphalt. Jordan reached in his belt and pulled out a small can of pepper spray, or actually, cayenne oil, a more powerful form of pepper spray that often causes severe swelling in the eyes and faces of those unlucky enough to get a dose. Clarkston Police Department regulations required officers to carry two bottles of water in their squad cars in order to rinse the substance from the faces of any suspects on which they'd had to discharge the chemical. Jordan placed the nozzle against Chime's face and eyes and pressed the button. Chime cried out, and was silent—he fainted, he believes. The video camera captured Jordan's next words to a now flaccid Chime.

"It's you—it's Africans," Jordan said. "I have nothing but problems from you guys. Always love to argue. That's why there's so much crap going on around here—because you guys don't understand I've got a job to do."

Chime felt his face and windpipe swelling from the cayenne oil. His head was throbbing from the flashlight strike. Jordan never offered to rinse the pepper oil from Chime's eyes. At one point on the tape, as Chime whimpered in the backseat of the cruiser and complained about the chemical, Jordan told him, "I hope it burns your eyes out."

At some point, Jordan apparently got spooked by Chime's condition. He called an ambulance. Chime remembers that it seemed to take forever to arrive. The medics rinsed Chime's face and flushed his eyes with water, providing some relief. When Chime revived, the medics gave Jordan the all-clear to take him away. Chime was booked on a variety of charges, including speeding and resisting arrest. It was a Friday night at the DeKalb County Jail, and in the confusion of his booking, no one told Chime that he might be eligible for bail. Chime had no one at home to notice his absence; he and his wife had separated. So he sat in jail for one night, and another, and yet another, essentially lost in the system. As he waited among a population of much tougher and younger men, Chime's greatest worry was not for his physical safety so much as for the business he'd worked twelve years to build.

"Some of my customers thought I was dead," Chime said. "And some of my tax customers thought I'd run away with their refund checks."

The incident involving Chike Chime and Officer Jordan underscored the degree to which tensions remained in Clarkston some fifteen years or more after resettlement began. While some sought to write off Jordan as simply a rogue cop with an anger-management problem, months later, in the relative calm of a lawyer's office during a deposition related to the incident, he was able to articulate the frustration he and many others felt toward people like Chime who were changing the social landscape around Atlanta and who, in his view, weren't doing enough to adapt to local customs.

"They're in America now," Jordan said of the immigrants and refugees. "Not Africa."

Chapter Nine

Get Lost

The Fugees themselves were not immune to the continued tensions between refugees and some locals. At about the same time as the incident between Chime and Jordan, problems began to develop between the team and its hosts at the Clarkston Community Center, where the Fugees practiced. Emanuel Ransom, a board member at the center who had long criticized the refugee community for not contributing more to the center's upkeep, thought the Decatur-DeKalb YMCA, which sponsored the Fugees, should pay more for the program's use of the field. And after some refugee teenagers got into a fight near the field, Ransom insisted that the Y hire security guards. The Y balked. While her sponsors and hosts squabbled, Luma tried to stay focused on her players and their families. But late in the spring season of 2006, she received a call from an executive at the YMCA who told her that the relationship between the Y and the center had broken down completely. The Fugees, Luma learned, were no longer welcome to play at the center at all.

Luma still had games to play that spring, so she scurried to find a place for her team to practice. She eventually found an unused field a few miles outside of Clarkston and managed to borrow a bus from the YMCA to shuttle her players back and forth from the apartment complexes to practice. It wasn't a long-term solution, financially or logistically. Luma didn't have unlimited use of a bus, and in the autumn season, a few months away, it would be dark by the time Luma could get the kids bused to a field outside of town. Luma didn't know what she would do for a permanent fix, so she focused on the remaining games, and vowed to work on the field issue over the summer.

AT THE END of a soccer season, Luma was usually exhausted. She liked to take a break to recover, to spend a little time visiting friends from Smith or go to the mountains of western North Carolina, where she would turn off her cell phone and lose herself in the cool air and calming perfume of the laurels and rhododendrons. In a quiet moment before leaving Clarkston to recuperate, Luma logged on to Google Earth and scanned a satellite view of the town for open spaces. From orbit, Clarkston is a jumble of rectangles around gray splotches of asphalt—all those apartment complexes—nestled alongside the white vein of I-285 and indistinct from the confusion of angular shapes and shadows that emanate from downtown Atlanta in a pattern of gradually decreasing density. Swaths of green were few and far between. There was a jade-tinted rectangle in the middle of Clarkston, however: Armistead Field in Milam Park. It was less than a half-mile from the old community center field, and easily accessible from all corners of Clarkston. Perhaps that would work. Luma would need permission from Mayor Swaney, who recently had been reelected to a second term. No telling what that would entail. But Luma resolved to take the matter up when she was rested. August, and the beginning of a new season, was still a long way off.

IN THE SPRING of 2006, about the time Luma learned the Fugees had been booted from the community center field, a twenty-six-year-old Sudanese refugee named Nathaniel Nyok decided to organize a soccer team in Clarkston. Nyok, who lived in Clarkston, was one of the Lost Boys, a group of young men from southern Sudan who had been separated from their families during a civil war between the Muslim and Arab north and the Christian and African south. The boys had endured unimaginable misery in a years-long hegira through the Sudanese wilderness—crossing rivers full of crocodiles and scrubland roamed by ravenous lions—before making it to a series of refugee camps across the border in Kenya and Ethiopia. Nyok had been separated from his family during fighting when he was eight years old. With other orphans, he had made it to Kakuma, a sprawling, water-starved refugee camp of more than seventy thousand in an arid corner of northwestern Kenya, where he lived for ten years before he was accepted for resettlement, along with thousands of other Lost Boys, in the United States. One hundred and fifty of the Lost Boys had been resettled in and around Atlanta, and many of them, like Nathaniel Nyok, ended up in the apartments of Clarkston. Resettlement had been hard on the Lost Boys, but they endured the difficulty by relying on one another. Their main escape was soccer, and so Nathaniel Nyok had no problem recruiting players for a club team he started and called simply the Lost Boys Soccer Team.

"We grew up playing soccer," Nyok said. "We are still young and so we just want to play and keep our game alive. Some of us still have this trauma of not having our family, our parents. So we just want to have a little fun."

Nyok and his team needed a place to practice and noticed that the field in Milam Park, which was owned and maintained by the City of Clarkston, was hardly ever used. Armistead Field, as it was called, was the town's general-purpose field. A large rectangle with a blanket of rich Bermuda grass, Armistead was surrounded by thick stands of pine trees and sat at the foot of a hillside that offered perfect, bleacher-like viewing. At opposite ends of the field, there were rusty chain-link backstops, the vestiges of a long-defunct Little League baseball program. Lately, there was almost no activity on the field at all. It was just a giant virginal pitch of green that to Nyok seemed almost to plead for soccer. There was one hitch: a small sign affixed to the chain-link fence around the field warned that no one was to use the field without permission from City Hall.

Nathaniel Nyok had been in the area long enough to know that Clarkston was a town of rules. Cops doled out traffic tickets to driv-

ers for violations that seemed impossibly arcane to many newcomers. One local refugee restaurant owner who had undertaken a small
remodeling project in his restaurant without the proper permit had
been handcuffed and carted away to jail. Signs in Milam Park noti-
fied would-be picnickers that they needed to obtain permission from
City Hall before so much as eating a sandwich in the shade of the
large wooden pavilions there, and as a result, the pavilions remained
mostly empty on even the balmiest summer Saturdays. There was
even a sign in Milam Park notifying visitors that simply walking a
dog on the park grounds, even leashed, would bring a fine of no less
than five hundred dollars. Clarkston, it was clear, was a town that
liked things just so.

Nyok didn't want any trouble for himself or for his team. Despite
the urge to hop the fence and start playing soccer immediately on
Armistead Field, he did as the sign there demanded: he called City
Hall to ask for permission. Nyok was referred by a clerk at City Hall
to a man known to most in town simply as Coach Cooper, a onetime
Little League coach who, Nyok was told, oversaw scheduling of the
fields in Milam Park. Nathaniel called Cooper, who was pleasant and
happy to schedule the Lost Boys for use of Armistead Field. So late
one afternoon, Nyok and his friends went to the park to scrimmage.
It wasn't long before the first squad car showed up from the Clarkston
Police Department.

"They claimed it was neighbors who called and told on us," Nyok
said. "We said, 'We don't drink, we don't make noise, we don't cause
any problems—why can't we play?' They said, 'We can't tell you, but
you have to leave the field.'"

Nyok and his teammates left the field, certain there had been some
kind of misunderstanding. Nyok called Coach Cooper, who confirmed that the Lost Boys had permission to play. Again they took
the field to practice, and again the police came. When Nyok asked for
an explanation, he said, the police refused to respond.

"The police were rude," he recalled. "They would intimidate us
every time they came."

Nyok was now annoyed and determined to get some answers. He
went to City Hall and asked to speak with Mayor Swaney. Swaney
denied any knowledge of the situation and told Nyok to take it up
with the police chief. The chief too claimed ignorance and told Nyok

that Coach Cooper handled the schedule for Armistead Field. Nyok called Cooper. Cooper gave the Lost Boys permission. The Lost Boys showed up to practice. The Clarkston Police arrived and told them to leave.

This absurd process went on over the course of several weeks, until the Lost Boys Soccer Team had been ordered off the field at least eight times. The last time, Nyok said, both he and the police were fed up. When the police arrived, he asked them why they were interfering with his right to assembly as guaranteed by the United States Constitution. The police were in no mood for a lesson on constitutional law from a Sudanese refugee.

"They gave us a warning that myself and some of my assistants would be arrested," Nyok said. "I wanted to talk to them but they'd tell me, 'Keep quiet or you will go to jail.' I was quite upset. I decided I don't want to get in trouble for soccer."

Nathaniel Nyok and his friends were worn down, and thought they finally understood the reason behind the treatment they were receiving from Clarkston town officials.

"It came into our mind that it's because we are not from this country," he said.

Nyok and his friends were disappointed not to have a place to play soccer. But they were more upset about what the whole strange episode seemed to tell them about their status in their new home. They didn't feel welcome, Nyok said. They felt like outsiders.

"When I came to America I heard it was the land of opportunity, and indeed it was," said Nyok. "But on that particular day, I was disappointed. It was too bad for me and my team. We live in Clarkston. If we can't play in our city, where can we play?"

IN JULY, A little more than a month before tryouts for the Fugees' fall season, a reporter from the *Atlanta Journal-Constitution* named Mary Lou Pickel caught wind of the dispute between Mayor Swaney and the Lost Boys over use of the field in Milam Park. Pickel interviewed the mayor and Nathaniel Nyok and published news of the dispute in a succinct 633-word article. "The Lost Boys of Sudan want to practice soccer in their new hometown of Clarkston," Pickel wrote. "But when the refugees play it usually ends with the police telling them to, well, get lost."

"There will be nothing but baseball down there as long as I am mayor," Mayor Swaney said in the story. "I don't have no beef with nobody. But I do have a problem with these big guys playing soccer because those fields weren't made for soccer."

The mayor's comments puzzled Nathaniel Nyok. In his conversations with the mayor over use of the field, he said, the mayor had never mentioned any prohibition on "big guys" playing there—or any ban on soccer at all. He'd simply referred them to Coach Cooper. Something didn't quite make sense to Nyok. Why would the mayor send him on a wild goose chase involving the police chief, Coach Cooper, and numerous Clarkston police officers if the issue were simply that there was a rule against adults playing soccer in the park? Something else didn't follow. Whatever a large green rectangle of grass has been *made for,* Nyok felt, it could probably sustain plenty of other activities—football, soccer, ultimate Frisbee, lawn bowling, doing cartwheels, sunbathing—without upsetting the cosmic order. But even so, there was a more explicit problem with the mayor's argument that, as he'd put it, "those fields weren't made for soccer." In the corner of the parking lot above the disputed patch of grass in Milam Park, there was a cracked and aged sign that in faded lettering proclaimed the name of this public space to any who might pass by—ARMISTEAD FIELD. Beneath those words, three simple, hand-painted illustrations, sun-bleached but still decipherable, declared exactly what sorts of games the park's founders intended Clarkston's residents to play on the field. There was a drawing of a baseball, a football, and, just as prominently, a patchwork orb of geometric shapes clearly recognizable as a soccer ball.

IN FACT, MAYOR Swaney was not alone among politicians around the country in his consternation over the "soccer problem." Controversies over the use of public park space for soccer have long been part of the game's history in the United States. But in recent years, disputes over soccer in public parks were occurring more frequently around fast-growing cities like Atlanta, due largely to the influx of immigrants—particularly Latinos—from soccer-playing cultures around the world. Unable to get field time on park space set aside for more traditional American sports like baseball and football, soccer enthusiasts around Atlanta were moving their games to whatever open spaces they could find. In Doraville, a suburb north of Atlanta, a group of Latino immigrants had provoked a public outcry by playing soccer in a town cemetery.

A group of local white kids tossing a Frisbee in a cemetery would probably not make the newspapers. But soccer seemed to be different, and indeed the Doraville cemetery incident—and the town mayor's angry reaction—received coverage in the local press. Soccer, perhaps more than ever, had become a conspicuous symbol of cultural change. The sight of a large group of Latino men taking over a public space as if it were their own—to play a foreign-seeming game, no less— seemed to gall those Americans who were growing fed up with immigration, legal or otherwise.

In justifying his soccer ban in Clarkston, Mayor Swaney had cited an argument public officials commonly deployed against the sport: the grass defense. It was a firmly held belief among soccer's detractors that the game was harder on turf than other sports. There was something to the charge. Americans typically played soccer in highly structured settings; kids joined teams, which were part of leagues, which scheduled games well in advance. Parents showed up a half hour before game time, bivouacked with folding chairs, blankets, and a picnic lunch, then, after the game, broke camp and headed home, after which the field—usually at a large, well-maintained soccerplex—had time to recover. Immigrants tended to play soccer more the way American youths play basketball in public parks—in spontaneous pickup games that went on all day. It was also true that many soccer-playing immigrants to America came from poor nations where the game was less likely to be played on grassy fields than on rectangles of bare earth on which grass could never take root for the constant use. Poor immigrants and refugees from war-torn regions, it's probably fair to say, do not share Americans' collective obsession with lawn care.

And yet, sorting out fair and responsible use of playing fields in public parks was not among society's more insurmountable problems. All around the country, in fact, progressive city and county governments were taking steps to accommodate soccer's growing popularity, by developing scheduling systems so that fields could be shared for multiple uses, and in the case of DeKalb County, in which Clarkston was situated, converting less trafficked fields for soccer-specific use. In Clarkston, accommodating soccer would have been easier than in most places for the simple reason that *there was no competition for field time in Milam Park.* The Little League baseball and football teams in town had folded. No adult sports leagues had asked City Hall for use of the field. No one besides the Lost Boys soccer team, it seemed, actually wanted to play sports on Armistead Field.

Of all the episode's strange details, this one puzzled Nathaniel Nyok the most. In the weeks following the *Atlanta Journal-Constitution* story, he would drive by Milam Park to have a look at the activity there, expecting to see all those baseball teams Mayor Swaney was looking out for. But Nyok saw no baseball teams or anyone else—just a beautiful green meadow, neatly mowed and seeming to cry out for someone to roll some kind of ball across it.

"It was empty," Nyok said, confusion still in his voice. "Indeed, there were no people on the field."

WHEN LUMA HEARD about Swaney's comments in the Atlanta newspaper, her heart sank. It was midsummer. Tryouts for the Fugees' fall season were fast approaching, and she had hoped to hold them on the very field that Swaney had declared off-limits to soccer. His statement that the park was reserved exclusively for baseball had seemed unequivocal. Luma concluded she would have to make other plans. She had just a month to find the Fugees a new home field within walking distance of the apartment complexes where her players lived. Since the Fugees had almost no budget, save the small amount the Decatur-DeKalb YMCA had put into equipment and occasional use of a small bus to get to away games, Luma wouldn't be able to pay much, if anything, to rent a field. Her options were few.

Administrators at the YMCA offered to help out, and after a few weeks, they called Luma to let her know they'd found a solution: a field out back of Indian Creek Elementary School, just across the Clarkston town line on one of the town's main drags. Luma had driven past Indian Creek Elementary School countless times without ever realizing that there was a field out back. One afternoon in July, she got in her car and drove to see her team's new home.

When she saw the field at Indian Creek Elementary, Luma was stunned. It was a rutted, gravelly moonscape of gray Georgia chalk, with a few tufts of grass and weeds on the fringes. The field and surrounding asphalt track were covered with glass from broken bottles, and there were no soccer goals—only a couple of rusting and wrenched chain-link backstops. Despite the field's condition, there was a crowd. Members of the Clarkston refugee community were taking their afternoon strolls around the track. Young men were playing their own pickup games of soccer on the field. There was a jungle gym alongside the track, where parents watched their toddlers tumble about. A basketball court alongside the field drew a crowd of young men who went back and forth between playing hoops and sitting in their cars, smoking blunts and sipping beer from cans in brown paper bags. As one of few open spaces in Clarkston available to the public, the field at Indian Creek Elementary was certainly well used, but it was a rotten place to run a youth soccer program.

"There was broken glass everywhere, electrical wires hanging down," Luma said. "And mass chaos."

LUMA LIKED TO run her practices in private, where her players were free of distractions. The field at the community center was in a secluded bog behind the town library, away from the social flow. The field at Indian Creek, on the other hand, was something like the refugees' town square. The field at the community center was fenced, and Luma had no problem running off her players' friends who stopped by after school to heckle them as they submitted to her regimen of running and calisthenics. At Indian Creek, anyone could wander onto the field, and there was little Luma could do about it.

The field did have a few things to recommend it. For one, it was easily accessible to the apartment complexes around Clarkston, some of which were visible through the gangly stand of loblolly pine trees on the field's northern side. The elementary school itself had classrooms, where Luma could run tutoring for her kids before practice. Perhaps best of all, the field was free. The principal of Indian Creek had given the Fugees use of the field with the understanding that she wasn't offering much: there were no lights, no soccer goals, no bathrooms.

Luma resolved to put the best face on the new field. There were no bathroom timeouts during soccer games, she would tell her players, for example, so there would be no bathroom breaks during practice either. But if pressed, Luma would admit the situation with the field made her angry—at Mayor Swaney, at the folks who ran the community center, and even at her sponsors at the YMCA, who, she felt, should've worked harder to meet the community center board's demands, even if they were unreasonable. Another thought nagged Luma. She knew that if a soccer team of well-to-do suburban kids were assigned to play on a field of sand and broken glass, their parents would call the team's sponsors, the league—or someone—in protest. The parents of the Fugees' players were seen as powerless, she believed, and unlikely to make much noise, so no one thought much about shunting the team off to such a dire environment. Her team would be playing at a marked disadvantage.

THE SITUATION WITH the field underscored a frustrating reality for Luma. She aspired to build the Fugees into a well-organized program that provided refugee children with the sorts of opportunities— athletic, educational, or otherwise—available to better-off American kids. But for now, the Fugees' organization consisted of one woman running practices on a ragtag field while scrambling off the field from one crisis to the next. Luma realized she needed help, and she began to recruit from the pool of volunteers she interacted with when dealing with refugee families. The catch, of course, was that Luma couldn't afford to actually pay a salary. She would have to find someone as passionate about the work as she was.

In 2005, through the Balegamire family, Luma had met a Nebraskan named Tracy Ediger who had moved to Georgia to work with refugees. Ediger had grown up on a corn and soybean farm west of Lincoln in a strict evangelical Christian family. She and her three sisters attended church three times a week, rarely watched television growing up, and had each enrolled at Christian colleges after high school. Tracy studied biochemistry and French as an undergraduate and had gone on to pursue an MD-PhD at the University of Nebraska Medical Center, an intensive eight-year degree that portended a career as a doctor or medical researcher. But the program had worn her down. Deprived of sleep and surrounded by the gravely ill and the dying, Tracy began to fear that she was losing her capacity for empathy.

"I was tired and exhausted and I started to feel like I was numb to everything," she said. "It was like, 'Uh-oh. What have I gotten myself into?'"

Tracy completed her degree but along the way realized that a career in medicine wasn't for her. But she didn't have the faintest idea of what else she might do with her life. After graduation, she got in her car and drove to Maine, where she worked temporary jobs and waited for a kind of eureka moment to give clarity to her career search. But that moment never came.

"I was trying to figure out what I was going to do, and I came up with nothing," Tracy recalled. "And I'm supposed to be making plans for the rest of my life."

Tracy headed south to be with one of her sisters, who had decided to volunteer at Jubilee Partners, a Christian-run facility in the woods near Comer, Georgia, that serves as a transition point for refugee families who have just arrived in the United States. Tracy joined up as well and spent time teaching English to just-arrived Somali Bantu refugees for fifteen dollars a week. The experience, she said, was cathartic. While Tracy fretted over her own career, she was working with people who had been through dislocation and war and who still managed to show kindness to the strangers around them.

"You'd sit on the porch, and you wouldn't be able to talk but somehow you always felt welcome," she said. "In spite of what they've been through and despite our lack of commonality, they were all generous and friendly and open. It's very different than the way that people live in the U.S. because we're so driven and we're so busy all the time."

At Jubilee, Tracy said, she began to see the stress she felt about her own career in a different light.

"It made me feel that my questions were not nearly as important as I'd made them out to be," she said.

Tracy worked at Jubilee on that fifteen-dollar-a-week salary on and off for the next year and a half. Along the way, she would go to Atlanta to check on refugees who had passed through Jubilee during their resettlement in Clarkston, people like Paula Balegamire from Congo, whose sons Grace and Josue now played for Luma on the Fugees. Through Paula, Tracy met Luma, who idly mentioned that she was looking for a coordinator for her soccer program—someone who could handle logistics and head the tutoring operation. Tracy was reticent; as a country girl she had no intention of moving to a big city like Atlanta, but she kept running into Luma through Paula's family. Each time, Luma mentioned that she was looking for help. As Luma and Tracy got to know each other, they found they had something powerful in common.

"We had the same feeling that with refugee families we felt at home in a way that we didn't feel in the rest of our lives," she said.

Tracy was still on the fence in the spring of 2006 when she went to watch the Fugees play and to cheer on Grace. She found the soccer mildly interesting, but there was a moment after the game that particularly affected her. The players were walking off the field at an old football stadium where youth soccer games were now played, when Tracy spotted Grace, a boy she had met just after his family had arrived in the United States and who she recalled as shy and scared.

"I was standing at the top of the stadium watching the kids walking up the steps and I saw the look on Grace's face and the way he was interacting with his teammates," Tracy said. "He was smiling this big smile and looked really happy. I thought to myself, 'I could do a tutoring program for these kids.'"

In the summer of 2006, Tracy agreed to join the Fugees for a year. She would have no salary—but she had no debts, and her car, an old 1990 Chevrolet S-10 pickup she'd bought from her father for $900, was paid for. Tracy figured she could pick up a part-time job in Atlanta to make ends meet. For the Fugees, she would serve as team manager, a job that included everything from driving the YMCA's bus to running tutoring sessions for Luma's players. She would also apply the research skills she'd honed in graduate school to ferreting out funding opportunities and grants for the program. Beyond that, Tracy figured she'd make it up as she went along. In retrospect, she said, she didn't quite realize what she was getting into.

"I didn't have any idea that this would take over my life," she said.

———

IN LATE JULY, Luma set about a familiar task. She called a few of her established players to let them know about tryouts, though for the most part, that wasn't necessary. Luma's voice mail was full of messages from her kids asking when soccer would begin. She returned the calls, and soon, word spread around the parking lots and apartment complexes around town. Tryouts for the Fugees' fall season would take place the second week of August, dust and chaos be damned.

Part Two

A NEW SEASON

Chapter Ten

"I Want to Be Part of the Fugees!"

For most of the Fugees, tryouts meant the end of weeks of tedium. There was little to do in Clarkston in the summers but sweat. Bienvenue, Alex, and Ive—the brothers from Burundi—for example, had no bikes with which to get around town to see their friends. The pool at their apartment complex was closed and sat empty. (A spate of drownings by refugee children in Clarkston had prompted many of the landlords to drain their pools—hiring lifeguards was just too expensive.) The boys had a television, but no cable. They mostly passed the time in the apartment with their mother, Generose, and baby sister, Alyah, watching blurry videos of Burundian drummers and Congolese choirs singing Christian hymns.

"We just stayed at home," Bien said, describing his summer. "We didn't do nothing. Without soccer, life was boring."

Bien could hardly wait for tryouts. There wasn't much drama in it for him—he knew that as a one-year veteran he would make the team. But he was curious to see what kind of new talent showed up from the complexes around town, and to see the team's new field. Bien had grown up playing soccer in a refugee camp in Mozambique on a patch of bare earth with goals marked by small piles of rocks. He had been impressed with the field at the Clarkston Community Center. It had grass, proper soccer goals with nets, and lights overhead that allowed for practice when the sun set early in the fall. And he appreciated the grassy fields of the Fugees' competitors. By far his favorite, though, had been a field of artificial turf he'd played on at one away match. It was fast, and shots and passes rolled especially true on the smooth surface. When Bien got the word that tryouts would be at the field behind Indian Creek Elementary, he stopped by to have a look.

"Wow," he thought. "It's like Africa."

AS WORD OF the upcoming Fugees tryouts spread around Clarkston, kids began to prepare. Some went jogging to get in shape. The pickup games in the parking lots around town began to attract more players and to get more intense. It wasn't just that the Fugees were the only free soccer program in Clarkston (even the teams at the public schools required fees these boys' families couldn't afford). More than that, the Fugees offered a chance to play the game the way the pros did—on a grand scale, in a big open space with room for beautiful crosses, arcing corner kicks, and long, elegant shots that blistered the tips of the keeper's fingers. The Fugees had practices and uniforms and they traveled all over the state, no small enticement to kids who rarely left Clarkston at all. As important to the boys, their parents understood that soccer with Luma was safe, unlike the games in the parking lots of the apartment complexes, which often took place in the menacing presence of drug dealers and young men with too much time on their hands.

AS TRYOUTS APPROACHED, Luma began to worry about her rosters. She would be coaching three different teams within the Fugees program—the Under 13 Fugees, for boys thirteen and younger, the Under 15s, and the Under 17s. There were veteran players returning to each squad—Bien, Grace, and Jeremiah on the Under 13s, for example, Alex Nicishatse, Bien's older brother, and Mandela Ziaty on the Under 15s, with team leaders Kanue Biah from Liberia and Nat-nael Mammo from Ethiopia. But Luma faced the perennial struggle of fortifying the ranks of each team with newcomers, few of whom had ever played organized soccer, and finding a way to get all of her players—rookies and veterans—to play together as a team.

First and foremost, Luma needed players who would show up to practices and games on their own, since their parents—who were already overwhelmed—would not likely be of much help. The boys had to be willing to walk long distances if necessary, and to wake themselves up and get ready for games early on weekend mornings, without the help of parents. They would have to be self-sufficient, or learn to become so.

After the trauma of war and relocation, many refugee kids had severe psychological and behavioral problems. Luma had to keep this in mind during her assessments. She had learned from experience that she needed about a third of her players to be well-adjusted kids from stable families. They would set an example for the others and give the team a foundation. Another third of the team would be boys who were for the most part dependable even if they had occasional problems at school or with other kids. The last third would be marginal cases, those with behavioral problems and unstable families. These were the boys who could be counted on to demand the bulk of Luma's energy and who would most likely threaten the cohesion of her teams. They were also the boys who needed the Fugees the most.

LUMA'S THREE TEAMS had their own needs and aspirations. The Under 17s were the most mature, and would cause Luma the least amount of trouble. In previous seasons, most of the problem players had left or been kicked off the team. A few players on the Under 17s had cars. Luma expected this team to take care of itself.

The Under 13 Fugees, Luma's youngest team, consisted of a group of boys who had been with her from her first season two years before. Some, like Jeremiah, had been with Luma since her very first week of tryouts. Others, like Bienvenue, had joined along the way and made the team the center of their new lives in the United States. Their youth made them the most malleable and the most responsive to Luma's strict discipline. She knew their mothers well, relationships that extended Luma's authority to the boys' homes, since she frequently coordinated with the mothers when the boys acted out or broke the rules. The Under 13s had a star left forward in Josiah Saydee, another Liberian, whose awkward, toes-first gait masked amazing speed, as well as an experienced center midfielder in Qendrim Bushi, a stylish, mosquito-legged Kosovar with a penchant for wearing bright-colored bandanas around his neck during practice. The Under 13s' weakness was on defense. The team's best defenders hadn't returned this season, and so Luma had to find replacements from the pool of boys who turned up for tryouts.

The team was also weak at goalie—desperately so—but that was a condition of Luma's choosing. Her goalies were Eldin Subasic, a Bosnian refugee and Qendrim's best friend, and Mafoday Jawneh, a heavyset refugee from Gambia with a halogen-bulb smile and a sentimental streak—his older brother teased him for his habit of getting teary-eyed during sappy episodes of *Oprah*. A goalie, even in youth soccer, needs both aggressiveness and a degree of recklessness, qualities utterly lacking in Eldin and Mafoday, both gentle, happy souls. Their combined vertical jump came to less than a foot. And yet, the two boys did everything Luma ever asked of them. They came to practice on time, didn't miss games, studied hard during the afternoon tutoring sessions Luma required her players to attend, and supported their teammates on and off the field, qualities that assured inclusion on the Fugees roster more than did simple athletic ability. If the boys created a weak link in the Under 13s defense, the rest of the team would simply have to work harder on the field to reinforce them. And if they did, Luma felt her team had a chance to win their division.

THE UNDER 15s were a different story. They had an incredibly talented pool of players—if they decided to show up. Earlier in the summer, Luma had sent the word around that she expected her players to get their hair cut short. Luma wanted the Fugees to look respectable. The news of the hair rule, though, hadn't gone over well with some of the Under 15s' best players. Prince, for example, a cat-quick Liberian and one of the team's best returning players, had spent the summer cultivating a crown of perfectly proportioned braids that traversed his head and dangled down the back of his neck in the style of Allen Iverson, the NBA point guard. The braids gained Prince a measure of respect among his peers at school; girls liked them, and they hinted at gang affiliation, or at least comfort with a dangerous realm of many of his American peers. Prince had no intention of cutting his hair. He knew he was talented at soccer, and he fully expected Luma to make an exception to get him on the team. Further, some of the other players—particularly fellow Liberians such as Mandela Ziaty and Fornatee Tarpeh—looked up to Prince. If he was kicked off the team, there was a chance they might quit in solidarity.

"Some people want short hair, some people want braids," Fornatee said. "We don't all want to be the same. We want to be different. And playing soccer doesn't have anything to do with your hair."

The hair issue spoke to the bigger challenges facing the Under 15s. They were in the throes of adolescence, their moods subject to the disorienting flood of hormones that can turn even the most well-adjusted kids into moody rebels. Like teenagers everywhere, they longed for the respect of their peers and craved a sense of belonging, a concept especially fraught for young refugees and immigrants who were caught between the world of their parents and the new world of their friends and schoolmates. The boys on the Under 15s felt the conflict between the two worlds more acutely than their younger siblings, if only because they had spent more time in their home countries, which was borne out in the older boys' thicker accents and fondness for the native dress of their parents, proclivities that sometimes drew ridicule from the American kids at school. Even choosing to play soccer had implications for a teenager's social standing in Clarkston. Soccer was the game of refugees, Latino immigrants, and white kids from the suburbs. American kids in Clarkston and inner-city Atlanta played basketball. Soccer wasn't cool.

And finally, there was the lure of gangs, which promised both belonging and status. There were gangs in all of the public middle and high schools around Clarkston—Crips, Bloods, even an African American gang that called themselves the Taliban. Luma had lost more than one of the teenage Fugees to gangs in the past; she knew she would be competing against the gangs again this season.

If Luma could find a way to keep the Under 15 Fugees focused, and if she could find a way to create a sense of belonging and camaraderie through the team that kept the boys away from corrupting influences in Clarkston, she felt the boys were capable of playing incredible soccer. It was this team that had beaten another 9–2 the previous spring, silencing that team's extra-vocal coach and drawing an expression of awe from the referee that afternoon. Luma thought the Under 15s might win their division, and she hoped to enter them at season's end in the Georgia State Cup, a tournament for the region's best clubs. But a couple of the team's leaders were not returning; they'd moved away from Clarkston, to new lives elsewhere in the United States. Luma would have to see what kind of talent turned up. Tryouts were a day away.

IT WAS A broiling August afternoon in Atlanta, the sort of weather that long ago prompted people in these parts to start drinking their tea on ice, when Luma stepped onto the field and looked over the group of boys who had turned up for tryouts. They were a raggedy bunch. These kids arrived in blue jeans, long T-shirts, and baggy shorts that looked like pajama bottoms. One wore ankle-high brown hiking boots, as if he were about to go mountain climbing, while another stood ready to play in his socks, which flopped like clown shoes when he ran.

Luma took down the names and ages of the prospective players, and with the help of the team manager, Tracy, wrote their names on strips of masking tape, which they plastered across the backs of the boys' T-shirts. Luma had a few extra sets of used soccer shoes; she waved over the young man in sock feet and placed her foot next to his as a reference. In two years of coaching the Fugees, Luma had learned to eyeball a young man's shoe size with the accuracy of an old cobbler.

"You're a seven," she said to the boy before tossing him a pair of shoes.

Luma divided the boys into two groups and told them she wanted to see them play. As the boys took the field, she cleared her throat, squinted against the platinum glare of an August afternoon, and tried to stifle the negative thought that had been nagging her since tryouts began: *This is a rotten place to play soccer.*

The "field" looked worse than it did the day Luma first saw it.

Summer thunderstorms had carved ruts into the baked earth, expos-
ing bits of gravel and shelves of sandstone in the process. A salting
of broken glass from edge to edge glinted in the summer sun. There
was a smattering of grass that took root in hard red clay around the
perimeter, but most of the playing surface was dug out of dry Georgia
chalk. White puffs of dust were released beneath the boys' every foot-
fall and pivot, until the field was obscured by a cloud of dry, choking
dust that resembled fog.

Every now and then, the dust coughed up a figure: a heavyset Iraqi
man whose gray dishdasha dragged on the ground, a Sudanese man
with a henna-dyed beard who walked laps on the track counterclock-
wise, a wooden staff in hand, and neighborhood kids who wandered
freely through the scrimmage as though the field were any other
right-of-way. The area behind Indian Creek Elementary was one of
only a few open spaces in Clarkston accessible to the public, and in
the afternoon, it seemed to attract nearly everyone in town who dared
to venture out into the leaden heat. The field was the crossroads of the
entire refugee community.

LUMA SAT CROSS-LEGGED on the edge of the playing surface, her
eyes calm and appraising beneath the bill of her baseball cap. There
were obvious attempts to gain her favor, but Luma wasn't easily impressed. When one young man took the ball the length of the field,
dancing and dribbling through a succession of defenders before tapping in a shot, he looked toward Luma for acknowledgment of his
prowess.

"Do you know how to pass?" she called out.

As the boys played, Luma glanced every now and then toward a
footpath that led through a stand of pines to the apartment complexes
where a star player from the previous season lived: Christian Jackson,
the Liberian striker who had lost his siblings in that apartment fire in
Clarkston the previous spring. Christian, the young man who scored
five goals in the first Fugees game I'd seen, still had not shown up.

"Where's Christian?" one of the boys asked.

"He's at home on the couch, watching TV," said another. "He said
he'd come when he felt like it."

It was distressing news. Maybe it was the rumored hair rule, or perhaps after all he'd been through Christian simply preferred staying at home on the sofa. Whatever the reason, Luma wasn't going to beg him to turn out. Luma felt she could teach kids a lot about soccer, but she couldn't teach them to want it.

The evening sun dipped behind the pines to the west of the field, casting a slanting yellow light into the clouds of chalk that hung in the air. A group of adults were playing a casual game now at the south end of the field, and refugee children, out for some playtime with their parents, dangled from the bars of the nearby jungle gym. A young Somali girl and her brother, a toddler, wandered onto the field and through the scrimmage. This was their field too. The boys played around the kids and paid them little mind. They were focused on the game, lost in it, even.

Luma watched from the sideline in silence. This was the sight that had drawn her to start the Fugees in the first place, two years back, on a lark and with little appreciation for what she was getting herself into: a group of refugee boys who had survived the unimaginable, strangers now in an unfamiliar land, playing the game with passion, focus, and grace that seemed, for a brief moment anyway, to nullify the effects of whatever misfortune they had experienced in the past. In such quiet moments, Luma would sense the responsibility she had taken on and find herself wondering, *Can I really get these kids to win?* Given what they'd already been through, the challenges they faced in creating new lives in America, the social turmoil in Clarkston, and the attitudes of many locals toward these newcomers, there was another question that for now was perhaps best left unconsidered: Would they at least get a fair shot?

LUMA BLEW HER whistle and summoned the boys in. Sweating, panting, and covered in dust, they formed a circle around her at mid-field.

"Prince," she said, addressing the Liberian veteran with a head of braids. "If your hair is not cut by the first day of practice, you're off the team."

The boys glanced at Prince, but no one said a word.

Practices would take place twice a week and would last three hours,

Luma said. The first half of practice time would be for homework and tutoring. Luma had arranged volunteers for that. Tutoring was mandatory. The second half would be for soccer—and running, lots of running.

"If you miss a practice, you miss the next game," she told the boys. "If you miss two games, you're off the team."

"I have eleven spots," she added. "I'm not looking for a superstar. I'm looking for players who are willing to learn."

The final roster for the Fugees would be posted on the bulletin board of the Clarkston Public Library by ten a.m. on Friday, she told the boys—no reason to call before then.

"If you don't follow the rules, you're off the team," she said. "There are plenty of kids who want to play. If you do follow the rules, you're going to have a lot of fun."

Luma held up a stack of paper and passed a sheet to each player—contracts she expected her players to sign.

"If you can't live with this," she said, "I don't want you on this team."

Hands—white, brown, yellow, black—reached for the paper. As the boys read, their eyes widened.

I will have good behavior on and off the field.
I will not smoke.
I will not do drugs.
I will not drink alcohol.
I will not get anyone pregnant.
I will not use bad language.
My hair will be shorter than Coach's.
I will be on time.
I will listen to Coach.
I will try hard.
I will ask for help.
I want to be part of the Fugees!

Chapter Eleven

Figure It Out so You Can Fix It

"Why you have to cut your hair?" Mandela Ziaty asked. "You play with your feet—the hair doesn't touch the ball."

"Who are you representing?" Kanue Biah said.

"I represent myself."

"No," said Kanue. "You represent your coach and your team."

Luma's hair rule had set off a debate between the veteran players on the Under 15 team. Prince had refused to cut his hair and wouldn't be joining the team. With Christian already out—he never turned up at tryouts—and the missing players from the previous season who'd moved away from Clarkston, the Under 15 team was suddenly very short on talent. The absence of Prince and Christian in particular upset Mandela and Fornatee Tarpeh. Neither Mandela nor Fornatee had long hair. Mandela's mother, Beatrice, wouldn't allow him to grow his hair long; that wasn't acceptable for young men in Africa, and she didn't care what the American boys did. And Fornatee kept his hair cut so close to his scalp that he nearly looked bald. But the boys had counted on playing soccer with their friends and fellow Liberians, and now that Prince and Christian weren't around, they blamed Luma and her rule that hair must be "shorter than Coach's."

Luma's hair *was* short—a couple of inches, maybe, trimmed above the ears and high on her neck—a length that didn't leave the Fugees much wiggle room to fashion their own personal hairstyles. But she had her reasons for the rule. The Fugees had come in for abuse from some of their opponents outside Atlanta—in the suburbs and in the country—for their accents and names; she didn't want to encourage hostility with hairstyles like the cornrows and braids that were worn by gang members in Clarkston and in the rougher sections of Atlanta. The issue of hairstyles was also important to Luma's relations with perhaps her most important constituency: the mothers of her players. Many, like Beatrice Ziaty, associated braids with black Americans—whom many African refugees further associated with Clarkston's street gangs, in the all-too-common habit of some new arrivals in America of adopting the worst of America's racial assumptions. In any event, these mothers would be far less likely to entrust their sons to Luma if they thought the boys would be in dangerous company. Respectable African men, Beatrice believed, wore their hair short and neatly trimmed.

There was a final reason Luma resolved to hold firm on the hair rule. The previous season, she had become so enamored of Prince's talent on the field that she allowed him to get away with skirting the team rules. He would leave tutoring early or skip it altogether, acts that undermined Luma's authority before the rest of the team. Players soon started to challenge her and to follow Prince's lead. Luma counted the episode as a hard lesson, and vowed not to let any player, no matter how talented, get away with flouting team rules.

"They idolized him and I idolized him," Luma said of Prince. "But it created a dynamic where he wasn't accountable, and I made excuses for him."

Luma didn't explain her rationale. She expected her players to figure it out for themselves. But Fornatee didn't see the point. All he knew was that the hair rule was putting him in the uncomfortable position of having to choose between his coach and his friends.

Fornatee had been in the United States for seven years, longer than most of his teammates, and was perhaps the most assimilated member of the team. Few refugee kids in Clarkston knew anything about American football, but Fornatee had been around long enough to develop a strong allegiance to the Atlanta Falcons, the local NFL team. He'd even considered playing football for his high school this fall instead of rejoining the Fugees, but he'd re-upped for soccer in part to play with Prince and in part because he knew he needed the Fugees, perhaps now more than ever.

Earlier in the summer, Fornatee's father had been in the backseat of a car driven by a friend when they were rear-ended by an out-of-control truck. He was critically injured, suffering broken ribs and severe internal hemorrhaging. Fornatee's father had been in the hospital for a month and was still weeks away from being sent home when tryouts came around. He faced a long recovery. Without his income, the family's situation in Clarkston had become dire. Fornatee's mother, he said, was in Africa. He had an aunt in Clarkston and an older brother who worked at the Atlanta airport. They were scraping by, but Fornatee wasn't sure how long they could make it without his father's income.

"I'm scared," he said. "My daddy can't work. I'm wondering where we gonna get the rent. They gonna put us out 'cause we can't pay the rent?"

Though he didn't like to admit it to his friends, Fornatee had come to trust and depend on Luma for support. She was one of few adults in Clarkston he trusted, a conclusion he'd come to after a simple gesture she'd made one day after practice. Fornatee had injured his hand when he fell during a scrimmage. When Fornatee hurt himself, he was used to just dealing with the pain and letting whatever hurt heal itself naturally. But after practice, Luma told him to get in her Beetle and drove him to a nearby CVS pharmacy for first-aid supplies, an act of concern Fornatee had never forgotten.

"That's why I want to be on the team," he said, referring to the trip to CVS. "She's more than a coach to me—she cares about you like she's your parent."

But Fornatee also felt loyalty to his fellow Liberians, Prince and Mandela, among others. It was a connection, he said, that was more powerful than the one he felt to his Fugees teammates from other countries, a reminder that the gelling of the Fugees into a unit was by no means a foregone conclusion, particularly for the Under 15 team. At times their differing backgrounds all but vanished in the shadow of things that bound them together as a team. But the possibility of fracturing into cliques based on country or tribe or language was always there.

"We're international and all that," Fornatee said of the Fugees. "But you hang out with people who speak your language and who come from your country. When we leave the field, I'm not going to call those other kids. They don't have my number, and I don't have theirs. That's just the way it is."

Prince was one of Fornatee's best friends. Both young men played offense. They'd planned to set each other up for goals and help each other on the field. And together they'd lobbied other Liberian friends to come out for the team, only to have them bail out when they realized they'd have to get their hair cut. Fornatee wanted Prince and Coach to work things out. But he knew Prince wasn't going to cut his hair. It was up to Coach, he thought, to give in.

"I guarantee you," he said, "if Coach said, 'Don't cut your hair,' all those guys—Prince, everybody—they would come back."

THE FUGEES' PRESEASON practices took place amid miserable conditions. It was late August. The Georgia sun was blast-furnace hot, and still high enough in the sky in the late afternoon that its rays were unimpeded by the tree line. And the dust was everywhere. The players inhaled clots of it as they played. It ground into their hair and eyes, and settled into their clothes, giving sweat-soaked T-shirts the feel of wet, sandy beach towels. Mixed with sweat, the dust formed an abrasive paste that collected in the clammy spaces between the feet and the simulated leather of the boys' cleats, gnawing blisters into their ankles. On the black skin of the African players, the dust turned to a gray sort of mud when soaked with rivulets of sweat, so that when the players wandered quietly to the sideline to take a sip of water, it looked like the shift change at a limestone quarry. And yet no one mentioned this quiet scourge—not Luma and not her players. It was as if all had made an unconscious pact to defy the shortcomings of their new home field by simply refusing to acknowledge them. Some problems weren't so easily ignored. There was broken glass and trash on the field that posed a hazard to players; Luma had her teams walk the field, scouring for such debris. And it was impossible to tune out the presence of the rougher element that hung around the field. At one early practice, a young man with a beer and a joint in his hand approached Luma as she coached on the sideline. She asked him to leave, but the young man refused, and in fact was joined by two friends, who hovered menacingly alongside the field. Luma took out her cell phone and dialed the police, but a squad car didn't show up for nearly half an hour, by which time the men had left.

"The Y isn't going to do anything about a new field until one of us gets shot," Luma said to Tracy, the team manager, afterward, half-kidding.

And there was another hard-to-ignore shortcoming of the Fugees' field: there were no soccer goals. The Fugees' sponsors at the Decatur-DeKalb YMCA had received a $9,100 grant to supply the Fugees with uniforms, equipment, and goals and had promised to have them put in place by the time the Fugees started fall practices. And yet no goals had arrived. The delay, Luma had been told, was due to concern that the neighborhood around Indian Creek was so bad that the new goals might be stolen. Luma had persuaded the elementary school's principal to allow the new goals to be cemented in place, but the Y still hadn't sent them. Luma registered their absence as another small sign of neglect and disrespect for her team, and one with practical implications. Soccer was a game played in three dimensions, and soccer without goals, Luma said, was "like playing basketball without a hoop."

After two weeks of practicing without goals, Luma got fed up. She called the YMCA and insisted that they offer some sort of temporary solution. A coordinator at the YMCA offered to loan Luma an extra set of goals the Y had in a park not too far from Clarkston, if Luma was willing to pick them up herself. So on a hot August day Luma and Tracy rented a U-Haul and drove to the park. There were three sets of goals in the park; a small set of the sort that was used for kiddie leagues, and two larger, regulation sets. The Fugees played with regulation-size goals, so Luma and Tracy got to work, disassembling a pair of the heavy metal frames into piles of individual tubes, which they loaded one by one onto the truck. They drove across town, carted the metal tubes up a hill and onto the field at Indian Creek, and put the goals back together.

Later, a panicked administrator at the YMCA called Luma to inform her that she had taken the wrong goals from the park. Luma would have to return them. Luma refused. If the YMCA wanted their goals back, she said, they could go pick them up themselves. It was a bluff—Luma hoped the Y would put as much energy into taking goals away from Indian Creek as they had into acquiring them. But in this case, the Y showed quick resolve; by the weekend the goals were gone, with nothing left to replace them. The field was once again bare.

THE REGIMEN FOR each of those early practices was the same. The Under 15s practiced on Tuesdays and Thursdays, the 13s and 17s on Mondays and Wednesdays. For the first half of the days on which Luma coached two teams, the Under 17s practiced first while the 13s received tutoring in a classroom inside Indian Creek Elementary from Tracy and whomever else she could find to volunteer to help the boys with their schoolwork. After an hour and a half, the younger boys came outside and ran their laps while the Under 17s scrimmaged in front of Luma. At the end of the scrimmage, the older players were dismissed to write in journals, an exercise they performed sitting on cross ties that surrounded a bark floor beneath the jungle gym. The Under 13s then finished their running and took the practice field for drills and instruction.

Practice for all the teams began with twenty-five minutes of running laps on the grass just inside the asphalt track. Luma had resolved that her teams would never lose because they were out-conditioned, and she found that running was the closest thing to a foolproof therapy for boys who acted out at school or at practice. When boys misbehaved, she'd run them to exhaustion.

The boys ran in silence, but they would jerk upright when they heard Luma call out a teammate's name for running too slowly. When the players had completed their running, Luma ordered them to line up on the fringe of grass at the field's edge. There she led them through sit-ups, push-ups, leg lifts, and bicycle kicks, walking up and down the line to push down the backs of players who tried to make their push-ups easier by bending up at the waist, or to stand over a player who was groaning theatrically during leg lifts, to make sure his heels never touched the ground. The spectacle drew laughter from the neighborhood kids who'd come out to play on the jungle gym alongside the track. Occasionally it seemed Luma would prolong the exercises to elicit a few more futile groans from her players for the entertainment of the younger spectators on the monkey bars.

After exercises, she laid out a line of small orange cones in an alternating pattern and ran the players through a series of drills: quick passes, headers, and chests—nothing fancy, just the rudiments of the game. As practices progressed, Luma would add a new twist at the end of the routine—a drill in which she fed balls to shooters, who were expected to volley the ball before it touched the ground, for example, or a new passing combination. Practice ended with a straight scrimmage—the unquestioned highlight of the afternoon for the boys. Luma divided the players into teams. The boys deposited two clumps of sweaty T-shirts in the dust at either end of the field, to delineate the goals. Luma blew the whistle and let them play.

Play they did. Young men who had seemed exhausted to the point of collapse after drills found miraculous reserves of energy once the game was on, and suddenly were capable of sprinting up and down the field without pause. Taciturn and withdrawn boys who hadn't so much as grunted for the first two-thirds of practice now shouted insistently for the ball. The commotion had a way of drawing in the rest of the neighborhood. Young children on the jungle gym climbed higher on the bars to get a better view. Their parents and some of the older Clarkston refugees who'd come out for their evening exercise turned toward the field as well, or sat down on the cross ties parallel to the track to watch.

AS LUMA WORKED to size up her players and to identify the best talent for particular positions, the boys too were subtly trying to size up their coach, to get a sense of her boundaries and what they could get away with at practice. Luma expected her players to work hard and take practice seriously, and above all to obey her during practice. A player shouldn't have to speak perfect English to understand that goofing off in practice wasn't allowed, and if there was any doubt about that, Luma's sharp intonation conveyed disapproval across

any language barrier. When she sensed she was being tested, she responded swiftly—sending kids home or ordering them to run extra
laps at the first sign of disobedience or lack of focus, with a fierceness
and absoluteness that sometimes made it difficult not to feel sympathy for the boys as they ran headlong into the futility of trying to skirt
Luma's iron rule.

One afternoon as the Under 13 Fugees were running, Luma heard
the boys cackling and shouting. A boy named Hussein, a small and
perpetually bemused Meskhetian Turk with big eyes set wide apart
near his temples, was skipping and thrashing his arms comically to
the amusement of his teammates.

"Hussein!" Luma barked. "Stop that—now!"

Hussein, though, spoke only a few words of English, and it was
unclear whether or not he understood Coach's order. Luma turned
her attention for a moment to the Under 17s, who were writing in
their journals at the edge of the field. She heard a few muted laughs
and turned back around to see Hussein still skipping and flapping
his arms.

"Hussein!" Luma called again, raising her arm in the air and pointing in the direction of the apartment complexes north of the field.
"Go home!"

Hussein came to a halt, and his expression knotted into one of confusion as the other players ran past him, suddenly quiet. He dropped
his head, then looked up, with pleading puppy-dog eyes.

"Go *home*!" Luma said, gesturing again with her arm for emphasis.

Hussein grimaced and slouched over in defeat. However poor his
English, he understood what his coach was saying. When he lifted his
chin finally, Hussein looked like he might cry.

"Go *home*," Luma said again, her voice softening only slightly. Hussein turned, lowered his head again, and began to traipse sullenly
toward the footpath that led to his apartment complex, just out of
shouting distance from the field.

LUMA SEEMED TO have the auditory acumen of a rabbit, and the
capability of hearing foul language, even spoken sotto voce, from a
field's length away. Kids who cursed usually were sent running after
a warning that if they cursed again, they'd be off the team—a threat

Luma had made good on in the past. Sometimes her ability to sense insubordination seemed almost supernatural.

Luma was watching the Under 17s scrimmage at one early practice, when the Under 13s emerged from the school building after tutoring to run their laps. The younger boys noticed Luma's absorption with the scrimmage and sought to take advantage. They ran vigorously for the 270 degrees of each lap that took place in Luma's field of vision. But once they passed into the blind space behind her lines of sight, the boys stopped running and began to walk. Just before they reappeared on the other side of her field of view they started running again. Luma was completely absorbed in the scrimmage. She never turned her head to catch the boys walking, to their extraordinary satisfaction.

Soon Luma blew her whistle and dismissed the Under 17s from practice. Normally at this point she summoned the younger players in from their laps and started them on their drills. This time, though, she crossed her arms and wandered aimlessly around the field, looking at weeds, picking up rocks, kicking the sand—killing time. The younger team kept running: twenty-five minutes, thirty minutes, thirty-five . . . and so on. Eventually, the boys began to look at her with plaintive expressions: they were confused, in pain. Luma remained impassive, and they kept running . . . and running.

"Coach—what we did wrong?" Bienvenue finally yelled out from across the field as he held his cramping midsection.

Luma looked at her watch. Forty minutes of running.

"It took them this long to figure it out," she said, shaking her head in disbelief.

Luma blew her whistle and called in the 13s. From now on, she told them, they would no longer run laps around the track, out of view. Instead they would run back and forth at one end of the field, in her direct line of sight, so she could keep an eye on them. The boys looked at each other with a mixture of guilt and anger, as if searching for the one among them who had suggested trying to pull one over on their coach in the first place. It hadn't been such a bright idea after all.

Later I asked Luma how she'd known the boys were walking when she couldn't actually see them. She scrunched her brow in thought for a moment, in the way of someone who is asked to explain an act that had been performed instinctively. Luma said she knew from experience how long it should take for the boys to reappear in her field of vision on one side after disappearing behind her on the other—if they were running. They didn't reappear when they were supposed to, she explained, so she knew they were walking. I asked her then why she hadn't called the boys on their infraction the moment she noticed it. Luma said she wanted to know if the boys would police themselves, to see what sort of team she was dealing with. Now she knew, and both she and her team would live with the consequences.

"They need to figure it out so they can fix it," she said.

If Luma's way of teaching these lessons to her players seemed harsh, she made no apologies.

"These kids face so many hardships," she said. "Some of them are taking care of their siblings. They don't have the mom driving them in the SUV. So I'm not going to baby them, because they're never going to get babied. They need to grow up."

THE UNDER 15S were also testing Luma in their own way. Even though he was no longer on the team because of his refusal to cut his braids, Prince hadn't gone away exactly. He had made a habit of stopping by practice and watching from a distance, his braids stylishly intact. He snickered as the Fugees groaned and sweated their way through laps and exercises as Luma barked instructions. He showed up one day with a group of friends—guys and girls—who laughed and cut up in view of the practice field before wandering off to hang out as they pleased. Prince's conspicuous displays of personal liberty during the Fugees' practice were a challenge to Fornatee and Mandela: Were they going to cave to the coach or hang out with their friends?

The challenge seemed to unnerve them both. Fornatee and Mandela began showing up late, talking back to Luma, grumbling and sulking through drills—small gestures of protest to register their unhappiness at having to play without their best friends. During one practice, Mandela simply wandered off and joined in a pickup soccer game at the far end of the field. Fornatee invited some girls he liked to come watch him at practice; when Luma saw him chatting with them, she sent him home.

"My daddy don't care if I talk to girls," Fornatee said. "So why does she care?"

Collectively, Fornatee and Mandela threatened to undermine Luma's authority over the Under 15 Fugees, an ominous sign heading into the team's season opener, just a week away. Luma had to decide on a course of action. Her first instinct was to blame her circumstances. The old field at the community center was fenced off and private. A kid like Prince who was intent on disrupting practice wouldn't even have been allowed on the property. But while practicing in the open field behind the public elementary school there was little beyond bluffing that she could do to run Prince off. She also felt a pang of . . . if not sympathy, then perhaps tolerance toward Prince. He was showing up as a way of acting out himself, she suspected, because on some level he did want to be on the Fugees, or at least to play soccer with his friends. There was a simple way he could accomplish that, and it involved nothing more complicated than a pair of scissors. On that, Luma wouldn't budge.

AS LIBERIANS, PRINCE, Fornatee, Mandela, Christian Jackson, and the others shared not just a connection but special challenges as well. Within the resettlement community in Clarkston, there were commonly held generalizations about the various groups of refugees who had come to town: Vietnamese were hardworking and valued jobs over education. The Lost Boys wanted to go to college before pursuing jobs. Afghans were tough and resilient; Somalis were quiet, proud, and uninterested in assimilation. The stereotypes almost always accentuated the positive. But with Liberians it was different. They were "a challenge," or "troubled," caseworkers would say. Fourteen years of civil war in Liberia—wars marked by unspeakable violence and cruelty—had taken their toll. Children who had grown up in that environment had little or no access to formal education, except for brief bits they might have received in refugee camps. Their social skills, such as they were, had developed in a crucible of fear and stress. Many young men had grown up fatherless because the war claimed so many men of fighting age. And many boys had been drawn into the

fighting themselves, usually by compulsion. Charles Taylor, the former Liberian president, after all, was arrested and charged with war
crimes in part because of his wanton use of child soldiers in waging
the bloody conflict that led him to power.

"Liberians have been through a conflict for almost thirty years,"
said the Reverend William B. G. K. Harris, a Liberian-born pastor at
the International Christian Ministries, a mostly Liberian congregation just south of Atlanta. "So you're talking about a group of people
who were born into a war-torn nation. All they have seen or known
is instability, war, crime. And some of them were fools for carrying
guns. They saw lots of different things happening to themselves and
to their families. So some of them never even stay in school for a
year. And nonetheless, even with minimal education, they come over
here, and they are an age where they should be either finishing high
school or almost finishing high school. So they come with no social
skills or education or background to help them move on. So those
are the challenges—coupled with the normal thing of just being an
immigrant."

What put Liberian refugees in Clarkston at special risk had to do
with not just Liberia's troubles but America's as well. More perhaps
than any other refugee group in Clarkston, Liberian boys and young
men were susceptible to the lure of the American gangs that flour-
ished in the public schools and in the parking lots of the apartment
complexes around town. For a young man who had grown up in Liberia during the war, the leap to the world of American gangs was not
a particularly big one. Most Liberians speak English, so they had no
trouble communicating with indigenous gang members in Clarkston.
The subset of hip-hop culture that glorified gangs and violence was as
popular in the streets of Monrovia as it was in Atlanta. And for young,
fatherless men, some of whom had been co-opted into violence themselves as child soldiers, or who certainly had brothers or friends who
had fought, a gang—with its promise of power and authority amid
economic and social dissolution—must've seemed an intensely familiar analog to the bands of fighters who roamed Liberia during the war.
Because Liberians were so familiar with American culture, they were
also keenly aware of the degree to which, as immigrants and refugees,
they were outside it. A gang offered a chance to bridge that divide, a
way to become, as it were, American.

For Liberian parents in America, the prevalence of gangs in Clarkston—and their potential allure to young Liberian men—created a bitter paradox. After succeeding at getting their children out of the war in Liberia, they were now charged with saving them from another low-grade but still deadly conflict on the streets of the United States, their "safe haven." And if they ever forgot about the dangers that lurked outside their doors in Clarkston, the periodic sound of gunfire cutting through the night and echoing off the walls of their apartment complexes would remind them. Beatrice Ziaty had heard the sound of gunshots puncturing the nighttime quiet around her apartment complex and was frightened by it. The sound was an echo from a haunting past. And as then, she worried about her boys. Jeremiah did what she said—he stayed inside when he wasn't with Coach Luma. Darlington, the oldest, could fend for himself, and spent most of his time watching TV in the apartment. But Beatrice worried most about Mandela. There was no telling what kind of trouble a fifteen-year-old could get into in Clarkston.

MANDELA ZIATY DIDN'T like thinking of himself as a refugee. Refugees, to his mind, weren't American. They were poor. It was true that there had been times when Mandela's mother, Beatrice, was too broke even to buy food for her three sons. Mandela didn't want people to know about that, not his friends especially. Like a lot of fifteen-year-olds, he worried about what people thought of him. On school days, Mandela wore what American kids wore—long T-shirts that hung halfway to his knees, blue jeans so big and baggy that they slid off his hip bones, and clunky high-tops that he left untied so the laces trailed behind him. But when someone pulled out a camera at home, Mandela would go to his closet and pull out his church clothes—his clean white dress shirt with the crisp collar, his smooth black pleated slacks, and his shiny black shoes. He didn't want to look like a poor person. You never knew who might see a photograph.

Mandela didn't ask for help, and if he ever felt sorry for himself, he didn't let on. Instead, he got mad. When Mandela got mad, he got quiet, the kind of leaden, ear-splitting quiet that made people ill at ease.

"When he would get mad, oh my God!" said Alex Nicishatse, Mandela's teammate. Alex laughed nervously at the thought. "Nobody would want to talk to him—they were afraid."

When Mandela's little brother, Jeremiah, began playing soccer for the Fugees, Mandela made fun of him. Soccer was whack, he said—for refugees. Jeremiah loved soccer and wanted his brother to play for the Fugees too, on the older boys' team. Mandela laughed at the idea.

"Mandela, from the beginning, he not wanted to play soccer," Beatrice recalled. "When Jeremiah come home, he would start mocking Jeremiah. Mandela say, 'As for me, I will play basketball.'"

Basketball was the popular game at school. Mandela had the frame for it too. He was tall, quick, and built like a punching bag—the physique of the perfect power forward. But in the summer, there weren't many options for basketball in Clarkston. Mandela was bored. Jeremiah kept at him. Beatrice had come to trust Luma, and she joined in.

"That lady—she's doing well," Beatrice told Mandela. "To keep you busy all the time is good!"

Restless, Mandela eventually gave in and joined what was now the Under 15s. He didn't know the game particularly well, but on the field his natural ability took over. He could outrun most of the other kids. He used his big frame, his softball-size shoulders, and his chiseled biceps to ward off defenders the way a basketball player might block out for a rebound. His shot was devastating. Goalies learned to run from it. Luma had once caught a stray shot of Mandela's on the top of her thigh. She was bruised and sore for a week.

And yet something weighed on Mandela. He never seemed fully comfortable. It often seemed as though he wanted to be someplace else. When he was in one of his moods, he acted out in practice—talking back, showing little effort. Normally, Luma might have sent a kid like Mandela away. But she had grown close to Beatrice, and she held out hope that Mandela was going through a phase, that he would behave and do what he was told, like his little brother. Mandela was one kid Luma was convinced she could help.

Mandela made friends on the Fugees—mostly with the other Liberian boys like Prince and Fornatee—and he made friends at school. But they weren't always the kind of friends Beatrice had hoped he would have. The boys hung out after practice, sometimes late into the night. Beatrice worried. She felt he was hanging out with the wrong crowd. She didn't like the way the boys dressed—the ghetto look, with those low-hanging pants, untucked T-shirts—or their braids.

"I say, 'Is that a way we can dress in Africa?' No!" she said. "It's not a way that the men, they can dress. You can't hang your trousers right here." She pointed low on her hips. "We can't do that in Africa. Men always have the low haircuts. Men can't grow hair—it's for ladies!"

If she were in Africa, Beatrice said, she would've set Mandela straight.

"In Africa, when you tell your kid something and he doesn't want to listen, you will beat him—take the rod to him," she said. "Next time when you say 'Shhh,' he will not do it. But here, nothing, you cannot do that."

America's sensitivity to corporal punishment ran counter to nearly everything that Beatrice and many refugee mothers had learned about keeping kids in line. The new rules favored her kids, she felt, and undercut her authority. She had learned this the hard way. A few months before, Jeremiah left his new winter jacket at school. Beatrice yelled at him for being so careless with something she had worked so hard to buy. She didn't feel he was sufficiently contrite.

"He make me mad, so I beat him," Beatrice said. "When he go to school, he say, 'My ma beat me! My ma hit me right here.' And his school have to send for me! The times I beat him, I say, 'Next time don't do that again,' and he say, 'Okay, I will not do it.' But from now on, when they ask him at the school, he say, 'My ma beat me!' And they have to send for me! When I'm in Africa, they can't do that. When your child misbehave in the school, you can go to the school and say, 'Teacher, you can give the child twenty-five lashes—twenty-five on his butt.' They will beat him sound. They will lay him on the bench and beat him. Fine! He won't do that again. He respect the teacher. When teacher say 'Shhh!' he won't talk. But here, nothing."

It was a common complaint among the newly arrived mothers in Clarkston. While their parents were at work—usually isolated, cleaning rooms in a hotel or working amid the din of a chicken processing plant—the kids were at school, vacuuming up the rules of the new culture, and sometimes deploying their new knowledge as leverage against their parents, with only a child's understanding of the potential consequences. This was particularly true of non-English-speaking families, in which the kids—whose English was almost invariably better—became the family interface with the English-speaking world, particularly with authority figures like police and teachers. But even in an English-speaking family like the Ziaty family, there could be an inversion of authority when it came to dealing with the world outside the family's apartment. Beatrice often felt she was at a disadvantage when dealing with Mandela in particular. And so when he stayed out late or acted up, Beatrice called Luma for help.

"When I have problems with the children I will call her," Beatrice said. "I say, 'Please come to my aid. Mandela—he's going out too much, Luma.' And she says, 'I will.' So right now, she's really a sister to me now. Because she take care of the children more than myself."

WHEN MANDELA ACTED out at practice, Luma appealed to Beatrice as well. The two women—a soccer coach from Jordan, a widow from Liberia—found themselves teaming up to try to keep Mandela out of trouble.

"Luma comes sometimes and says, 'I didn't like Mandela's way,'" Beatrice said. "Then I will apologize to her, and I will set Mandela down to make him to understand the life we passed through."

The life we passed through. Mandela, Jeremiah, and Darlington heard that phrase all the time, especially when their mother was angry. Unable to discipline them the way she liked, Beatrice would instead sit them in a chair and tell them once again the story of the life they'd passed through. They knew it well by now, and exactly how she would tell it.

"We went from Monrovia, got to Ivory Coast, then stay in Ivory Coast for five years," Beatrice would preach to them. "You forgot. As for me, I didn't forgot.

"While you're sitting, you forgot all the bad things we passed through—you and myself!" she would say. "I think you forgot. But I not forgot. You forgot that we could go in the bush to look for food— you forgot. But I not forgot."

"Our country's here," Darlington, the oldest, would sometimes protest.

But Beatrice would go on: she'd remind them of the mud hut she'd built for them in the refugee camp, and how she used to break a single nutritional biscuit handed out by aid workers into four pieces, so they could all eat. She would remind them of what she had to go through to get asylum in the United States—the countless interviews with UN officials and their attempts to ferret out lies and exaggerations by asking her the same questions over and over again, sometimes months apart—and of all the worry she had that some small mistake, some forgetful error, would doom them to that refugee camp for years more. In Atlanta, she'd been working ten-hour days as a maid at the Ritz-Carlton Hotel all the way across town—one hour by bus, each way—cleaning sixteen rooms a shift. All for her family.

"You forgot," she told her boys. "But I not forgot."

Beatrice would go on until she got the acknowledgment her up-bringing demanded: she wanted her boys to be quiet, to bow their heads and lower their eyes. That was all. Just a simple gesture, an act of submission that acknowledged her authority and the sacrifices she'd made.

"When you make a face like this"—Beatrice scrunched her brow, narrowed her eyes, and puckered her lips. "It means disrespect.

"When you bend your head down," she said, "you're *thinking*. You're *remembering*."

Beatrice wanted her boys to remember. Remembering meant re-spect for all she'd done, and respect, she hoped, would keep her boys out of trouble. That was her hope. But Beatrice was never sure the message was getting through.

"Sometimes they listen," she said. "Sometimes they don't."

Chapter Twelve

Meltdown

With no lines or goals, the field at Indian Creek Elementary wasn't suitable for league games. So through the YMCA, Luma arranged for the Fugees to host their home matches at Ebster Field, a perfectly maintained grass pitch in Decatur, a fifteen-minute drive from Clarkston toward downtown Atlanta. Luma secured the use of a YMCA bus to shuttle her players back and forth between Decatur and Clarkston, and gave them instructions to meet at the Clarkston Public Library at one p.m., an hour before game time. Anyone who was late, she told them, would be left behind.

The Under 15s' first regular-season game was on September 10 against the Gwinnett Phoenix, a club team from Lilburn, Georgia. Lilburn was only ten miles from Clarkston, but in many respects it was a world away. Lilburn was the very model of the modern Atlanta suburb: a mostly white, middle- and upper-middle-class enclave that had sprung up around the old town center of a long-defunct railroad stop. With its open spaces and relative affluence, it was also soccer country. The Gwinnett Soccer Association was founded in 2000, and was home to girls' and boys' teams of all ages that together had won more than a dozen state championships as well as a 2001 national championship in girls' soccer.

Soccer games were social events for the families of Phoenix players. An entourage of parents, siblings, and friends accompanied the team to Decatur and set up camp on a near sideline with folding chairs, blankets, coolers, and picnic lunches, as their boys warmed up with a complement of shiny new soccer balls. The Fugees sideline, as usual, was empty. The Fugees, it was safe to assume, wouldn't enjoy much in the way of a home-field advantage.

Luma drove to Ebster Field in her yellow Volkswagen, the backseat full of soccer balls, shin guards, and cleats, which she planned to hand out to her players who couldn't afford their own soccer shoes. The visitors faced equipment challenges of a different kind. Before warm-ups, a young man from the Phoenix stepped on the pitch and rubbed his hand across the turf, testing its depth and thickness.

"I think I should change my spikes," he said to his dad, who was standing nearby.

"You better pick the right ones," the dad replied. "I paid three hundred dollars for those shoes."

LUMA EXPECTED THE YMCA bus to show up at Ebster Field by 1:15. At 1:30 p.m., though, the bus was still nowhere in sight. Luma looked at her watch and shook her head in frustration. The Phoenix took the field and began warming up. Luma took out her cell phone and called the bus's driver to see what was going on. Some of the players hadn't shown up, he reported. He'd waited as long as he could and was now on his way, but without the full roster.

A few minutes later, the bus hurtled into sight and then stopped abruptly alongside the field. The Under 15s began to disembark. When the bus had emptied, Luma did a head count. Only nine Under 15 Fugees had shown up, two short of a full roster.

Mandela Ziaty had made the bus. He sat on the bleachers, counting heads as he tied the laces of his cleats. Disgusted, he shook his head.

Mandela had hoped that Fornatee and the others had simply hitched their own rides to the game. It was only now settling in that they simply hadn't shown up. Mandela was angry. Playing nine against eleven was not the way to win soccer games. Not only that—it was close to 95 degrees and stultifyingly humid. With no substitutes, each member of the Fugees would have to play the whole game in the heat without a break. The Under 15 Fugees stood not just to lose, but to lose in particularly exhausting fashion.

Mandela sat next to me on the bleachers and asked to borrow my cell phone. I obliged, and he began frantically calling his absent teammates to see where they were. He reached Fornatee at his apartment; Fornatee had missed the bus and was now stretched out on the sofa, watching television. Mandela asked me if I had a car. My bright midsize rental car was parked in view. He wanted to know if I would drive him to pick up Fornatee and two other members of his team. If we left immediately, he thought we could make it back by game time.

I hesitated, weighing the need for journalistic detachment against the desperation on Mandela's face. I also worried what Luma would think—if my helping Mandela round up his teammates might in her eyes look as though I was enabling their truancy. Tracy, the Fugees' team manager, was nearby. I asked her advice; she said she thought it would be all right. Mandela and I jogged to the car and were off.

At 1:55 p.m., we pulled back alongside the field, with three additions to the Fugees roster, including Fornatee, in the backseat. The boys sprinted onto the field to join warm-ups, which were already in progress. Luma, though, wasn't with her players. Instead, she was standing in a corner of the field, far removed from the action and offering no instructions to the team.

"Coach," shouted Kanue Biah, the Liberian veteran, "why you not talking to us?"

"Because there's nothing to say," Luma replied. She turned her back on her players, walked to a set of bleachers in the shade at the far end of the field, and sat down.

Only Kanue seemed to fully understand that something serious was going on. He was a veteran member of the Fugees and was devoted to the team. Kanue was always on time, and more than any other player had bought into Luma's system. He decided to take charge. He told his teammates to hurry up, to get on the field and start jogging.

A moment later, the referee summoned the players to the midfield stripe to go over their player cards. He called their names haltingly. One by one, the boys stepped forward and acknowledged their names, correcting the referee on his pronunciation. The teams took their positions on the field, the Fugees in dark blue shorts and light blue jerseys with orange trim, the Phoenix in white jerseys and white shorts. The referee blew the whistle, and the game was under way. Luma was still sitting far from the field in the shade, arms crossed, silent.

Minutes into the game, the Fugees were called for a foul in the box, setting up a penalty shot for the Phoenix. The Fugees' goalie dove left; the ball went right. The parents on the Phoenix sideline jumped to their feet and cheered. Before they'd even had enough time to get comfortable in their folding chairs, the Phoenix led 1–0.

The Fugees responded by playing more desperately, and aggressively. They were called for one offsides penalty, then another, and yet another. Fornatee shouted at the referee in protest and in the process drew a yellow card, to cheers from the Phoenix sideline. A moment later, the Phoenix scored again: 2–0.

Mandela was angry now, and determined to get a shot on goal with or without help from his teammates. He took the ball on a pass from Fornatee and dashed up the middle of the field, fighting his way through the Phoenix defense and shielding the ball with his large frame. He dribbled to his right across the top of the box and blasted a shot high and to the right—score: 2–1. The Phoenix responded minutes later, on a crisp cross to an unmarked forward right in front of the goal. It was now 3–1, and the Phoenix had the momentum. But just before the half, Fornatee got free up the middle. He had an unusual way of controlling the ball; he put his back toward his defender and then moved his way down the field by gently rolling his foot over the top of the ball. It was almost like a center in basketball, dribbling his way toward the basket just before taking a turnaround jumper. Fornatee made his move, quickly tapping the ball into an open space to his right: he had a wide-open shot. Inexplicably, he hesitated—for a bit of showy footwork, a juke to the left, a feint back to the right. It was just enough of a pause to let the Phoenix goalie move out to cut off the angle.

"Shoot it!" his teammates yelled.

Fornatee took the shot, but it was blocked. The whistle blew twice, signaling the half.

THE FUGEES GATHERED near midfield and as a group looked toward Luma, awaiting her halftime instructions. But Luma stayed where she was, head down, in the shade, refusing even to make eye contact with her players.

"You see our coach right there?" Fornatee fumed to his teammates. "She's got a job to do. I can't be the coach. You look at her—she's sitting right there!"

"Play on," Kanue said. "You've got to play on. You've got to come together."

"When you get the ball, kick it!" someone snapped at Fornatee.

"Coach has never did this to us," Fornatee said. "She's got a job. That's why she's a coach. This is her job!"

He paused and took a breath. The other Fugees stood in silence. "We're not going to worry about that," Fornatee said, collecting himself. "We're just going to play. Three to one isn't that much. I'm sorry, I had a shot. That won't happen again. If I'm open like that, I'm going to score, I promise y'all."

At once, everyone started shouting.

"One at a time!" Fornatee said, before taking the floor again himself.

"Let me tell you something: Coach is just a coach. She cannot show us how to play soccer. Is she playing? No—we are. The skills we got, we don't need her. She's just going to talk. She cannot come on the field and play for us. We gotta play for ourselves. It don't make no difference if she's sitting down because she's *not playing for us*! Don't no coach play. They coach, but they don't come in the game and play. We gotta do that for ourselves.

"She's trying to make us think that we can't play without her," he continued. "She's trying to test us, man. She's trying to make us realize that we need to win this.

"When the second half comes—we start scoring," Fornatee said. "We can win this, man. There's gotta be a reason why she's not coaching now. But it don't matter, man. We gotta win this game, man. We gotta *win this game*."

"Get your hands in here," Kanue yelled. The young men formed a circle and stacked their hands one on top of the other.

"One, two, three," they chanted. "Go Fugees!"

MINUTES INTO THE second half, the Phoenix forwards methodically and almost casually picked their way through the Fugees' defense and tapped the ball into the left side of the net for an almost embarrassingly anticlimactic goal. It was now 4–1. The Fugees were yelling at each other now, their halftime enthusiasm instantly drained. After another offsides call, Fornatee cursed at the referee, drawing his second yellow card and an ejection. The Phoenix parents and friends were quiet now; there was no need to pile on. The Fugees were exhausted, and without their coach, they were lost. The Phoenix scored again, and kept scoring. When the referee blew his whistle three times to signal the end of the game, the score was 7–2, Phoenix.

After the game, the Fugees gathered on their bench in silence, guzzling water from plastic cups until Luma called to them from across the field to get on the bus. As the players filed off the field, I asked her what was going on.

"They show up to tutoring late," she said. "They're disrespectful. They show up to practice not dressed to play, their pants hanging down. I tell them practice is at five-thirty, they show up at six-thirty. I tell them, 'You have to be at the field at one o'clock for a two-o'clock game,' and they're coming, what, like ten minutes before the game?

"It's not going to work," she said. "So I was like, 'You know, the way they're behaving is the way I'm going to behave. They're being irresponsible, and I'm not going to be accountable for them.'" She told me that she'd thought about going to get a hamburger, but the referee told her before the game that if she left the field her team would have to forfeit. So she decided to sit and watch what she knew would be a meltdown, especially on the part of Fornatee.

"He can't handle it when I get mad at him," she said. "They don't have the discipline to hack it. They don't show up to practices. They don't show up to the game. You can't compete like this."

With that, Luma walked away, trailing behind her players as they walked toward the bus. She waited for them to board and to take their seats. A moment later, she climbed onto the bus to address her players and to give them the news. Luma had decided to cancel the Under 15s' season. They would forfeit the rest of their games. There would be no more practice or tutoring sessions. The Under 15 Fugees were finished.

Chapter Thirteen

"How Am I Going to Start All Over?"

Luma's decision to cancel the Under 15s' season was hard on many of the team's players, but it was especially wrenching for fifteen-year-old Kanue Biah.

Kanue was from Nimba County, in eastern Liberia, though his family fled the war there when he was just two years old, for refugee camps first in Ivory Coast and eventually Guinea. Kanue kept the circumstances of his upbringing to himself; for reasons he rarely revealed, he was separated at some point from his parents and taken in by his uncle, a stern and demanding man named Barlea, and a great-aunt, whom he called simply Grandma. In 2004, Barlea was accepted for resettlement in the United States and placed in Clarkston. The plan was that he would eventually bring as many members of his extended family as possible into the United States. A year later, Kanue was accepted for resettlement as well, and joined Barlea in a two-bedroom apartment in Clarkston, a dreary place with bare walls, tattered old carpeting, and in the kitchen, warped particleboard cabinets and uneven linoleum floors. Asylum for those family members left behind did not come easily, or at all. Months passed, and none were granted entry into the States. So Barlea and Kanue, uncle and nephew, did the best they could on their own.

To support the two of them, and to have money left over to send back home, Barlea shouldered an almost inhuman work schedule. He took two jobs in back-to-back night shifts at the Atlanta airport, an hour's commute by rail. He left the apartment each evening at seven p.m. and worked a shift cooking burgers at a fast food restaurant at the airport. When that shift was over, Barlea then worked a second shift at the airport in the morning, as a porter. He returned home each day around three p.m. and collapsed into bed for a few hours of sleep before waking up for another double shift. He was perpetually exhausted and bleary, and a little cranky, particularly when dinner wasn't ready.

Kanue's role was to cook and keep the apartment. After classes each day at a public school called Avondale Middle, he went home and got to work making African food from recipes he'd learned from Grandma: beans and spicy stews of spinach and cassava leaves, which he poured over rice, and his favorite, peanut butter soup. He stored the meals in the refrigerator so they were ready for Barlea when he came in the door from his long night and morning of work. Barlea would heat the meals in a microwave and quickly eat—often too tired to exchange more than a few words with Kanue—before dashing off for his few hours of sleep. Kanue had kept up this routine from the age of thirteen. He was not allowed to play soccer, do homework, or leave the house until the cooking was done. So the food was always there. Kanue never complained. In fact, his duties at home had imbued him with a sense of responsibility and self-reliance that belied his age and set him apart from his peers.

These qualities came in handy in the halls and classrooms of Avondale High School, a rough and failing public school where American kids could be cruel to new arrivals, particularly refugees. Kanue was fortunate that as a Liberian he was fluent in English. But his thick accent set him apart from American students, who frequently teased him. Once, while reciting his lines in a school play, Kanue was mocked by an American student because of his accent. He lashed out. There was a tussle, and Kanue was briefly suspended. But it wasn't in

Kanue's nature to seethe or hold grudges. Instead, he tried a different tack, engaging kids who made fun of him so that he could learn from his mispronunciations and grammatical mistakes.

"They say, 'You don't know how to speak English,'" Kanue said. "So I always say, 'When I speak wrong English, don't laugh at me—just correct me.'"

Not long after Kanue arrived in the United States, he was playing soccer in the parking lot of Southern Pines when one of the other kids told him he should come to practice with the Fugees. It was summer, and tryouts were two months away, but the coach, Kanue learned, would let kids join summer practice so long as they understood that they weren't guaranteed a spot on the roster. They'd still have to prove themselves at tryouts. Kanue was determined to make the team. He crafted his own conditioning program, running to and from practice each day, to get in better shape. At practice, Luma would ride her bicycle around the track for half an hour, setting the pace for her players, who ran behind her. In his mind, Kanue imagined himself overtaking her, and he tried his best each day to catch up with Luma. His endurance improved by the week.

The Fugees offered a welcome opportunity to get out of the apartment. Kanue made friends. He honed his cooking routine to free up time for soccer practice. And he was determined to stick around, even if a slot didn't open up on the roster.

"I said to Coach, 'If I don't make the team can I just practice with you?'" he recalled.

An opening did arise, eventually, at goalkeeper. It wasn't the most desired position for someone as physically fit and eager to participate in the game as Kanue was, but he happily accepted. He gave the position his all and quickly developed a reputation among his teammates for toughness bordering on recklessness in his efforts to keep the ball out of the net. In his entire first season as keeper, Kanue gave up only three goals.

Once, the Fugees showed up to a game three players short of a full roster. Luma could have forfeited, but instead she decided to make adjustments and play eight against eleven. Thinking that she needed her best athletes up front if she hoped to stay in the game, Luma moved Kanue from keeper to striker. Kanue knew it was his chance. As a keeper, he had watched and learned the tricks and moves of successful offensive players, and had noted how the best had worked to keep a goalie off-balance. He was determined to put that experience to work. In that first game as striker, Kanue managed to score his first goal. He was so elated that his celebratory dance drew a yellow card. The Fugees went on to win that game 4–2, despite playing down three players. In the process Luma had discovered a new offensive weapon.

Over the course of his two years with the team, Kanue's devotion to the Fugees and to Luma had become complete. He showed up early for practices and was always on time to the bus for games. He rode his bike from his apartment complex near Clarkston to Decatur to watch the younger Fugees team play, and to help Coach carry gear. If the Fugees held a team car wash to raise money, Kanue washed more cars—and more thoroughly—than any of the others. In games, he would frequently chase the ball from one end of the field to the other, switching from defense to midfield to offense and back, of his own accord, running himself to exhaustion. Luma's biggest challenge with Kanue was preventing him from doing too much. She learned that his teammates would sometimes slack off, knowing that Kanue would step in to make up for their lack of effort. She had even benched Kanue midgame simply so that her other players didn't become too reliant on him. And she helped him too with Barlea. Once when Barlea told Kanue he couldn't play soccer because he hadn't yet made dinner, Luma stopped by with a roasted chicken for Barlea so Kanue could leave the apartment.

With no siblings in the United States, and a guardian who was hardly ever home, Kanue began to view the team as his family.

"The Fugees—it's really important to me," he said. "When I play on that team, I'm with my brothers."

Luma's decision to cancel his team's season hit Kanue hard. She offered to let him join the Under 17 Fugees, but for Kanue it wasn't the same. Those boys were older and bigger than he was, and anyway, he wanted to play with the boys he'd become close to over the previous two years.

"I was feeling really bad," Kanue said. "I was thinking, *How am I going to start all over?*"

THE SUNDAY AFTER Luma canceled the 15s' season was rainy and listless. On such days, the apartment complexes of Clarkston were especially dreary. Televisions blared and echoed menacingly in the empty hallways. The footfalls of upstairs neighbors shook the thin walls and rattled the ceiling lights. Children could be heard crying amid the clanging of pots and pans. In the parking lots, teenagers scurried between buildings, slouched, heads bowed against the rain, on the way to see friends, or else they stood under the eaves, poking their heads out to check the sky, waiting for the rain to cease. Every now and again, a crowded automobile would dart into the lot and an adult would hop out and run through the rain toward a front door— carpools of refugees on the way home from weekend shifts at local commercial bakeries, packaging or poultry processing plants. Kanue was at home by himself, bored, and upset about the demise of his team. The phone rang. It was Luma.

Luma asked Kanue if he wanted to see a movie; she was picking up Mandela and Natnael, another team leader and a close friend of Kanue's. Kanue said sure, and he went outside on the balcony to wait for the sight of Luma's yellow Volkswagen.

The ride to the theater was quiet. No one mentioned the team. The movie was *Invincible,* a true story about a South Philadelphia bartender who went on to play for the Philadelphia Eagles. Luma didn't care much for American football, but she thought the boys might enjoy the plot. In truth, their minds were elsewhere. They were thinking about the Fugees.

It wasn't until they got back into Coach's car after the movie that Kanue finally broached the subject. He asked Luma not to cancel the season. Luma told the three boys that she couldn't coach a team of players who weren't committed enough to even show up on time for practice or games. If she cut the bad apples from the team, there wouldn't be enough players for a full roster, she explained. And it wasn't fair to ask the remaining players to play an entire season with a short roster and no substitutes. Without a full roster, she told them, the Fugees would probably lose every game.

Kanue was ready with his own arguments.

"Canceling the whole team wouldn't be fair to us," he said. There were good kids on the team who followed her rules, he said. They shouldn't be punished because of the others. Kanue understood Coach's argument about playing with a short roster, but he had a solution. He, Mandela, and Natnael could round up a new roster of players. They could knock on doors in Clarkston and find good kids— kids who would follow her rules. They could start all over again, with another day of tryouts. They would go back to the old players and tell them that if they weren't willing to obey the rules, they shouldn't show up. Kanue told Luma that he would read the contract to new recruits himself. If he had any doubts that they would abide by her rules, he wouldn't let them try out. Luma presented the counterarguments: It would take the boys ten days to get players and hold tryouts, by which time they would have had to forfeit two games—their season would be shot. And even then, how would a bunch of kids who had never played together compete with teams from Atlanta's best soccer academies—teams that had been playing together for years?

As the boys and Luma debated, Kanue took Luma's cell phone and quietly began to scroll through her contacts list, writing down the phone numbers of his teammates and other kids whose names he recognized.

Luma, uncharacteristically, was torn. Canceling the team would send a clear message about her expectations to players on all of her teams, and she was anxious about seeming to cave in. She was also worried about encouraging Kanue, Natnael, and Mandela to recruit new players, knowing that such a hastily conceived team faced the prospect of humiliation against a schedule of well-coached and well-prepared teams in their division. She feared what might happen if her players got frustrated and lashed out during play.

On the other hand, Luma thought about the good kids, the ones who had done all she'd asked, like Kanue. She thought of Mandela, a kid on the fence for whom the Fugees were a lifeline. She shuddered to think of what kind of trouble kids like Mandela might get into without the Fugees to keep them busy.

Luma mulled her options and decided to try to bide her time. There was a possibility that Kanue, Mandela, and Natnael might not round up enough new recruits to even force her into a decision. She told the boys that if they convinced the committed players on the team to return and rounded up new players who would follow her rules, she would be willing to hold another day of tryouts. She'd make her final decision about the team's season based on how those tryouts went. There were no guarantees, she said.

The boys were quiet for the rest of the ride home. Luma dropped them off one by one. When they got to Southern Pines, Kanue said goodbye, climbed out of the car, and dashed through the rain to the front door of Building D, where he lived. Barlea was at work, so Kanue had the apartment all to himself. He picked up the phone and began to work his way through the numbers he'd taken from Luma's phone.

"Bring all friends who want to join the team," he told everyone he called. "We're going to have tryouts. Coach is giving us another chance."

THE 15S' SEASON was on hold, but Luma still had two other teams to coach, and on Monday afternoon she stood on the field at Indian Creek Elementary as the younger of those, the 13s, completed their running. Luma summoned them in with a blast of her whistle. The boys were joking with each other as they approached, but when they got close enough to read Luma's expression, they sensed that her mood was gloomy, and fell quiet.

"You're supposed to all line up and start running nonstop for twenty-five minutes—no walking," she said by way of a greeting. "See how many of you are here? I don't have to take you all to the game on Saturday. I only have to take eleven. So if you decide to cuss, Jeremiah"—her bionic hearing had apparently picked up on some foul language from across the field—"you will be sent home.

"I don't know if you all know, but we no longer have an Under 15 team, and the reason is because of their behavior. So if you want to follow in their footsteps, go ahead—I don't have a problem with that. But then you too will no longer have a team. If you want to come out here and have fun, then play hard. If you want to take walks around the track, then go home. You're only practicing twice a week, so twice a week you run the whole time. No jogging. Real quick—if any of you lag you're going to take five more laps."

The 13s' first two games had not portended well for their season. They tied their first game 4–4, and then gave up a one-goal lead in their second, to lose 3–1. The team wasn't passing well. Players weren't holding their positions, and they weren't talking to each other on the field. They had a long way to go. But the 13s seemed to get the message from Luma. It was time to get serious. Their Monday practice was quiet and intense. Two days later, on Wednesday, the boys showed up on time, ran hard, and were focused during their drills. The 13s seemed to determine to let their coach know they weren't like the 15s. They were willing to do what she said, and they wanted to win.

THE 13S' THIRD game of the season took place on a sweltering Saturday afternoon at Ebster Field, the Fugees' home ground in downtown Decatur. The opponent was the Triumph, a mostly white team from nearby Tucker, Georgia. Luma gave her players their positions—Josiah, the tall, slightly bowlegged Liberian with deceptive speed at left forward; Jeremiah Ziaty on the right. Qendrim, the small, spindly-legged Kosovar, would play center midfielder; Bienvenue, the happy-go-lucky Burundian, would direct the defense from the middle in back. The 13s had heeded the precedent set by Luma's cancellation of the 15s' season; a full roster had turned out for the game. So in the early going, Luma was able to substitute freely, to keep her players fresh in the heat. To his astonishment, even Santino, a quiet ten-year-old Sudanese boy who had arrived in the United States only a few weeks before the season, found his way into the rotation.

Only minutes into the game, Jeremiah took a throw-in on the far side, near the corner. He heaved the ball to Josiah, who captured it neatly beneath his cleats and passed it back to Jeremiah, who fired a long, arcing shot that flew across the face of the goal and just inside the opposite pole: the Fugees were up 1–0. Before the half, tiny Qendrim dribbled through the defense ten yards out and tapped a slow roller past the goalie's left foot. The Fugees were up 2–0.

Luma, though, wasn't satisfied.

"We've got one big problem going on," she told her team at halftime. "You guys are starting to play like them. You're starting to kick the ball wherever it goes. You're starting to walk around. You're starting to get lazy."

It was a theme I would hear countless times during the season:

when the Fugees played poorly, or slowly and without zeal, Luma would tell her players they were playing the other team's style of soccer—playing "like them." It was a clever bit of psychological manipulation; while ostensibly a criticism, the line contained the implication that the Fugees themselves were special. The only way they could lose, her argument suggested, was by adopting the ordinary ways of their mostly American opponents. It was as close as Luma ever came to pointing out to her players that as refugees, they had not just a connection to one another, but a special quality that set them apart.

"Start spreading the ball, looking up, and taking more shots on goal," she said. "You haven't won this game, and the way you're playing you're not going to win it.

"You need to go in with the game zero-zero and you need to play hard," she continued. "You're better than them. We all know you're better than them. But you're not going to be better if you start playing *like them.*

"You guys ready?" Luma asked her team finally.

"Yes!" they shouted in unison.

In the second half, the Fugees put on a show. Josiah slipped around his defender on the left side, and dribbled downfield at a full gallop before taking a clean shot into the right side of the net: 3–0, Fugees. Luma moved Bien from defense up the field to offense, and he quickly executed an amazing bicycle kick over his head. The ball flew straight to the goalie, but the move was so remarkable that the parents of the Triumph players applauded in appreciation. Jeremiah scored again, and late in the second half, Bien lobbed an elegant cross across the face of the goal. Qendrim dove headfirst, arms at his sides, like a spear, and executed a perfect header, deflecting the ball and freezing the goalie—another score. When the whistle blew three times to signal the end of the game, the Under 13 Fugees had won 5–1.

"Guys, you had a good game," Luma told them afterward. "It wasn't your best game, but a good game.

"We're going to keep working on our crosses, because we're getting there," she added. "Not bad. Next week will be a much better game—okay?"

Chapter Fourteen

Alex, Bien, and Ive

The apartment where Bienvenue lived with his brothers, Alex and Ive, his infant sister, Alyah, and his mother, Generose, looked scarcely more lived-in than it did the night they arrived from Burundi, a year and a half before. The walls were still bare but for a photograph of Bienvenue that he himself had hung with tape in the living room, as well as a large abstract drawing in black crayon on a wall leading into the kitchen—a mural young Ive had started and abandoned but that had not yet been washed away. There was a TV on a stand in the corner, with rabbit-ears antennae on top and a VCR underneath, and three old sofas around the perimeter of the living room—all items that had been donated to the family by a local church. Off a small hallway to the right, there were two bedrooms—the boys shared one and Generose and Alyah slept in the other. The living room opened onto a modest kitchen with bright fluorescent lights in the ceiling and tawny linoleum tiling on the floor. A glass sliding door at the back of the kitchen remained closed most of the time; it opened onto a small concrete slab and a thinly wooded hillside that sloped down to the ever-thrumming interstate below.

It was impossible to visit Generose's family without having a large meal cooked in one's honor: rice or foofoo heaped with cassava leaves the consistency of creamed spinach, potatoes soaked in tomato broth, beans, greens stewed with sardines, and often fried whole fish or beef in a sauce of onions, tomatoes, and garlic—though the family would have rarely had whole fish or beef on their own. Fresh meat was simply too expensive for any but special occasions.

Like many refugee parents I met in Clarkston, Generose was eager to meet an actual American. Meeting Americans was a rare occurrence for newcomers. Refugees and locals went through their days in full view of each other—a stream of thousands of Atlantans passed by on the interstate each day on the other side of Generose's glass sliding door—but the two groups rarely interacted. Instead, they lived along the borders of two inaccessible but transparent worlds, separated by some invisible border, like birds from fish.

The first time I visited Bien and Alex at home, things got off to a rocky start. I introduced myself to Generose by saying that I worked for a newspaper in New York and had come to Atlanta to write about the Fugees. Bien translated into Swahili and listened to his mother's response.

"My mamma say she don't like newspapers," he said.

I asked why, expecting to hear a version of the seemingly universal distrust of journalists, but instead Generose quickly stood and disappeared into another room. A moment later, she emerged with an envelope, which she handed to me: it was a $136 bill for daily delivery of *The New York Times*—my employer. I was puzzled; it didn't make sense to me that a Burundian refugee who spoke no English should have a subscription to the *Times*. Generose was equally confused.

"Why they bring newspaper every day and ask for the money?" Bien said, translating for her. "We don't want. It's too much."

Generose had never ordered daily delivery of the *Times*—aside from the language issue, the cost was well beyond her means—and yet the paper had been piling up at her front door for weeks. I said I would take the bill and call the company myself to sort things out. When I called the *Times*' subscription department and explained the situation, the company dropped the charges and a supervisor chalked the situation up to a misunderstanding on the part of one of the tele-marketing companies the *Times* used to sell subscriptions.

It was an insight that helped explain a recurring problem I heard about from refugees in Clarkston over the next weeks and months: they were constantly getting calls from telemarketing companies of-fering free subscriptions, vacations, legal help with immigration is-sues, and the like. Telemarketers, resettlement officials surmised, had figured out that dialing numbers located in the Clarkston zip code produced an excellent chance of reaching someone who spoke little or no English. With a few inducements that broke through the language barrier—repeating the word "free," for example—and by playing on the hopes of the newcomers, marketers could get them to sign up for just about anything. Signing up a new customer required only a sim-ple yes, a word most refugees knew and often used as a substitute for "what" or "pardon." It was a regular task of aid agency caseworkers and volunteers to extract refugees from agreements and arrangements they'd inadvertently signed up for, and there was no way of knowing how many refugees simply paid the bills out of fear. The transactions came with an additional cost to the sense of security and optimism refugees felt toward their new home, as I was reminded a few months later when I received a call from Bienvenue's older brother, Alex. The family had received a letter in the mail offering them a free car, he said. He wanted my help in claiming it. I called the number on the circular to confirm what I knew—that it was a scam. I called Alex back with the news, which he relayed to Generose while I was still on the phone. The long silence that ensued left no mistake about her disappointment.

Despite my affiliation with the company that kept sending newspapers—and bills—to Generose's apartment, I was invited to sit down on a tattered sofa in the living room. I dropped my weight on the sofa, but instead of landing on a soft cushion, I collided with a piece of wood framing that hid beneath the fabric. When the boys saw me wince, they laughed hysterically. The coccyx-busting sofa frame had become a family joke, and had claimed another victim.

Generose covered the coffee table with a piece of beige fabric and brought out a stack of small plates and a fistful of forks from the kitchen. The boys followed with the food: a large plastic bowl full of steaming rice and smaller ceramic bowls containing warm helpings of cassava, beans, potatoes, and stewed greens. Generose pressed Play on the VCR beneath the TV, and the screen came to life with the blurry images of a Catholic choir from Congo, singing hymns outdoors against changing backdrops of mountains and green forests.

In at least one respect, Generose and her boys perfectly fit the profile of the typical refugee family in Clarkston. Their English skills were in inverse proportion to their ages. Generose, who spoke Swahili, some French, and Kirundi—the language of Bujumbura and western Burundi—knew only a few words of English. Alex, fifteen and the oldest, understood English, but spoke haltingly and with a thick Burundian accent that, combined with his deepening and sometimes cracking adolescent voice, made him sometimes difficult to understand. Sensing this, perhaps, Alex was shy and quiet and spoke mainly in Swahili to his family. Bienvenue—Bien or Bienve to his family—was two years younger, a difference in age that had helped him pick up a new language more quickly than Alex. Luma had managed to get Bienvenue accepted into a nearby charter school with a curriculum designed for immigrants and refugees, extra help that had improved Bien's English quickly. He spoke with a less pronounced accent than Alex, and though he struggled with writing and reading, his natural desire to make jokes and to engage powered him through spoken English. When he occasionally got hung up searching for an elusive word or phrase, Bien would lower his chin, place his open palm on the crown of his head, and rotate it in small quick circles, the same motion, I learned later, that Generose had used to soothe him when he cried as a child.

Ive, who was seven, spoke English fluently and with no accent. His favorite TV show was *The Simpsons,* and not by coincidence, he spoke in a slightly high-pitched intonation and sometimes with a surprisingly knowing tone that sounded a lot like Bart Simpson himself. It often fell to Ive, as the best English speaker in the family, to answer the phone and to have conversations with Americans—the landlord, billing agents from the phone and power companies—who were decades older than he was.

Having to rely on her seven-year-old son as her interface with the outside world had its frustrations for Generose. But the more pressing impact of her inability to speak English was in the job market, where it limited her options significantly. She had managed a part-time job as a stocker at a local drugstore for a while, but since giving birth to Alyah six months before, she had been unemployed. She had no money, she said. Alyah's father, in Canada now and without immigration papers to get into the United States, helped out as much as he could by sending money, and a well-to-do Atlanta woman who volunteered to help refugee families through the International Rescue Committee donated groceries and helped Generose make ends meet while she looked for a job. But working presented its own economic challenge. Having a job would require Generose to find day care for Alyah. To come out ahead after childcare costs, Generose figured she would have to find work that paid thirteen or fourteen dollars an hour. If such work existed in Atlanta for unskilled applicants who spoke no English, Generose had yet to find it.

Rent for the family's two-bedroom apartment was $650. Power and phone bills amounted to nearly $200 a month. Food was a relatively cheap but not inconsequential expense; Generose bought her rice in bulk, in large, fifty-pound plastic sacks from the DeKalb County farmers' market, just down the road. She was open to a job at night, she said; that way the boys could babysit Alyah when they returned from school while she worked, and she could sleep and stay with the baby during the day.

It was a measure of Generose's desperation that she was willing to leave her six-month-old daughter in the care of her three sons, ages seven, thirteen, and fifteen. While in a refugee camp in Mozambique, Generose had lost a daughter not to war or famine, but to a domestic accident. The girl had accidentally knocked over a pot of boiling potatoes that was propped over a fire on an arrangement of rocks. The girl was badly scalded, and Generose, too poor to afford transportation out of the camp to a hospital, was left to tend her daughter's burns with wraps of leaves. For a time it seemed the girl might be fine, but eventually she succumbed to her wounds and probable infection, and died at just nine years old. Generose was constantly shooing her younger children out of the kitchen, and allowed only Alex, the eldest, to cook on the stove. She feared the idea of leaving her children alone at all. But she had to find a way to provide for them.

Generose hadn't anticipated that life in the United States would require her to decide between work and watching after her children. Like many refugees in Clarkston, she had put so much of her energy and hope into getting out of a refugee camp that she hadn't thought much about what life might be like after she arrived in a new country.

"I thought America would be paradise," Generose said, through Bien.

"We thought America would be like this," Alex said, pantomiming a magician with a wand and flicking it at the table to conjure something out of the ether.

"Soda!" he said, then, flicking the wand again: "Food!"

Bienvenue, Generose, and Ive guffawed along with Alex. In just over a year in the United States, they had come to see their blind faith in America's bounty as naive to the point of comedy. Disappointment on this count was common among the refugees in Clarkston and drove home the reality that however much the United States' reputation had suffered around the world in recent years, most refugees arrived here with the image of America as a land of plenty. Over time, a more complicated reality set in.

"No worry, no worry," Generose said in her sparing English, and raising her hands to stifle the pessimistic conversation about money. "God very, very good."

Generose turned her attention to the hymns still playing on the television, closed her eyes, and rocked her head back and forth gently, singing along in a hushed falsetto.

Chapter Fifteen

Trying Again

When Luma called the team's sponsors at the Decatur-DeKalb YMCA to let them know she had folded the Under 15s, administrators there were incensed. They called her in for a meeting, which took place around a table in a small upstairs conference room. As long as the YMCA was sponsoring the Fugees, Luma was told, only YMCA officials had the authority to cancel the team's season. In particular, administrators at the YMCA were concerned about how folding a team after a season had begun would affect the Y's reputation within the Georgia Youth Soccer Association, the large and sometimes political overseer of some seventy-five thousand youth soccer players in the state. The administrators argued that Luma should simply kick the troublemakers off the team and continue with the core of committed players.

Luma's counterargument was simple. She was not going to waste her time coaching kids who wouldn't show up on time for practice or games. It was true that there were some committed players on the

Under 15 Fugees, but if she kicked off the troublemakers she would be left with just eight or nine players, short of the full complement of eleven. She would have no substitutes, so each player would have to play entire games in the Georgia heat with no breaks. It wasn't safe, she argued. And if a kid got tired and frustrated and started fouling, Luma would have no one to put in his place until he cooled off. It wasn't fair to the players who would remain, she said.

To join league play, the Fugees needed affiliation with an established organization, and the Y had stepped in. The Y provided use of the bus to get the Fugees home after practice and to away games, and helped with scheduling and logistics. But resentments had built up on Luma's part. There were still no goals on the field at Indian Creek Elementary School. Luma had spent hours looking for quality leather soccer shoes that were affordable under the team's paltry budget, so that her players didn't have to play in the cheap, uncomfortable plastic shoes she knew the YMCA would likely purchase for them if given no guidance. She passed the information on the affordable leather shoes to the youth sports coordinator at the YMCA, but the coordinator had gone ahead and bought the cheap plastic shoes anyway. Luma's players were now paying the price with their blistered feet. On successive nights the previous week, the YMCA bus had failed to show up after practice, leaving Luma to ferry two teams' worth of players home four at a time in her Volkswagen. It was Luma's firmly held belief that the YMCA would never simply forget to send a bus to take home the well-to-do American kids in its other athletic programs. And no one from the Y ever came out to games or practices or showed any particular involvement or support.

Luma had started the Fugees on her own, and had committed herself to the program. She worked as a volunteer; she received no salary from the YMCA and had no official position there. If Luma decided not to coach the 15s, the team would simply cease to exist. There was no other coach in the wings to take over her position if she simply decided not to show up at practices or games, and no committee of team moms to fill the breach. The Y was essentially telling Luma that she was compelled to volunteer—"like they own me," she fumed.

"They tell me, 'You don't have the authority to make those decisions,'" she said after the meeting. "They don't have the authority to make me show up!"

Administrators at the YMCA were beginning to believe that Luma was simply too difficult and demanding to work with. They read her relentless advocacy for her players as haughtiness, and a lack of appreciation for what the YMCA had provided the Fugees: use of its bus, as well as financial and logistical support.

For Luma, the dispute was in part about issues of authority and control. She felt strongly that if she was going to run a soccer program, she had to do it on her terms. If she thought it was both unfair and unsafe to field a depleted team, she did not expect to be questioned by people who worked behind desks and who had rarely, if ever, seen her teams play. The Y's incompetence with the bus, the shoes, and the goals, she figured, all but disqualified them as advisers on how to run her soccer program. Luma also feared that if she gave in and went back on her decision to end the season, players on her other teams might try to see what they could get away with. She could lose control of the whole program.

But more infuriating to Luma than simple matters of control or authority was her belief that the YMCA had simply failed repeatedly to follow through on its word. In her worldview, there was no greater flaw.

"She still has this high expectation that people will do the right thing, coupled with a very strong sense of right and wrong," Tracy said. "She won't work with someone that she thinks lacks integrity or the proper motivation to do what's right."

Aside from the battles of will with the Y and with her players, there was a much more practical concern that Luma had taken into account in deciding to fold the team, one that went more or less unspoken: she was exhausted. She was coaching three teams—the Under 13, the Under 15, and the Under 17 Fugees—in addition to running her cleaning company, which employed refugee mothers. She had forty-eight players in all, and she spent her evenings and weekends driving around Clarkston visiting and helping their families—shuttling them to doctors' appointments, making sense of their phone and power bills, explaining the meaning of the countless forms that arrived from school and from various government agencies. Even for someone of her commitment and zeal, it was depleting work. Luma rarely had any time for herself. She might occasionally make time for a weekly night of trivia at a local pizza parlor with friends, but for the most part

her social life consisted of short two- or three-line e-mails to friends
and a slew of unreturned phone calls. By jettisoning the Under 15
team, Luma still wouldn't have time for herself exactly, but she could
focus her energies on the kids who were reciprocating her commitment to the Fugees. She had agreed to hold new tryouts for the Under
15s if Kanue, Mandela, and Natnael managed to round up enough
new players, but her mind was more or less made up.

TRYOUTS FOR THE possible revival of the Under 15s were set for
Monday afternoon on the sandy field behind Indian Creek Elementary, as chance would have it, during a reprieve from the late-summer
heat. Luma had agreed to attend if Kanue, Mandela, and Natnael did
the recruiting and organizing. They had come through—new faces
were arriving from the footpaths through the surrounding woods—
although there had been some confusion about the starting time. The
boys had told their teammates and potential players to show up at
five-thirty p.m. and absentmindedly told their coach to show up at six
p.m., an instruction the boys later forgot. So for half an hour the boys
stretched, jogged, and passed a ball around, all the while glancing
anxiously at the parking lot for sight of Luma's yellow Beetle. Perhaps,
someone wondered aloud, she had changed her mind.

As the boys waited, members of the other two Fugees teams began
to show up as well, to see what sort of talent Kanue, Mandela, and
Natnael had unearthed from the apartment complexes around town.
Word that something was up with the Fugees seemed to have seeped
out to the other kids in the neighborhood, even those who didn't play
soccer; boys and girls who normally would have unhesitatingly run
across the field in the middle of practice gathered quietly beside the
running track and climbed atop the big orange and blue jungle gym
to watch.

At five minutes to six, the yellow Volkswagen pulled into the lot.
Luma got out, opened the trunk, and wrestled out a mesh bag full of
soccer balls. She heaved the bag over her shoulder and made her way
to the field.

Luma surveyed the young men who had turned out. There were
six familiar faces; four from the current Under 15s—Kanue, Natnael,

Mandela, and Bienvenue's older brother, Alex—and two other boys who had come out for practices with the Fugees in the past. The rest were unknowns. Notably absent was Fornatee; when the other boys had called him, he had explained that he intended to play for the Under 15s if Luma reinstated the team. But he felt strongly that he had tried out once before and shouldn't have to try out again. It was an insult, he said.

Luma gathered the newcomers, asked their names, and wrote them down on a sheet of paper. Then she divided the group into two teams and told them she planned simply to watch them play. As the boys took the field, Luma noticed that one boy was wearing sandals. She called him over and placed her foot alongside his: they were close to the same size. Luma kicked off the black Puma soccer shoes she wore each day to practice and offered them to the boy, who stepped out of his sandals and slipped them on. Sock footed, Luma sat on the ground and watched the scrimmage in silence.

"It feels like our first season," she said finally. "There's no base for the team. If we could practice five days a week we might be able to make it—"

She cut herself off. With two other teams to coach, that wasn't possible. If Luma decided to reinstate the 15s, they'd have perhaps three practices before their first game. She'd be lucky if her players learned one another's names. She had her concerns too about some of the new kids; she didn't know yet who they were, or if they were the sort of kids she wanted in her program. And Luma feared that by going ahead with the season, she might be setting her kids up for failure. The thought of it all put Luma in a brooding mood. She was weak from hunger as well. It was Ramadan, the Muslim month of fasting from sunrise to sunset, and though Luma wasn't an observant Muslim, she observed the daily fast for the lessons it provided in humility, sacrifice, and patience. But she was worn down. For the first time since I'd met her, she seemed unsure of herself.

"What would you do?" she eventually asked me.

Luma didn't wait for an answer. She dropped her head and sighed.

"I don't know," she said. "I just don't know."

LUMA STUDIED THE players. Kanue was leading the scrimmage, calling out to his teammates, urging them to pass, and sprinting desperately for each free ball. The new players responded. There was a pair of Somali Bantu brothers, Hamdu and Jeylani Muganga, who were relentless on defense. Mandela charged his way through traffic, using his large frame to shield the ball, and scored a goal. Natnael flicked a series of clever passes across the field to players he'd never met before. The boys were playing with desperation, as if they were trying to will their team back into existence.

Luma watched intently, making occasional notes next to the players' names on the sheet of paper she held in her hand. She drew a soccer field on the back and began to write names in specific positions: The Mugangas were quick and determined; Luma wrote their names on the back line, on defense, and put Alex in between. She put Kanue at center midfielder, Natnael at left mid, and Mandela at striker. There was a quick-footed young Bosnian player named Muamer—easily spotted by his thin black mustache that made him look ten years older than his actual age of fifteen. He was an excellent ball handler, even though he was raw and seemed never to pass. Perhaps he could be brought along; Luma put him at right forward. She wrote other names down, erased them, and wrote them down again at other positions—an exercise she repeated until the sheet of paper was a nearly illegible jumble of names and smudges.

After an hour or so, Luma blew her whistle and summoned everyone in. The boys formed a semicircle around her and waited for Luma to speak.

"Out of the sixteen players here today I have only coached six," she told them. "So only six of you know how I am as a coach, and only six know what kind of players I expect. And only six of you know what rules I am going to make you have.

"If we go in with this team," she continued, "we're probably going to lose the majority of our games. I say we might win one or two if we're lucky."

One of the newcomers groaned in disagreement.

"Are you guys going to be okay going into a season and losing most of your games?" she asked.

There was no response.

"You're playing teams that have been together five years," she said. "We're not going to play this weekend. You play the weekend after—you will have been together one week. So five years against one week."

Luma pointed out that they'd have just three practices to get their team together.

Kanue spoke up. They could get an extra practice in early Saturday morning, he said. The other kids nodded—they'd be there.

"We can do this," Kanue said.

"If you still want it, then I'll see you Thursday at five," Luma said. "And if you don't—don't show up Thursday.

"Practices are not going to be easy," Luma added. "You're going to be running more than the other teams, kicking the ball a lot more. And I'm not going to be nice. So if you thought I was mean these past two weeks . . ."

Luma let that thought hang in the air for a moment, and then turned to walk from the field.

KANUE DROPPED HIS head in relief. His team was alive. He had vetted the newcomers and let them know Coach's rules—he'd read the contract to many of them himself—and he was going to make sure everyone was there on Thursday afternoon, on time. He also believed the team could get in yet another practice, early Sunday morning—he planned to talk to Coach about that later. But for now he simply wanted to let her know what was on his mind, and he did so quietly, when no one else was around.

"I told her I appreciate her," Kanue said later. "I told her thanks, and that we were going to do everything to follow the rules and give her the respect she deserves."

Chapter Sixteen

The Fifteens Fight

There was plenty of raw talent among the group of boys who had come out for the second edition of the Fugees' Under 15s, but there was little in the way of cohesion. The boys came from Liberia, Kosovo, Sudan, Somalia, Burundi, Bosnia, Ethiopia, and Afghanistan, and while most spoke functional English, they had little in common with one another. With just nine days to go before their first game, Luma figured her best shot at getting this disparate group of boys to bond was to make them face adversity together. After two standard practices that focused on the basics of passing and ball handling, she scheduled a scrimmage between the new Under 15 Fugees and their counterparts on the Under 17 team. The 15s stood little chance, which was the point; their reaction to the frustration of playing a much better opponent would give Luma a better sense of whether or not she would proceed with the rest of the games on their schedule. If the Under 15s lost their cool against the older Fugees, she figured, they stood little chance against the more hostile competition to come.

In truth, she was skeptical that they could actually pull it off. Mandela, one of the three anchors of the team along with Natnael and Kanue, was a particular worry. Although he'd contributed to the recruiting effort to find new players, at the practices following tryouts he was taciturn and irascible. Mandela was still angry that his friend Prince wasn't on the team because of the hair rule, which he considered stupid. And now Fornatee, his other close friend on the team, hadn't shown up for the new round of tryouts. Of his clique, Mandela was now alone on the team, which apparently now would include Bosnians, Kosovars, and Somali Bantu kids he'd never met before. That wasn't what Mandela thought he'd signed up for. He seemed to have little interest in getting to know the new players. Before practice, he hid within his headphones and juggled a ball, content not to speak to anyone. In practice, his body language now conveyed his deepening dissatisfaction; his posture was slumped and his arms flopped unenthusiastically as he labored through drills. He snapped at kids who made bad passes or who missed the opportunity to set him up for a shot during scrimmages. Again, Mandela simply wandered off in the middle of practice, once for no discernible reason and another time to join a pickup game of older players from the neighborhood at the far end of the field.

Luma hadn't challenged Mandela on his attitude or on these disruptions. She sensed that he was upset and disappointed that his friends weren't playing, and she thought he was waiting to find out if the team was any good before he really committed to it. She decided to ride out his moods, hoping that he would come around and that in the meantime her indulgence of him wouldn't cost her the respect of his teammates.

FORNATEE TARPEH HAD gotten wind of the scrimmage through the kids in his apartment complex. Though he had not shown up at the second tryouts or at either of two subsequent practices, Fornatee thought that scrimmage day was the right time to make his approach to Coach Luma, to ask to get reinstated to the team. He knew he was talented and figured this was his leverage. The Under 15s needed someone like him up front.

Among the absences of Liberian boys from the second tryouts, Fornatee's had been the most surprising. He respected Luma and the impact she'd had on his life. He was passionate about soccer. Fornatee had closely cropped hair, so he wasn't affected by the short hair rule, which had driven Prince and some of the other Liberian boys away. Standing on the field on scrimmage day, waiting to speak to his coach, he said he had skipped the second tryouts as a matter of pride.

"I wasn't going to come to tryouts," he said, "because I *tried out*.

"I love playing soccer," he added as he waited for Coach. "I love playing with my friends, but my friends aren't here. It's like you break up with your family. And this is why: Don't nobody want to cut their hair. I want to play on the team, but I want to play on the team with my friends."

I asked Fornatee what it felt like to be off Luma's team.

"I'm not *off* the team," he snapped. "She hasn't called me, and I haven't called her. So in my opinion, I'm still on the team."

A few minutes later, Luma arrived. Members of the Under 15s and 17s were warming up when she walked onto the field past Fornatee, without making eye contact. Luma blew her whistle and told the two teams to gather at opposite ends of the field.

"She's more than a coach—that's why," Fornatee said, almost to himself. "She's a great person. I'm going to go over there and tell her, 'That's my team.'"

Fornatee hesitated. I asked him if he was nervous about talking to Coach. He laughed anxiously, then composed himself.

"Nah—I'm not nervous," he said.

A moment later, Fornatee made his way toward Luma. She was standing in the midst of a huddle of Under 15 players, assigning them their positions, when he approached. Fornatee tried to blend into the group as if he expected to get a position assignment himself.

"Fornatee," Luma said when she saw him, "go away."

Fornatee was startled. He froze as the other players turned to look at him.

"Coach, can I talk to you after?" he managed, feebly.

"Yes—go away," Luma said before continuing with her position assignments.

Fornatee padded sullenly back to the jungle gym, where Prince and some of his other friends had gathered to watch the scrimmage. He would watch and wait, and try to persuade Coach to take him back.

THE 17S WERE not just older and more mature than the 15s; they were much more talented. They were led by a talkative and self-confident Iraqi refugee named Peshawa Hamad and a quiet, graceful Sudanese player named Shamsoun Dikori, whose younger brothers Idwar and Robin played on the Under 13s. Luma had no doubt who would win the scrimmage, but she wanted to see how the 15s would react to the challenge of a superior team—to see if they would crumble and lose their composure or if they would keep fighting. She handed out red mesh pullover jerseys to the 15s; the 17s wore white. The YMCA still had not delivered soccer goals, so Luma designated the two chain-link baseball backstops on the field as goals instead.

Luma blew the whistle, and soon a white cloud of dust began to rise from the scuffling feet of the two sides.

The field at Indian Creek was more chaotic than usual. There was a pickup game of older boys at one end of the field, and children wandered from the jungle gym into the Fugees' playing area. In the parking lot beside the field, teenagers drank beer from cans in paper bags. Luma tried to focus on the scrimmage while simultaneously keeping an eye out for trouble.

From the outset, the 15s displayed a new energy and determination, and took control of the ball. On an early run, Mandela set up Muamer, the new, mustachioed Bosnian forward, with a touch pass off the back of his foot, but Muamer missed the shot.

"Man!" Mandela shouted in frustration.

Moments later Peshawa slithered through the 15s' defenses and fired a shot that clanged into the chain-link fence of the backstop. The 17s were up 1–0.

The 15s didn't give up. Soon Mandela dribbled through a seam in the 17s' defense, got a clear view of the goal, and fired a perfect shot: *clang!* The 15s had tied it 1–1. Luma blew the whistle for halftime. She left the 17s to strategize on their own, and summoned the 15s.

"You're outhustling them—keep it up," she told the 15s at the break.

On the 17s' side of the field, Peshawa had grown angry, and embarrassed: he had no intention of getting shown up by the younger team.

"Wake up!" he said to his teammates. "They only have Mandela. Shut that down and they don't have anything. Control the middle. These players—they're nothing. Let's finish it off!"

In the second half, the 17s took advantage of their size and experience. Their passes were crisp, and they chipped their way downfield methodically, using their elbows to control the movements of the younger, smaller team. Again Peshawa juked around the 15s' midfielders and a toddler who had wandered onto the field, then tapped the ball around Hamdu Muganga, one of the two Somali Bantu brothers who had joined the 15s on defense. Peshawa scored; 2–1, the 17s now led.

A few minutes later, Kanue was dribbling downfield and had just passed the ball when one of the older players took him out with a vicious tackle. Kanue rolled forward violently on his right shoulder and tumbled to a stop in the dust. He looked up for a whistle, but there was none. Luma was letting them play. Kanue was furious. He set his sights on the young man who had tackled him, and with the ball clear across the field, Kanue slid into his ankles, cleats up—a move that almost certainly would have drawn a red card in a regulation contest.

"Hey!" Luma shouted. "Kanue! Take a lap."

When Luma blew her whistle a few minutes later, the final score was 3–2 in favor of the 17s. Luma waved the 15s over.

"U-Fifteens—you played a decent game," she told them. "Kanue, if I see you lose your temper again, you're off the team. They're going to foul you in a game and you'll get red-carded." Kanue shook his head in disappointment at himself. He knew he had made a crucial error, the kind that could put the very existence of his team in jeopardy. Coach had let him off easy with a lap.

AFTER PRACTICE, LUMA wasn't despairing. She had concerns: Kanue's outburst had been troubling, and she wasn't happy that Mandela was lashing out at his new teammates when they made inevitable mistakes. But the 15s' effort had been heartening. They had managed some clever runs on offense, thanks to their newfound speed on the wings. The Muganga brothers had played well on defense, chasing down loose balls and catching up with the 17s' more experienced front line when they had managed to get free. Mainly, though, the Under 15s hadn't quit when they fell behind. They wanted to win.

There was one more order of business before Luma could wrap up her day. She had agreed to hear out Fornatee's case for why he ought to be allowed back on the team. Luma turned and looked toward the jungle gym where Fornatee had been watching the scrimmage with Prince and the others. But the boys were no longer there. At some point during the scrimmage, they'd walked off, and, in Fornatee's case, away from his team for good.

After the scrimmage Luma gathered her soccer balls into a mesh sack, which she slung over her shoulder and carried toward her car in the parking lot below. The lot was still teeming with young men who had come to hang around the basketball court, smoking blunts and drinking beer. She kept her head down and walked straight to her Beetle. She opened the hatchback and heaved the sack of balls into the backseat. Truth be told, she was growing tired of the whole scene at Indian Creek—the chaos on the field as well as the menacing crowd in the parking lot.

There was a safer place for the Fugees to play, of course: Armistead Field in Milam Park, the park Mayor Swaney had declared a soccer-free zone. Besides offering the luxury of grass, Armistead Field was set away from the flow of pedestrians in and out of the apartment complexes around town. The field was in a hollow, surrounded by chain-link fence. Clarkston police cars frequently patrolled the park. Granted, they came in part to make sure no one was playing soccer on the field, but the effect of the police presence meant that there was little in the way of beer drinking, pot smoking, and hanging out in Milam Park. The thought that such a perfect resource was sitting unused had previously struck Luma as absurd, annoying, and perhaps frustrating; now it simply made her angry. She resolved to do something about it.

The next day, Luma got in her yellow Volkswagen and drove to City Hall to ask Swaney once and for all to change his mind and let the Fugees use his field. Swaney was in his office when Luma arrived, and agreed to speak with her. She spoke calmly; she didn't want the mayor to get his back up. Luma pointed out that her program kept kids off the streets after school, at no cost to the city. It was exactly the sort of the program, she argued, that Clarkston should support.

The field in Milam Park was completely unused; it seemed little to ask that the Fugees be allowed to practice there four days a week.

Lee Swaney took it all in. Her appeal put him in a tough spot. He'd catch hell from the old Clarkston residents, especially those who lived around Milam Park, if he gave a group of refugees free run of the place. Milam Park, surrounded by the neat houses of old Clarkston, was one of the few defining landmarks of the town, and seeing its pristine fields overrun with soccer players would be an alarming sign for some in town. At the same time, the mayor hadn't enjoyed the fallout from his treatment of the Lost Boys Soccer Team, and he had no appetite for another round of negative publicity in the newspapers. So Swaney did what any conflict-averse public official would do when faced with two unpleasant options: he passed the buck.

Swaney told Luma that he couldn't unilaterally allow her to use the empty field, but that she was free to make her case to the Clarkston City Council. Swaney seemed unaware of the contradiction in his position: the mayor who had earlier claimed an outright authority to ban soccer in Milam Park now disclaimed the authority to allow it. And yet, there was an opening. The Clarkston City Council met on the first Tuesday of each month. As it happened, the October meeting was just five days away. Luma planned to attend and make her case. But while there was pressure on Luma to be persuasive, the more significant voice on the matter belonged to Swaney himself. The soccer field issue had been his pet cause, for all it said about Clarkston's identity. The city council would likely go along with whatever he recommended. On the first Tuesday of October, Swaney would have a fresh chance to let his constituents know what sort of town Clarkston was becoming.

Chapter Seventeen

Go Fugees!

On the morning of the Under 15s' first game back after their suspension, Luma woke up in her small two-bedroom apartment in Decatur, hurried down a short hallway to the bathroom, hunched over the toilet, and threw up.

Luma had never become sick before a game until now. Her nerves were frayed, her stomach roiling with stress. She was terrified that her hastily assembled team stood a good chance of getting humiliated by their opponents. Luma understood she was dealing with a group of boys with fragile egos and with little self-esteem to spare. Kanue, Natnael, and Mandela, especially, had put their hopes and energy into this new version of their team, and against her better judgment, Luma felt she was enabling their blind optimism by keeping the season alive. She feared she was setting them up for failure, and Luma didn't know what she would say or do to comfort them if they got blown out. She looked outside; the skies were clear. There would be no postponement due to weather. The game didn't begin until five-thirty p.m., so Luma had all day to worry. A half hour before game time, she got sick again.

The game was set for Ebster Field in Decatur, on a late-September Saturday. A cooling northerly breeze rolled over the foothills east of Atlanta, displacing the wet, stagnant air of summer. It was perfect soccer weather. The white YMCA bus arrived on time, and to Luma's relief, a full roster of players disembarked and jogged onto the field.

The Fugees ran laps around the perimeter to warm up, Kanue in the lead. He led his teammates through a stretching routine, and then had them take the pitch to practice penalty shots. The competition was the AFC Lightning from Fayetteville, Georgia, a mostly white middle-class suburb south of Atlanta. The Lightning came from a well-established soccer program with a history of sending teams to both state and national championships. The players on this particular Lightning team were big, and looked on average a good two years older than the Fugees. Their coach barked commands in a booming voice that rang off the brick buildings of the housing projects across the street. The Lightning wore red and gold, and traveled with a modest entourage of parents, friends, and siblings, who had made the fifty-minute trip to Decatur and who had set up camp on the sideline across from their bench. The Fugees had exactly three fans, a couple who volunteered occasionally to help Luma with tutoring and transportation, and a young Liberian named Tito who had been recruited late by a Liberian player named Osman and who hoped someday to make the team.

Luma called her players in. She gave no hint of the anxiety that had had her retching earlier in the day, and her pregame instructions were spare: no cussing, and no tackling from behind. She didn't want any players getting carded or losing their cool. The Fugees nodded in acknowledgment.

"Are you ready?" she asked them.

"Yes" came the reply.

Luma extended her arm and her players formed a circle around her and stacked their hands on hers. She counted to three and the boys responded with a chant of "Go Fugees!"

The Fugees began the game tentatively. They turned the ball over early on clumsy passes, and then let the Lightning sneak past for a pair of early shots that went wide. Luma subbed her players frequently, to keep them rested and to see which lineups were more effective. Not ten minutes into the game, a Lightning player settled a pass on the wing and sprinted down the line past Kanue and into open space. From twenty yards out, he pivoted and quickly took the shot, catching the Fugees' goalie flat-footed. The ball sailed beneath the crossbar and into the net. The Fugees were down 1–0.

Kanue urged his teammates to keep their spirits up. While most of the newcomers lacked the confidence to call out instructions to each other, Kanue calmly encouraged his defenders to move up the field, his midfielders to spread out, his forwards to attack. Soon, the Fugees made a run down the right side, but Muamer, the mustachioed Bosnian forward, drew the linesman's flag for offsides. The Fugees made another go; Muamer was called offsides again, to groans from his teammates. Kanue didn't snap at Muamer; he simply gestured reassuringly with his hand to encourage his new teammate to stay on sides, to be patient. The Fugees seemed to gain confidence from the assaults. Soon they made another run; this time Mandela took off down the right line. He powered through the Lightning defenders and worked the ball back toward the middle of the field before blasting a shot that hit the right post and ricocheted in: 1–1.

As the half wore on, the Fugees charged once, twice, and then a third time, at one point racing down the field unimpeded and at a full sprint, like kids chasing an ice cream truck. Finally, they were getting somewhere. Kanue floated a pass downfield to Mandela, who traded passes with Hamdu as they attacked the Lightning defense. When the defense converged, Mandela flicked the ball to Sebajden, a wiry but tenacious Kosovar midfielder, who volleyed the shot: goal. At the half, the Fugees led 2–1.

At halftime, Luma tried not to let her relief show. Her mind was brimming over with adjustments she felt her team needed to make to win. She gathered her players in a corner of the field and quickly ran through her observations.

"Listen up," she told them. "You're playing well, but it's getting sloppy. What they do is they get the ball and they either cross it or switch the field and they overlap. They do the same thing over and over and over again. Don't let them do it. Don't let them do it."

Her players nodded. They understood.

"The midfielders need to get in there and squeeze them out before they can cross it in. Okay? Don't give them any crosses, because they could finish them off.

"Next thing: Mandela—they're going to mark you this half," she said. The strategy now, she told him, was to head in to the box, draw the defenders, and kick the ball out wide to the open player. After doing that a couple of times and conditioning their defenders, she told him, he should take the shot himself. But not until then.

"A good soccer player is not going to let them know what he's going to do every time," she said.

Mandela nodded. Kanue tapped him gently on the back, a quiet gesture of assurance. They could win this.

"You guys have been doing great," Luma told her players. "When you guys have been going in for the attack, there's like eight of you charging through. They're not going to be able to defend eight of you going through. Okay? You need to keep it up at that level. All right? It's two to one. We need two more. It's your first game. You need to set the tone for the season today."

THE FUGEES TOOK the field in the second half with a renewed sense of energy and confidence—self-assuredness that grew as the second half bore out each of Luma's halftime observations to eerie perfection. The Lightning marked Mandela, as she had predicted. In frustration, Mandela pushed off, drawing a yellow card. Kanue patted the air with his palms, gesturing to Mandela to calm down. Mandela nodded, seeming to remember what Coach had said. On the next trip down the field, Mandela powered through the hulking Lightning midfielders and dribbled toward the box. The defense collapsed around him, just as his coach had told him they would. Mandela jabbed a pass out on the wing to Muamer, who was open. He tapped the ball, altering its angle and freezing the goalie. The ball rolled clear, and into the net: 3–1 Fugees.

With twelve minutes to go, the Lightning drew within a goal, on a penalty kick. Time was winding down, and the Fugees were getting tired. Kanue encouraged them to keep fighting; Coach had told them to get two more—they had one to go. Moments later, Mandela broke free again up the middle of the field. This time he charged the box, and when the defenders marked their men on the wings, he followed his coach's advice again and took the shot himself: goal. Tito, the Liberian recruit, and the two volunteers shouted in celebration. It was 4–2, Fugees.

The final minutes of the game were desperate and dangerous. Kanue caught a finger to the eye and crumpled to the ground, only to rise up moments later in anger. Luma shouted to him to keep himself under control; he took a deep breath and walked away from a confrontation and possible card. The Fugees were exhausted. The Lightning made a run, took a shot, and appeared to score, but the linesman raised his flag to signify offsides—a ruling that provoked jeers from the Lightning and their parents on the sidelines. Angry now, they made another run, and set up the overlap and cross on the right side—the very sequence Luma had warned her players to shut down. Kanue called out to his teammates to cover the overlap, but it was too late. The Lightning forward was in the open; he leaned into his shot and blasted the ball into the upper-right corner of the net. It was 4–3. The Lightning had seized the momentum. Their parents and coach were urging them on. There was a sense that the Fugees had run out of energy.

"No, guys!" Tito called from the sideline. "Don't let it happen!"

The Lightning would have their chance to tie in the final moments, when Hamdu Muganga, now on defense for the Fugees, was called for a foul at the top of the penalty box. The Lightning were awarded a free kick from fifteen yards out. A lean, blond-haired striker set up to take the kick. His teammates lined up on the left and right of the goal. He gave the signal, and his teammates charged just as he connected with all his might. The ball sailed on a head-high line drive toward a mass of bodies in front of the goal. Unable to see the ball, the Fugees' goalie was frozen. From the midst of the scrum, a light blue jersey leaped into the air; it was Kanue. He cocked his neck and thrust his head into the speeding ball. There was a violent thud, and the ball ricocheted back toward the lanky striker who had kicked it, sailing over his head and bouncing into the empty space at midfield. The ball was still rolling when the referee blew his whistle—once, twice, and again—to signal the end of the game. The Fugees had won.

Luma dropped her head in relief. Her players, some of them still strangers to each other, were high-fiving and shouting joyfully at the sky as they ran toward her on the bench. They seemed as surprised as she did. Luma raised her head, pulled her shoulders back, and smiled for the first time in two weeks.

"You guys floored me," she told her players when they had settled down enough to hear her speak. The Fugees broke into applause, for each other and for their coach.

"To tell you the truth, I didn't think you guys were going to come through today," Luma said finally. "But you played a beautiful game."

Chapter Eighteen

Gunshots

The gunshots sounded at first like small firecrackers rather than anything dangerous or deadly. They came in quick succession: one, then another, and another, and possibly a fourth—witnesses would disagree—echoing between the buildings of the apartment complexes behind Indian Creek Elementary at about ten-forty Sunday morning. When the shooting was finished, Tito, the Liberian whom Osman had recruited to the Under 15s and who had cheered the Fugees on to victory the day before, was covered in blood, shot in the face.

The exact circumstances of the shooting were murky, lost in the fog of competing rumors around the complexes. A few details were corroborated to police by witnesses. Tito and some fellow Liberians were walking up the street when they encountered an African American teenager they knew, walking with his mother and her boyfriend. An argument ensued. The kids on the team heard that the argument had to do with territory and gangs. The shooter was in a gang of American kids; Tito and his fellow Liberians, who identified themselves as members of a gang called the Africans, were walking on the wrong turf. The argument had been brief, cut short by the appearance of the small-caliber pistol the American teenager whipped out and began shooting. Everyone ran, including the shooter, who dashed back to his apartment.

When the police arrived a few minutes later, they found the American kid's mother at the scene of the shooting, picking up the shells that had discharged from her son's weapon. She claimed her son had been in their apartment all morning, asleep; but eyewitnesses to the shooting identified the sixteen-year-old as the shooter, and DeKalb County police officers handcuffed him and loaded him into the backseat of their black and gray squad car. Tito himself was lucky: the bullet had crashed into his chin and ripped through his jaw. A fraction of an inch lower, and it would have cut through his neck, spinal cord, or carotid arteries; a few inches higher, and it might have entered his brain. Tito, on this day, would survive.

LUMA WAS SHAKEN by the news. Her immediate concern was for her other players. Rival gang members certainly knew that Tito had been practicing with the Fugees, with his close friend Osman, and everyone in Clarkston knew exactly where and when the Fugees practiced. Luma feared gang members might show up to try to take revenge for their friend who had been arrested. She canceled practices and got the word out to her players not to show up at the field at Indian Creek until further notice. She drew a hard line with Tito and Osman as well. None of the Fugees had heard of a gang called "the Africans," and several thought that any declaration of membership in such a gang was little more than a bluff meant to frighten away the boys' American tormentor. Luma wasn't sure, but she was not prepared to discount the idea. And anyway, even pretending to be a part of such a group was enough for her. Tito and Osman were to have nothing to do with her soccer program ever again.

The shooting pointed up an unpleasant reality for refugee boys around Clarkston. While they experienced hostility from older white residents in town who believed the refugees were altering Clarkston's identity, they also faced hostility, often more acute and more violently expressed, from the poor Americans with whom they shared the same apartment complexes. Just as poor whites in the South had felt threatened by the prospect of fair competition from blacks in the years leading up to the civil rights struggle, poor blacks in Clarkston—who made up the majority of the American residents of those apartment complexes where the refugees lived—saw the newcomers as rivals. The contrived turf war that a sixteen-year-old African American used to rationalize the shooting of an African refugee was a make-believe corollary of the more realistic competition over limited resources— housing, jobs, government aid—that fueled identity-based hostility in Clarkston among adults. The shooting, after all, had taken place in front of two adults, one of whom had gone out of her way to cover up the crime.

For Luma, the shooting had immediate implications for how she would run her soccer program. It was difficult for her to imagine ever feeling safe again on the field at Indian Creek Elementary. The field was next door to the very apartment complex where the shooter lived, which Luma now knew was also considered the sovereign territory of a street gang—a gang that now seemed to be embroiled in conflict with some of her own (now former) players. The field at Indian Creek was a free-for-all in the afternoons; there were no fences around the property, and neighborhood teenagers were constantly popping out of the surrounding woods. It would be impossible to sort out a particular stranger who was simply taking a shortcut by walking across the field from one with bad intentions. The teenagers who hung out in the parking lot beside the field, smoking pot and drinking beer out of paper bags, suddenly seemed no longer just a nuisance but a threat. Luma had no idea who they were. She felt vulnerable and compromised. Luma promised her players' parents that she would keep them safe; she wasn't sure she could keep that promise at Indian Creek.

On Tuesday night, Luma would have a chance to improve things for her team if she could convince the Clarkston City Council to let her use the city's field in Milam Park. She would face a tough audience, but Luma resolved to give it her best shot.

Chapter Nineteen

Getting Over It

While the city government of Clarkston—and Swaney in particu-lar—struggled to deal with radical demographic change, a hand-ful of institutions in town had stared change in the face and found ways to embrace it. Indeed, when looking for a successful model for coping with—and benefiting from—Clarkston's diversity, one needed to look no further than the local supermarket, Thriftown.

Thriftown was owned by a man named Bill Mehlinger, a Florida native who grew up working on a chicken farm and whose family had moved to the nearby town of Tucker, Georgia, when he was fourteen. Mehlinger's mother was a schoolteacher and his father made a living as an egg salesman. Tucker, like Clarkston at the time, was a typically homogenous white southern town. Integration had only just begun when the Mehlingers moved to town, and the only nonwhites young Bill Mehlinger encountered were the handful of black students en-rolled at Tucker High School.

After college at Georgia Tech, Mehlinger went to work for Winn-

Dixie, the supermarket chain. He began as a meat cutter trainee, and worked his way up through the ranks as a stocker of produce and dairy, store manager, and eventually district manager. That's when he heard about Thriftown.

It was 1990, and Thriftown, a privately owned grocery store in the Clarkston Shopping Center, was up for sale. Mehlinger and a fellow Winn-Dixie employee wanted to be their own bosses and thought they knew enough about the grocery business to run a store at a profit. They paid nearly a half million dollars for the store—most of it borrowed from a bank. It was risky to take on so much debt to buy a supermarket in a middle- to low-income neighborhood of Atlanta, but Mehlinger thought the place could make money if he just worked hard enough.

At the time, Thriftown's customer base was roughly half white and half black. The store sold "all-American stuff," Mehlinger said—Jif peanut butter, Bama jelly, Campbell's soups, gallons of milk, and loaves of sliced white bread. The meat department sold steaks, chicken, and pork chops. The store did okay. But within a couple years, Clarkston began to change. The incoming refugees—from Southeast Asia, eastern Europe, Africa, and the Middle East—and had little interest in Mehlinger's traditional southern- and middle-American fare. And soon, Mehlinger's American customers began to move away. Business began to suffer, at first gradually, then precipitously. Mehlinger's partner bailed out, and Mehlinger himself fell behind on his payments to the bank. Eventually, as he fell deeper into debt, the bank issued an ultimatum: Come up with ten thousand dollars in ten days, or face foreclosure. Mehlinger borrowed the money from his father, but it was a temporary fix: he didn't see his way out of the bigger problem.

"Our sales were just going south," he said. "And I owed the bank an awful lot of money."

It was during that dark time when one of Mehlinger's employees, a teenage Vietnamese refugee named Hong Diep Vo, came to him with an idea. Hong was concerned for her boss, who had been understanding about her poor English and who let her keep flexible hours to accommodate her schedule as a student. At the same time, Hong knew that the nearest market offering Vietnamese food was a thirty-minute drive from Clarkston.

"Business was way down—big-time," Hong recalled. "I thought I wanted to help him by bringing people to his store. And I thought, 'Why don't we have the opportunity for these people to get their food close by instead of so far away?' "

Mehlinger had nothing to lose, so he got in a van with Hong and drove across town to the store that carried Vietnamese food. There, Hong showed him the sorts of things he should carry—fifty-pound bags of Asian rice, hot sauces, coconut drinks, and fish sauce, which Mehlinger described as "the most awful-smelling stuff you've ever smelled in your life."

Nevertheless, Mehlinger loaded up his van and stocked the goods on his shelves. Hong spread the word to Clarkston's community of Vietnamese and Laotian refugees, and pretty soon the shelves were bare. Mehlinger quickly set about trying to fill them up again.

"I drove around in my van picking up stuff here and there, found suppliers—even called embassies to get suggestions," he said. Hong served as a culinary consultant, urging Mehlinger to buy more of this and less of that, and when she wasn't around, Mehlinger himself would spend time wandering the aisles of that Asian specialty store on the other side of town, noting the buying habits of customers. The food kept selling, and Thriftown's bottom line began to improve.

"Within six months I was making enough to make my payments to the bank," Mehlinger said. "Things picked up from there."

With each new wave of resettled refugees into Clarkston, Mehlinger had new opportunities and new challenges. Bosnian refugees liked certain types of chocolates that were hard to find. African refugees wanted cassava powder to make foofoo. Refugees from the Middle East had no interest in pork—pork sales declined—but couldn't get enough whole lamb and goat. And each culture had its own preferred type of rice, which Mehlinger began to stock by the pallet, in huge burlap and plastic sacks. Mehlinger has become a wizard at ferreting out suppliers for hard-to-find culinary offerings from around the world. And he eventually hired members of each new ethnic group that arrived in Clarkston to work not just as stockers or clerks but as food consultants for each group's cuisine. These days, thirty-five of Thriftown's forty-three employees are resettled refugees, from twenty different nations.

As a result, the shelves at Thriftown are a mélange of exotic breads, grains, candies, and produce. In the meat department, whole lamb and goat have displaced beef as a favorite, and most fish is sold whole. Mehlinger ultimately had to separate his pork section from the rest of the meats to avoid offending Muslim customers.

The clientele reflects the diversity on the shelves. There are African women in colorful gowns, Middle Eastern women in hijabs and black chadors, and Bosnian men in blue jeans and white sneakers. Many arrive and leave on foot, and carry their groceries back to their apartments in the complexes nearby, piled high on the handlebars of old bicycles or even, in the case of some African refugees, on women's heads.

Thriftown's clientele is mostly poor, and Mehlinger has had to price his groceries accordingly, at low margins. Even so, the store is a thriving business again. Mehlinger has kept up with his payments and repaired the store's standing with the bank enough to establish a line of credit that helps him buy whole New Zealand lambs by the truckload, to the tune of seventy thousand dollars per order. Since Mehlinger changed his business to accommodate the refugees, a Publix and a Kroger have opened nearby. The stores cater to his old American clientele and could have easily undercut him with cheaper prices and a broader selection that surely would have put Thriftown out of business.

"If it wasn't for the refugees knowing us and knowing we go out of our way for them, we'd be gone," Mehlinger said. "I'd be working at Publix."

Hong Diep Vo stayed at Thriftown for nearly nine years, working part-time as she studied. She graduated from high school, and eventually college. Nowadays, Hong is the director of accounting for a large Atlanta-area real estate firm and oversees thirteen employees. She speaks perfect English, her Vietnamese accent now flecked with a Southern twang. She still shops at Thriftown, and sees Mehlinger often.

"Without Bill, I wouldn't be here," she said. "He was one of the people who helped."

Mehlinger feels the same way about Hong, who he says taught him a valuable lesson about running his store—and life.

"If you don't change," Mehlinger said, "you're gone."

ACROSS THE RAILROAD tracks from Thriftown, there was another dramatic example of reinvention and embrace of change—at the old

Clarkston Baptist Church, the center of Clarkston's spiritual life since its founding in 1883. As refugees moved to Clarkston in the 1990s, many members of the church's white congregation became so uncomfortable with their changing surroundings that they decided to move away. In the course of a decade, membership in the church plummeted from around seven hundred to just over a hundred. On Sundays, the pews sat mostly empty, and the church was on the verge of going broke. It was then that a group of church elders met to discuss the congregation's future. They looked to the Bible for guidance, and read a passage in which Jesus described heaven as a place for people of all nations. Some of the elders, including a former army lieutenant colonel and longtime Clarkston resident named William Perrin, argued that the words were a sign that the church should change and open its doors to the newcomers who were moving into Clarkston's apartment complexes.

"We realized that what the Lord had in store for that old Clarkston Baptist Church was to transition into a truly international church and to help minister to all these ethnic groups moving into the county," he said.

Perrin was an unlikely advocate for a multiethnic congregation. He was a staunch conservative who voted twice for George W. Bush and whose faith in God was matched only by his deep distrust of liberals and the news media. As someone who'd grown up in Clarkston, Perrin admits that he had absorbed local prejudices against blacks. But as he witnessed the slow-motion death of his church, Perrin began to believe that God was punishing the congregation for not living by the ways Jesus had prescribed. If the church changed, Perrin was convinced, God had great plans for it. The solution, he argued, was that the church remake itself as an explicitly international congregation that reflected the diversity outside its doors. It would have to make changes in its services, particularly with music, to accommodate a broad array of worship styles, and it would have to reach out to the small congregations of Liberian, Sudanese, and Ethiopian Christians and others who were meeting around Clarkston in borrowed spaces.

Perrin's proposal divided his already weakened church. Some, like Brenda and Robert White, members of the Clarkston Baptist Church for more than twenty years, left in protest.

"I know it's the twenty-first century and we have to change and do things differently," Brenda White said. "But I don't think it's fair that we had to cater to the foreign people rather than them trying to change to our way of doing things.

"It just wasn't a Baptist church anymore," she added.

Ultimately, Perrin's plan was adopted, and to reflect its new identity, the Clarkston Baptist Church renamed itself after 125 years: it's now the Clarkston International Bible Church. On Sundays, separate congregations of Liberians, Ethiopians, French-speaking West Africans, and Sudanese meet at various times throughout the day to worship in their native styles, and a bigger, come-one, come-all service takes place in the main sanctuary in English. In the main service, immigrants and refugees from Togo, the Philippines, Afghanistan, Liberia, and Sudan, some in colorful native garb, worship alongside silver-haired white southern women in their Sunday best. Since making the change, the church has become reinvigorated. Pews in the sanctuary, once nearly empty on Sunday mornings, are now near capacity, and membership has grown to over five hundred.

Phil Kitchin, the current pastor, said a multinational congregation presents all sorts of problems that a more homogenous church would not. There are disputes over the style of music that should be played during services, and there is a fear among the various ethnic groups that by joining the main congregation they might also give up elements of their own worship styles, and by extension ties to their old countries and cultures. But Kitchin believes these occasional headaches are a small price to pay for creating a church community that fulfills the teachings of Jesus.

"Jesus said heaven is a place for people of all nations," Kitchin likes to say. "So if you don't like Clarkston, you won't like heaven."

As head of an international church, Kitchin, who ministered to refugees in Belgium before taking the job as pastor, said he frequently hears complaints from people who long for the time when life in Clarkston was simpler.

"I tell people, 'America is changing,'" Kitchin said. "'Get over it.'"

THE CLARKSTON INTERNATIONAL Bible Church was only a few doors down from City Hall on Church Street. But there was another example of a less fearful approach toward Clarkston's diversity in even closer proximity to Mayor Swaney—just outside the doorway of his office in City Hall, in the warren occupied by Clarkston's new police chief, Tony J. Scipio.

Scipio, a black man of Trinidadian descent with an imposing upright frame and a broad, disarming smile, had been hired by Swaney to replace the recently retired Charlie Nelson, the old-school police chief whose office had borne the Barney Fife poster and who had hired Timothy Jordan, the problem officer who would beat Chike Chime. Scipio was working for the DeKalb County Sheriff's Department when he heard about the opening in Clarkston, and he went online to research the town. Scipio immediately grasped the challenge: a cultural maelstrom of more than a hundred nationalities in an area slightly larger than one square mile, poverty, and a haphazard layout—sprawling apartment complexes with countless dark corners and wooded thickets where drug dealers could hide or dispose of weapons or stash—that put criminals at an advantage. Scipio, though, was ambitious; he hoped someday to run for sheriff of the entire county. The Clarkston job offered an opportunity to establish his bona fides as a reformer.

A reform-minded chief fit into Mayor Swaney's ambitions as well. He had taken a political hit from Chief Nelson's sometimes ham-fisted methods, and Nelson's apparent lack of empathy for refugees had come to weigh on Swaney himself.

"We had our task force putting pressure on a lot of people, and a lot of it wasn't in the way that it should have been," Swaney said. "They were being . . . I guess you'd call it mean."

Hiring a black police chief intent on shaking up the Clarkston Police Department was an uncharacteristic act of boldness on Swaney's part, and another indication that perhaps attitudes in Clarkston were not fixed but fluid.

Scipio accepted the job, but on a condition. He told Swaney he wanted two weeks before his hiring was announced to spend time anonymously in Clarkston, speaking to residents and gauging their relationship and attitudes toward the police. He eschewed his uniform for blue jeans, tennis shoes, and a T-shirt, and made his way around town in his old Ford 150 pickup truck, talking to longtime residents and new arrivals alike. He heard about all the traffic tickets refugees had been receiving, the verbal abuse from officers, and complaints about the way police seemed to react with extreme aggression at the slightest provocation. His incognito tour only confirmed his hunches about what was going on in Clarkston.

"I found out I had my work cut out for me," Scipio said. "There wasn't a lot of public trust when it came down to the police department here."

When Scipio was finally announced as the new chief, he moved into Nelson's old office in City Hall next door to Swaney's. Upon arriving, Scipio issued a mandate that his officers should follow a simple code he called CPR—"courtesy, professionalism, respect"—and began to ask anyone who filed complaints against his officers if they had been treated according to the code.

"If any one of those three elements is missing," Scipio said, "then there's a problem."

Scipio instituted diversity training, and established a policy that allowed any Clarkston resident who asked to ride along in police squad cars. He went on patrol with his officers and watched the way they interacted with the public. More than once, he was taken aback by what he witnessed. At the sight of a Middle Eastern man whose car was broken down on the side of the road, one officer remarked that the man was probably more adept at riding camels than fixing cars. Scipio wrote him up for a violation of department policy. Another officer used a slur against homosexuals: Scipio wrote him up as well. Another used the phrase "you people" when referring to a group of refugees; it wasn't courteous, Scipio said: violation. Over the course of the next few months, nearly every member of the force was written up for some sort of department violation.

"There were some times that I felt that *I* could have easily become a victim because they didn't know who I was," Scipio said of his own officers, referring to those days when he roamed Clarkston undercover in civilian clothes. "So I approached all officers and asked them certain things, and they didn't like that."

Indeed they didn't. Three officers quit by the end of Scipio's first week on the job. By the end of the first month, four more were gone.

One incident sticks out in Scipio's mind as encapsulating the problems he found between refugees and his officers. Soon after he'd taken over the force, Scipio was walking the beat near the center of town when he spotted a group of African immigrants, talking excitedly into a cell phone they were passing among themselves. A short distance from the men, a Clarkston police officer watched from his squad car, Scipio recalled. The group, it turned out, was waiting for the arrival of a long-lost cousin from Gambia, who was on his way from the Atlanta airport to Clarkston to reunite with his transplanted family. The cousin was in a rental car, and the family was giving him directions to Clarkston via cell phone.

"They're telling me how excited their cousin is to get here," Scipio said of the family members. "And they're talking to him, telling him how to get off the interstate, what exit number to take, where to turn left and right, and he's only a few minutes away from here. They haven't seen him in ten, fifteen years, and now here he is in America! And he can't wait to get to Clarkston, because this is where everybody is."

Soon, the just-arrived relative pulled up in his car, and at the sight of his long-lost family, stopped the vehicle in a fire lane before jumping out to embrace them. Scipio was touched by the scene of reunification.

"He's so excited. Everyone's speaking in their native language. Everybody's jumping, and they're happy," he said.

But as the family celebrated, the Clarkston police officer got out of his car and approached them. The cousin had parked his car in a fire lane, and the officer began to write him up for the violation. When the cop walked over to hand the cousin the traffic ticket, the man mistook the ticket for some kind of gift, and went to hug the officer, who freaked out.

"He takes the officer and hugs him because he thinks the officer loves him," Scipio said. "And the officer wants to arrest him for assault and battery because the man hugs him!"

Scipio eventually intervened, but the incident pointed up the ease with which routine interactions could get out of hand, and also to his mind showed the need for the authority figures in Clarkston to take a more forgiving approach to situations that arose out of misunderstandings as opposed to blatant disregard for the law. It was no mystery, he argued, that refugees didn't yet fully grasp every nuance of the American judicial system, or understand every last bit of local traffic code. They'd just arrived. Most didn't speak English. They had no money and little education. And they'd been through hell. Why not, Scipio asked, cut them some slack?

Some officers, particularly white ones, thought that with his constant write-ups, Scipio was singling them out for discipline because of their race. Some saw themselves as pawns in a broader scheme by Scipio to paint himself as a reformer to bolster a possible run for sheriff. One of the white officers who thought Scipio was engaging in something like reverse discrimination was Timothy Jordan, the cop who had arrested Chike Chime and who had been hired by Nelson before Scipio took over as police chief. In his first few months on the job, Scipio and Jordan had already clashed. Scipio wrote up Jordan for an incident Jordan maintained was a harmless prank—he'd hung some plastic toy guns on the locker of a fellow officer with whom he had a series of running gags. Jordan didn't like Scipio's approach to dealing with refugees either. They were in America, Jordan believed, and they, not the police, should be the ones adjusting to new customs.

After Jordan arrested and beat Chike Chime, the Nigerian immigrant, Scipio decided to review the video of the arrest from the camera mounted on the dashboard of Jordan's police cruiser. When Scipio viewed the video, Chime was still languishing in the DeKalb County Jail, four days after his arrest. As he viewed the video, Scipio was shocked at what he saw. Not only had Jordan not treated Chime with the requisite courtesy, professionalism, and respect; he had plainly brutalized Chime with the metal flashlight. Scipio called the local district attorney and brought in outside law enforcement officials to review the tape. Then he went to the DeKalb County Jail.

Chime was surprised to hear that he had a visitor, and shocked to see that it was the Clarkston chief of police. What he heard from Scipio proved even more surprising. Scipio apologized to Chime for the way he had been treated. The chief added that he'd found the arrest video, as he put it, "strange," and said he was turning the tape over to investigators. Scipio then told Chime he was free to leave the jail. A few days later, Chime received a call letting him know that all charges against him had been dropped, and further, that Officer Jordan had been fired and arrested for the beating.

Chime, like any well-adjusted American, soon hired a lawyer. He sued the town of Clarkston, arguing that the town should never have hired Jordan given his troubled past. The town settled the suit for a modest sum, and Chime went back to work. Jordan eventually pleaded no contest to two counts of battery and violating his oath of office and was sentenced to two years' probation.

THESE WERE BIG examples of people and institutions embracing change in Clarkston. But every day there were countless smaller examples taking place between citizens intent on negotiating their own peaceful place amid the social and cultural confusion. Perhaps my favorite example of the strange nature and surprising outcomes of these negotiations took place between an Afghan family I came to know and their neighbors, a group of African American drug dealers. The Afghan family lived next door to the men, on the second floor of an apartment building off Memorial Drive outside Clarkston. In the evening, the drug dealers would set up shop on the stairwell, with a view of the parking lot below, where they would sit smoking pot and drinking beer with pistols in their laps, conducting a robust drug trade in the open. The dealers' friends frequently came over to join the fun and splayed themselves across the staircase that the Afghan family used to get back and forth between their apartment and the parking lot. In the evenings, the Afghan family's mother would come home and have to negotiate her way through a gauntlet of gun-wielding thugs, through clouds of pot smoke. The men made no effort whatsoever to accommodate her or to show her respect by sliding out of her way. One evening when his mother came in complaining about the men, her teenage son decided he'd had enough. He was small, perhaps five feet, seven inches tall, with narrow shoulders and a thin build, and he spoke little English. But he marched outside and approached the neighbor he knew to be the man in charge. In his culture, the young man explained in halting speech, when a woman walked by on a staircase, men stood and stepped out of the way, as a sign of respect. It was no good, he said, that his mother was not receiving respect from her neighbors outside of her own home. The drug dealer listened impassively through his lecture but didn't retaliate or argue with his strange-seeming neighbor. Instead, he seemed to take the young man's case under advisement. And from then on, whenever the young man's mother walked down the stairs, the men quietly stood, cupped their joints in their hands, and stepped aside.

IT WAS INTERESTING to consider what the examples of Bill Mehlinger, William Perrin, Tony Scipio, and even these drug dealers said about the possibilities of building community in Clarkston. In the cases of Mehlinger, Perrin, and Scipio, their embrace of their new communities was certainly informed to some degree by morality—a feeling of obligation to live by the Golden Rule. But in all these cases, there was an undeniable element of self-interest as well. Mehlinger's business was failing until Hong Diep Vo suggested he carry Vietnamese food, and his embrace of refugee employees from various cultures had only strengthened his bottom line. Perrin's church was about to fail as well; by embracing refugees the church found new vitality, and of course, as evangelicals, members of the old Clarkston Baptist Church were able to successfully proselytize among Muslims and other non-Christians. They were acting, in other words, out of spiritual self-interest. Chief Scipio was looking for a way to bolster his résumé for an intended run for sheriff of DeKalb County. It was certainly in his self-interest to gain a reputation as a man who had cleaned up an outmoded police department, and indeed, some officers driven out by Scipio maintained that they were victims of his ambition—not bad actors. The drug dealer probably made a conscious decision that he didn't need any trouble from his neighbors, and if stepping aside for their mother was all it took to keep his business running smoothly, he was happy to oblige. There was even an element of self-interest in Luma's starting the Fugees—of the emotional kind. Thousands of miles from home and estranged from her family, she had embraced a group of strangers, as she herself admitted freely, in part to fill a void in her life.

And yet, while self-interest—economic, spiritual, emotional—might have been a motivating factor, or even a prime mover, in these examples of cultural connecting in Clarkston, what was most interesting was what happened once the connecting kicked in. Bill Mehlinger found himself with barely a free weekend because he was so busy going to weddings of his current and former employees—events he found he genuinely enjoyed, even if he didn't understand the particularities behind the rites. William Perrin found himself looking forward to his church's potluck dinners because he so enjoyed the exotic meals brought by members of the various African congregations. Scipio, even if motivated in part by a desire to bolster his résumé when he sought the job of police chief in Clarkston, came to identify with the refugees during his first week on the job, when it dawned on him that as a black man, without his police uniform he could have easily been singled out by Clarkston cops. And of course, Luma had come to see the Fugees and their parents not as refugees from different cultures so much as family members. Self-interest might have put these disparate souls into close proximity, but proximity bred human connections that, while occasionally complicated and certainly complex, were real and elastic, able to withstand the normal tensions that characterize all human relations without losing their shape.

IN 2005, A British researcher named Steven Vertovec coined a term to describe the incredible cultural complexity that had taken hold in places like Clarkston, Georgia: super-diversity. In a paper he wrote about super-diversity in the United Kingdom, Vertovec put down his own thoughts about strategies for making super-diversity work, or at least, work better. He noted that top-down efforts to impose contact and understanding between various groups were likely to fail; connecting was something that individuals would have to accomplish organically and on their own. At the same time, he wrote, it was important to remember that a sense of belonging was not a zero-sum game. Immigrants who came to define themselves as British did not do so at the expense of natives who already defined themselves that way.

Vertovec proposed a simple three-step process for building connections between members of different cultures within a "super-diverse" society. The first was that rather than ignoring the various categories that distinguish individuals, one should instead consider *all* the categories an individual belongs to. A Liberian refugee might be a woman, a Christian, a worker, a single mother concerned about neighborhood crime and the safety of her children, and so on. When you become aware of every affiliation a person has, Vertovec argued, broad categories break down and individuality emerges. The listing of every category a person might fit into renders any single category less meaningful. Vertovec and other social anthropologists call this process decategorization.

The next step, Vertovec proposed, was what he called recategorization, whereby individuals recast themselves not in terms of their differences, but in terms of what they have in common. That Liberian refugee and a white southerner might seem to have little in common if categorized according to race and place of origin, but they might share gender, religion, their identity as single parents, and most powerfully, a concern for the safety of their immediate environment. They might also, for example, both care equally for their jobs at, say, a privately owned small-town grocery store. Vertovec describes this process as redefining the categories of "us" and "them."

Next, he suggests what he calls mutual differentiation, an acknowledgment of interdependence that takes into account various group identities. The idea is not that everyone needs to be the same, but that members of various groups respect members of other groups to which they themselves might not belong.

If it all seems a bit theoretical, Vertovec and other social anthropologists point out that there are already many well-functioning examples of large communities that have successfully gone through this process: practically every cosmopolitan metropolis in the world. People in New York, London, Cairo, Mumbai, Hong Kong, Moscow, and other large cities don't expect each other to be the same, and yet these cities function with an extraordinary degree of civility, because it's in the interests—economic, social, and psychological—of the various groups to get along. Super-diversity in New York isn't viewed as a new, threatening force but rather as the normal state of things. It's understood that people—perhaps even next-door neighbors—have different backgrounds or beliefs, and yet the universality of this situation essentially puts everyone on even footing. Citizens in such places therefore come to exhibit what Vertovec calls "civility towards diversity." As diversity becomes the norm, in other words, people cease to focus on it. Diversity becomes "no big deal." The key to making super-diversity work, in other words, may have less to do with embracing it than ignoring it. Or as the sociologist Lyn Lofland wrote in a book about city life, "Civility probably emerges more from indifference to diversity than from any appreciation of it."

186 • Outcasts United

Of course, many older residents of Clarkston didn't want their town to become New York City or Mumbai. What they missed was precisely the simplicity and clarity that had once characterized a place where everyone looked the same, spoke the same language, and went to the same church. Garry W. McGiboney, a longtime Clarkston resident who now worked at the DeKalb County board of education, believed it was the loss of this sense of familiarity—more than xenophobia or racism—that explained opposition to the refugees in Clarkston.

"If you lived in the same community, on the same street, for all these years, and you know everybody on the street," McGiboney said, "and one house at a time, they're either moving away or aging out of their house, and the person who's moving in is from another country . . .

"The small-town community over time was just fading away," he added. "And that created more of a problem than accepting the diversity."

The situation in Clarkston backed up Vertovec's argument that top-down efforts to promote the embrace of diversity were unlikely to succeed. A group of people mourning the loss of one reality were unlikely to embrace a new one, particularly when that new reality had been imposed on them. And yet, at Thriftown, at the Clarkston International Bible Church, in the police chief's office, and on the gravel-strewn field behind Indian Creek Elementary where the Fugees played, there were groups of people with a growing comfort toward—if not quite an indifference to—the extraordinary diversity that had come to Clarkston. These pockets of acceptance had arisen organically, out of shared need and from the experience of getting close enough to others to see them not as members of broad social categories but as individuals.

Chapter Twenty

The "Soccer People"

In early September I'd stopped by to talk to Mayor Swaney about the soccer field issue. His office in Clarkston City Hall, down a short hallway with plaque-covered walls, fluorescent lighting, and gray, low-pile industrial carpeting, looked like the Hollywood rendering of the workspace of a small-town mayor. A modest gold rectangular sign reading MAYOR adorned the door frame. Inside, the official flag of the City of Clarkston—a green banner with gold tassels and cording—drooped nobly in one corner, opposite the Stars and Stripes in another. A gold-painted ceremonial shovel for groundbreakings leaned against a wall. Swaney's official portrait, a sober three-quarter profile of the mayor in a blazer, hung behind his desk. On an adjacent wall there was a framed print of a bald eagle and an American flag floating majestically in the heavens against an ominous cloudscape.

Swaney invited me in and asked me to sit down. He was heavyset, but fit-looking, with a barrel chest and bulky midsection that had the effect of making him sigh when he sat down. Swaney's face had soft, wind-worn features, and with his gray mustache and carefully combed-back thatch of white hair, he projected a grandfatherly air. When I explained I was in town to write about the Fugees and the effects of refugee resettlement on Clarkston, he did his best to dissuade me. Everyone, he said, was getting along just fine.

"The refugees, the communication between the old residents in the city of Clarkston, is better now than it's ever been," Swaney said. "A lot of the longtime residents have learned to get involved with these people, and them people—the different nationalities—get involved with them. And so, it's really not an issue today.

"Refugees is like me and you—they're people," Swaney continued. "And they come to this country to try to make a better way of life. And I am willing to help them—if they're willing to help themselves.

"We've tried to get them involved with us," he added. "But let's face it—they don't want to get involved. In their country, I guess, they didn't have council meetings or get involved with city governments or any kind of governments."

Swaney's words echoed a common belief among many longtime Clarkston residents that few in the refugee community contributed much to the life of Clarkston, and conveyed a common misperception: that the refugees were a monolithic group of strangers from faraway lands. When these new arrivals didn't band together to get involved in the town, this way of thinking went, it was evidence of a collective failing by the entire refugee community. The refugees, though, didn't think of themselves as a monolithic group. To a refugee from Burundi, a neighbor from Bosnia or Afghanistan was every bit as culturally and linguistically different as a longtime Clarkston resident like Lee Swaney.

Swaney's critics—local progressives and members of the resettlement community for the most part—tended to view him more as a bumbling good ol' boy than as overtly malicious. As mayor of one of the most socially complex towns in America, they contended, he was simply in way over his head. But this view seemed to underestimate Swaney's political acumen. The fact was, there was an obvious rationale for any politician in Clarkston to side with locals over refugees. Few of the refugees had been in the U.S. the five years required of citizenship applicants. Though here legally, they couldn't yet vote, so longtime residents had a disproportionate say on election day.

In 2005, Swaney had run for reelection against an American-born Muslim candidate named Abdul Akbar. While campaigning, Swaney sent not-so-subtle signals to longtime residents that he understood their fears and concerns over the direction of their community. He pledged, for example, to work hard to recruit a good old-fashioned American restaurant to town. In the end, Swaney won by a vote of 288 to 102 over Akbar. The mayorship of a town of over 7,200 was determined by just 390 voters. And while Akbar's religion had not become an overt issue during the campaign, it was certainly on the minds of at least some of the voters. On AboutClarkston.com, an on-line bulletin board where Clarkston residents discuss town goings-on, an anonymous poster celebrated news of Swaney's victory with a post headlined, "No Muslims in Office, Thank Jesus Christ."

When I asked Swaney about the controversy involving soccer in the park and his comments in the *Atlanta Journal-Constitution*— "There will be nothing but baseball down there as long as I am mayor," Swaney had said. "I don't have no beef with nobody. But I do have a problem with these big guys playing soccer because those fields weren't made for soccer."—he displayed deft skills as a bureaucratic obstructionist that further belied his reputation as a simpleton.

"We don't have soccer fields—not in the city," Swaney told me. "We got baseball. Little League baseball. And they want to play soccer on our baseball fields. And when the land was given to the city it was given for Little League baseball—twelve and under. And this is one of the things they find hard to understand."

The mayor's argument was a red herring. Nathaniel Nyok and the Lost Boys had never played soccer on the town's baseball field. He and his friends had played on Armistead Field, a big green rectangle of open space, described on the official town website as "a multiuse field." So why couldn't they play soccer there? I asked.

"A lot of these big guys—grown people—grown men, I call it, wearing cleats and all this stuff—they really work on a field," Swaney said. "So we don't have a place for 'em."

The mayor seemed to be changing his argument on the fly. It wasn't that there wasn't a soccer field in Clarkston, exactly—it was that there was no soccer field for grown men. So what about youth soccer? I asked.

The mayor seemed momentarily caught out, but he quickly changed tack once again. There was a narrow set of circumstances, he told me, under which he would allow soccer at Armistead Field in Milam Park. If the players were twelve years old or younger, and if they were supervised by an adult who had undergone extensive background checks conducted by the city, the mayor said, he would allow them to use one half of the multiuse field at Milam Park.

I was beginning to understand what Nathaniel Nyok must have felt when he met with Swaney months before. The mayor's rules were constantly shifting. First, there were no soccer fields—period—in Clarkston. When that argument collapsed, the problem became soccer played by "big guys, grown people, grown men," as the mayor had put it. By big guys, we now learned, the mayor meant anyone over the age of twelve. Finally, even if a group of twelve-and-under kids showed up with an adult who had passed some undefined series of background checks, they would be able to use only *half* of Armistead Field. The other half, the mayor said, had to be reserved for Little League baseball. At the same time, the mayor admitted there was no Little League baseball team in Clarkston, and hadn't been for at least three years.

It was of course highly unlikely that anyone would meet the mayor's freshly conceived criteria. His rules were not published anywhere; they existed only in his head, where they could be altered later if necessary. And anyway, there were no twelve-and-under youth soccer teams in Clarkston, as the mayor surely knew. Luma's youngest team consisted of boys thirteen and under, a year too old to play soccer in Mayor Swaney's park.

As frustrating as it was to listen to the mayor's excuse-making, I actually found myself developing a degree of sympathy for Swaney as he fumbled through his rationalizations. He was sixty-eight years old, and had spent much of his life in a community to which he could no longer fully relate or even recognize. As an old-guard mayor, he had the impossible task of trying to maintain the status quo in a town that was changing radically all around him. He was sure to fail at that task—Clarkston was changing more every day, as new refugee families arrived—and he was equally sure to disappoint his constituents, who had counted on him to succeed in preserving their town's identity. The sheer clumsiness of his arguments for keeping soccer off the town fields hinted at a kind of desperation. It was also clear from Swaney's defensiveness that he didn't relish his reputation as the mayor who banned soccer. Swaney, like most politicians, yearned to be liked. The issue, I sensed, was eating at him.

And yet the mayor seemed almost unaware of the contradictions he'd articulated. He seemed to feel that he had succeeded in explaining the soccer field issue with perfect clarity, and evinced no hostility toward me for my bothersome questions. He even suggested we meet sometime for lunch. I accepted the invitation and asked Swaney where he liked to eat in town. With all the ethnic restaurants, he said, he was down to just one spot where he could get the traditional American fare he liked: a hole in the wall across the railroad tracks called City Burger.

"Whatever they fix, it's good," the mayor said as I stood to leave. "It's cooked right then—for *you*."

The exchange gave me some insight into the confusion and isolation Lee Swaney must have felt toward the town he'd lived in for twenty or so years and that he now governed. It turned out that City Burger, the best American restaurant in town, was now owned by an Iraqi.

ON THE FIRST Tuesday night in October, Luma went to City Hall to make her case for the Fugees' use of the field in the town park. She had a lot riding on the council's decision. The fields at Clarkston High School and at nearby Georgia Perimeter College were booked for the fall. The Clarkston Community Center was no longer an option given the rift between the center and the YMCA, and the field behind Indian Creek was too dangerous given Tito's shooting, Luma believed. She refused to put her players at risk. Her best bet if the council turned her down was to find a parking lot someplace where the boys could play, or else to cancel practices altogether.

The chamber at City Hall where the Clarkston City Council held its monthly meetings had the feel of a small country church at a weeknight service. Half-full rows of wooden benches, arranged like pews, faced a raised dais, where the mayor and six council members sat framed by flags. The town attorney and a clerk sat at desks off to the council's side. A low ceiling gave the room an air of intimacy verging on the claustrophobic. There was a microphone and a lectern in the gallery, but it was hardly necessary. A conversational voice would suffice in so small a space, and if not, one could always yell, as happened more than occasionally at city council meetings in Clarkston.

On this Tuesday evening, as on most, the meeting had drawn a small group with city business to transact and a larger group of the usual cranks and conspiracy theorists who had come to complain about slights from neighbors, disrespected property lines, and in one case, the threat that electronic voting machines posed to the institution of democracy worldwide. Chief Scipio was in attendance; Mayor Swaney wanted to commemorate the end of the chief's first year on the job with a plaque he'd had made for just the purpose. Luma sat quietly in the back.

The meeting was called to order and began with a heartfelt recitation of the Pledge of Allegiance. Various committee reports were asked for and delivered. Chief Scipio received his plaque, to applause. The council then moved on to the people's business. The first to address the council was an Ethiopian woman who owned a restaurant across the tracks from City Hall. She had come to petition for the right to sell beer on Sundays. Council members grilled her with a series of pointed questions focusing on the restaurant's proximity to the Clarkston International Bible Church, and seemed on the verge of rejecting the request when a lawyer in the gallery—a local citizen with no particular authority—pointed out laconically that the council had no authority to rule on the matter one way or the other, as liquor licenses were issued by the state. A council member asked the Ethiopian woman sharply if she had such a license, and when the woman said yes, council members looked at each other in a dumbfounded way and fell silent until someone suggested they move on to other business.

Soon, another conundrum presented itself. A man rose and pointed out that there was that sign in Milam Park threatening a fine of five hundred dollars to anyone who should walk a dog on park property, leashed or not. Had the city council ever actually passed a law, the man wanted to know, establishing a fine for walking a dog in Milam Park? There was another round of mumbling and puzzled expressions among the mayor and council members before the town attorney spoke up to declare that there was no such law on the books. Mayor

Swaney, who'd apparently ordered the sign put up, turned red in the face around his white mustache and sheepishly agreed to take the sign down. A theme was emerging in the matters the people were bringing before the council: those who governed Clarkston had a tendency to overreach their authority, at least until called to account by the citizens.

Against this backdrop, Luma rose and approached the lectern. She spoke in a soft, uncharacteristically meek voice, taking care not to offend, and introduced herself as the head of a soccer program for Clarkston's youth.

"We'd like to request the use of Armistead Park as our field to practice on, Monday through Thursday from five till sunset," she said.

"Why?" a councilwoman asked.

"Indian Creek Elementary is all gravel," said Luma. "It's also not controlled. Anyone can go on there and play, so unsupervised kids are out there playing. Unsupervised adults are out there playing. And it's not a healthy environment for kids."

A barrage of questions followed: What would it cost the town? How old were the boys? Were they local? Would they be supervised? What kind of equipment would they be using? What about insurance?

Luma parried the challenges and maintained a supplicant monotone that would've amused the boys on the Fugees, who knew what she sounded like when she wanted to make a point. But this was a different audience. These weren't kids, and they held all the cards. Luma said she would always supervise; the team would supply its own equipment; the program would be insured; the players were all local.

"Are these mixed teams for both boys and girls?" another councilwoman asked.

"No, it's just boys right now," Luma said.

"Just *boys*," the woman said, repeating the phrase for emphasis, like a trial lawyer who had just scored a point with a hostile witness.

An awkward silence followed, broken eventually by Mayor Swaney.

"This lady came and talked to me about using the lower end of Armistead Field—using the end for soccer," he said. "She knows that you don't play soccer on a baseball field. And we got the lower end of this field that we do not use and have not used. And the only time it was used was when grown people—grown soccer people—come in there with cleats and everything else, and was tearing the field up."

The council members leaned forward to look at the mayor to see where he was going with all this. He had been the one obsessed with policing the playing fields of Clarkston, after all.

"So, you know," he said finally, "I don't see anything wrong with this lady using the lower end of Armistead Field, doing a little soccer to get our kids off the street. How does the council feel about letting this lady use the lower end of Armistead Field for a trial period, and let's see what happens?"

The mayor's comments seemed to surprise the council members on either side of him at the dais. Luma stood stone-faced, trying not to reveal her own disbelief at the mayor's expression of support. Swaney's proposal had the effect of changing the energy in the room. The council's questions became more agreeable. They talked among themselves and agreed that six months sounded like a reasonable amount of time for a trial period. One council member even asked if they should forgo a formal vote and simply agree in principle to approve the idea. Mayor Swaney didn't take the bait on that one; he wanted a vote, with everyone on the record. If anything went wrong at the park—if these soccer people caused any kind of trouble—the mayor didn't want to have to shoulder the blame himself.

There was a motion, and a second. At that moment, the mayor's wife, Joan, seated in the front row of the gallery facing her husband and the council members on the dais, shook her head, to indicate her opposition to the idea. Over the years, Joan Swaney, who worked at the Clarkston Community Center, had come to be identified with the older residents in town who had organized against resettlement. She was no advocate for the refugees. But looking directly at his most powerful constituency—his wife—Mayor Swaney called for all in favor.

The motion passed unanimously. Luma nodded in thanks and stifled a smile. The Fugees, for now at least, had a home.

Playing on Grass

"What makes people join a gang?" Luma asked the boys.

"Race," said one.

"Money."

"Protection."

"To be cool."

"To be men."

"What makes a gang different from the Fugees?" Luma asked.

"They fight."

"They shoot each other."

"Once you're part of a gang, you can't get away."

"In a gang, you have to do whatever they want. Otherwise, if you don't do it, you get shot."

After Tito's shooting and her meeting with the city council, Luma called separate meetings of the Under 13s and 15s, which she held in a classroom at Indian Creek Elementary during practice time. At Luma's invitation, Chief Scipio met with the younger team while Luma addressed the 15s. It was quickly apparent that the Fugees knew more about gangs than Luma might have hoped.

"How many here would know where to join a gang in their neighborhood?" she asked.

"I would," said one boy, without hesitation.

Luma called Kanue to the front of the room, pulled an iPod out of her pocket, and offered to give it to him if he agreed to carry something for her. Kanue hesitated. The boys responded with nervous laughter.

"They give you money—they say, 'Oh, here's five bucks, walk this across the street for me,'" Luma said. "They say, 'I know Kanue wants an iPod.' Or 'Mandela wants a new pair of Air Jordans.'

"Why do people do that? Because they're the ones who don't want to get caught," Luma said. "They want you to do the dangerous work. And once you do it once, once you do it twice, you're in their gang. You're a part of them. And you're not going to get out. Okay? Because they would rather kill you than have you get out and maybe tell the police."

Luma asked the boys what sorts of things they could say if someone offered them money or an iPod to carry something.

"I would say, 'Give me the iPod first,'" one kid said. The boys laughed.

"What else could you say?" Luma asked.

"I'm sorry, I'm going the other way."

"You said if you do it, like, three or four times and you're in," said another kid. "So Tito did it three or four times?"

"I don't know if Tito ran drugs," Luma said. "I don't know if Tito joined a gang to be cool, or for protection, or because he didn't want to walk down the street and get jumped."

Grim faces fell on several of the boys. This last point was one they could relate to. Walking through the complexes around town could be treacherous, since you never knew when you might be treading on someone else's turf. Who wouldn't want some form of protection against such a random and unseen threat? Luma sensed the boys' discomfort.

"If I got beat up, I would want someone helping me out—to beat them up," she said. The boys laughed.

"I would," Luma said. "But what other ways could I look at it? What other things could I do?"

The boys called out in response: You could tell someone. You could tell the police. You could take another route.

"Right," Luma said finally. "And if you keep getting beat up on the same road, take a different road."

Luma let the message sink in for a few moments. The classroom quieted, and several of the boys lowered their gazes to the floor in a quiet signal that they understood: If you keep getting beat up on the same road, take a different road.

Luma had an announcement that proved she planned to practice what she had been preaching. The Fugees, she said, were finished playing soccer at Indian Creek Elementary. Beginning on Tuesday, she said, practicing would take place across town at Milam Park. The field was flat, she told them, with grass and no other soccer teams. Practicing there would offer a chance to play without distractions or fears for their safety. But it came with responsibility.

"You are the first soccer team to use that field," she said. "So you have to set an example so other people can use that field for soccer."

Everyone would be expected to pick up trash in the park so no one in town blamed the Fugees for any mess. To get to the field, the boys would have to walk past houses of older Clarkston residents in the neighborhood behind the library and community center. Luma told them she'd better not hear any reports of yelling or cussing or turning over trash cans. There could be no disruptions. And no one was to go on the field until Luma was there.

"I need you guys to be responsible and respectful," she said.

"I know where the field is," one of the kids said. "But I'm not sure if I can walk there."

"You don't walk, you don't practice," Luma said. "Nobody here is in perfect shape. You all could use the exercise."

"Nobody has an excuse not to get to that field," she added. "You don't want to play, don't show up. That's the field we're going to be playing on, okay? We're not going to be playing on this field—ever again."

———

THE BOYS COULD hardly believe their eyes when they showed up for their first practices in Milam Park. Compared to the dust bowl at Indian Creek Elementary, Armistead Field was Eden: A thick blanket of soft green grass covered the playing surface and itched their backs when they splayed out for sit-ups and stretches. The field was surrounded on three sides by tall trees draped in a tangle of vines and kudzu, forming nature's equivalent of an indoor arena. On the fourth side, running parallel to the field, there was a steep hill bisected by a crumbling set of concrete steps. The hill offered a stadium-like view of the field below. A decrepit chain-link fence formed an oval boundary around the circumference of the field, forcing visitors on their way to the playgrounds and picnic tables on the far side of Milam Park to take a detour around the playing area. The Fugees truly had a home field to themselves.

The main drawback of the move, from Luma's point of view, was having to give up the classrooms at Indian Creek Elementary, which the Fugees had used for tutoring and homework sessions before practice. There was a sheltered picnic area in Milam Park, not far from the field, with long wooden tables and benches. Luma resolved to hold tutoring sessions there for now. Later in the season, when it got too cool, or when the sun began to set earlier in the evenings, she figured she could hold practices slightly earlier and then move the teams to the Clarkston Public Library, about a half-mile away, for homework.

The bucolic quality of the Fugees' new home was so extraordinary that it almost seemed like a kind of elaborate joke. At an early practice, as the boys were scrimmaging, a gaggle of geese took flight from a pond on the other side of the woods. They flapped and honked noisily as they flew low over Armistead Field, startling the Under 13s, who then began laughing hysterically at the idea that they had been spooked by a flock of birds. At another practice, the Under 15s had gathered in a circle at midfield to stretch, when they heard noises in the woods—snapping twigs and the crushing of dry leaves. As the sound grew louder, the puzzled members of the 15s quieted and turned their heads in the direction of the hill alongside the field, just as a small herd of deer wandered into the clearing. The boys could hardly believe their eyes.

"We should chase after them," Hamdu Muganga whispered eventually to his teammates as they peered at the grazing animals.

"Nah, Hamdu," deadpanned a lanky Sudanese midfielder named Kuur. "We're not in Africa anymore."

EVEN AS THE boys were getting used to the idea that this was their team's new home, there were reminders that the Fugees were not entirely welcome. The Under 13s' first practice at Milam Park had just begun when an elderly man appeared at the top of the hill overlooking the field. He was short and thick, with a shuffle for a walk, and though it was nearly nightfall, he looked as though he had just gotten out of bed. The man shouted something, but his voice was raspy, weak, and unintelligible to the boys on the field below. The Fugees kept practicing. The man called out again, angrier now. The boys grew quiet. In the lull, he called out a third time.

"Y'all got a permit?" he shouted.

Luma motioned to her players to keep practicing.

"Without a permit they can't do it," the man called out again.

I introduced myself. The old man declined to give his name but said he owned six acres alongside the park and had lived in Clarkston for thirty-seven years. He knew the mayor well, he said, and shared Swaney's near obsessive concern for the turf in Milam Park. He was particularly galled by one resident who showed up in the evenings to walk his dogs in the park, under cover of darkness.

"He knows he isn't supposed to do it," the man grumbled. "Comes at night."

I mentioned that the soccer team on the field had been granted permission to play there by the city council. The man seemed surprised by the news.

"For how long?" he asked.

Six months, I told him.

He thought on the news for a moment.

"They have to get a permit," he grumbled.

An awkward silence followed. I tried to make small talk by suggesting that in his years in Clarkston, the man had probably seen a great deal of change.

"Oh, yeah," he said. "We have more break-ins than we did. Lot of people walking the streets late at night. A lot different."

In the old days, he said, people played baseball at Armistead Field.

There was a rusted-out old scoreboard still standing from that time, along with a couple of twisted and misshapen old chain-link backstops. People used to come out to watch.

"They used to have a stand right here," he said, gesturing to the grassy hillside below, which now looked eerily empty, like the slopes around the ruin of some ancient stadium. The man turned his gaze to the field and took in the sight of the Fugees in midscrimmage, shouting at one another in a confusion of accents. The man shook his head, whether in disbelief or disapproval it was hard to know.

"That was a long time ago," he said.

Part Three

FULL CIRCLE

Chapter Twenty-two

Who Are the Kings?

The Fugees all had their own soccer idols: David Beckham, Ronaldo, Ronaldinho, and the Ivorian Didier Drogba, the stars they wanted to emulate on the field. Qendrim Bushi's soccer idol was none other than his grandfather, once a famous goalkeeper at the highest level of play in Kosovo, and later, a well-known referee and the author of a definitive Albanian-language soccer rule book. The Bushi family kept a tattered copy of the rule book in their apartment just outside of Clarkston, one of a few things they had managed to bring with them to the United States, and one of Qendrim's most prized possessions.

"He was very famous in my country," Qendrim explained as he thumbed through the book one afternoon. "He used to be one of the best goalkeepers in Kosovo, and everybody wanted to be like him."

Qendrim—everyone on the Fugees called him "KWIN-drum" but his family pronounced it "CHIN-drim"—was a tiny but talented midfielder for the Under 13 Fugees. He had crisp features, a slight overbite, and narrow eyes that often seemed lit with some impish knowledge, as if Qendrim alone were in on some long-running and yet-to-be-revealed joke that the rest of the world would come to appreciate later on. He had pencil-like legs that packed surprising power, and he was a student of the game, which his father also played. He studied his grandfather's rule book and talked strategy with his dad. Soccer was in Qendrim's blood.

The Bushi family came from Kacanik, an ethnically Albanian town of twenty-eight thousand in the mountains of southern Kosovo, not far from the border with Macedonia. Qendrim's father, Xhalal—pronounced Ja-LAL—owned two small grocery stores there with his brother and father, one of which was located in the lower floor of the Bushis' home. Together the stores provided the family with a comfortable life in Kacanik, until ethnic violence tore their homeland apart.

Kacanik was one of many towns in southern Kosovo that became battlegrounds in the 1990s in the struggle between the Serb-dominated Yugoslav army of Slobodan Milosević, which was trying to assert Serbian control over the mostly Albanian-inhabited region, and the Kosovo Liberation Army, the ethnically Albanian militia that was fighting for independence against Milosević's iron rule. Civilians in Kacanik were victimized by both sides in the conflict. KLA soldiers had put sometimes violent pressure on fellow Albanians in Kacanik to flee the town for refugee camps in Macedonia, with the aim of provoking sympathy from the international community and—they hoped—a military response.

The NATO bombing, which was ordered by President Bill Clinton and which would eventually prompt the withdrawal of Serb forces from Kosovo, began on March 24, 1999. To avenge the military intervention, Milosević's army unleashed a wave of destruction and brutality on some sixty towns and cities in Kosovo. Kacanik's time came three days after the bombing began, on March 27, when Milosević's forces ransacked the town's commercial district, stealing food and valuables from residents and cleaning off the shelves of grocery stores, including those owned by the Bushis. The Serbian army holed up in Kacanik, but two weeks later, on April 9, a swarm of KLA militiamen attacked the Serbian soldiers there. The battle, which took place largely on Kacanik's main street, left some seventeen dead. The next day, Serbian reinforcements came to take revenge for the attack. As they approached, many Kacanik residents fled along a canyon path that ran along a stream.

Eyewitnesses said that Serbian police drove an armored vehicle equipped with a twin-barreled antiaircraft cannon through town, shooting all the way. Sharpshooters fired on those fleeing through the canyon. There were bodies everywhere. The summer after the fighting ended, NATO troops discovered a mass grave containing the remains of ninety-three people just outside of Kacanik. Some were KLA soldiers, but most were town residents, identified from scraps of clothing they'd been wearing the day they were gunned down.

XHALAL BUSHI HAD managed to get his wife and children to Macedonia before the fighting, but he and his brother had gone back to Kacanik to look after their homes and stores. Their presence had little effect; their stores and homes were completely destroyed by the Serbian army.

"My house is burned," Xhalal said, sitting on a sofa in his apartment outside Clarkston. "They put some bomb in it and destroyed everything." He flung his hands in the air: "Boom!" he said.

Xhalal and his brother fled Kacanik on foot and trekked for two days over mountains toward Macedonia. They drank water from streams as they walked, and went without food, until they were apprehended by Macedonian soldiers, who placed them in a refugee camp. Xhalal was reunited with Qendrim, his wife, and his daughter, and together they lived in the camp for three months, awaiting placement by the United Nations High Commissioner for Refugees. The Bushis were grateful when they learned they had been granted asylum by the United States, but the news was bittersweet. Xhalal's extended family was broken up, sent to a variety of Western countries that had offered to accept refugees from Kosovo. His relatives from Kacanik are now scattered from Norway to England and to Australia, a world away, quite literally, from both Kacanik and his new home outside Atlanta.

Xhalal was given a $2,275 loan for his family's one-way plane tickets to America. He spoke no English, and knew nothing at all about Atlanta when he arrived. The family's resettlement was handled by the resettlement agency World Relief, which helped Xhalal get a job at the Decatur-DeKalb farmers' market, stocking shelves and hauling groceries. Xhalal eventually got a job working for a company that made industrial conveyor belts. After a lifetime living above his store in a small Balkan village, Xhalal said the strangest thing about America was the idea of getting in a car and driving long distances for work. But he adjusted, using public transportation and getting rides from friends. The food took some getting used to as well.

"I never eat Chinese food before in my country—never know Chinese people," Xhalal said. "Now, I like it. I like Mexican food a lot. You know Mexican buffet?" His eyes lit up at the thought.

The biggest change for Xhalal from life under Milosević was a happy one: no checkpoints, no one stopping him to ask his intentions or to interrogate him for no reason. He was so used to living that way that he found his sudden liberty unsettling.

"When I live over there, for example, when it was Milosević in power, it was very very dangerous," he said. "If you go somewhere, for example, if you stay longer, and you come in the dark in the evening, they stop you—too many checkpoints.

"It was very different when I come here," Xhalal said. "You can go where you want. You can do what you want. You can open business— nobody can stop you. If you want to go somewhere—nobody can stop you. I was in a different city, different people—everybody go to the store and nobody check. Nobody watch what you're doing."

Qendrim was not quite six years old when his family arrived in Georgia. Now twelve and a half, he still remembered his first day of school, at McClendon Elementary. He knew no English, and none of the other kids.

"I was scared," Qendrim said. "I didn't know what to do. I didn't know where to go."

Qendrim's first friends were other Albanian and Bosnian Muslim kids he met in his apartment complex. As he learned English, he made friends at school. Xhalal took his son to the kids' soccer program at the Clarkston Community Center, where Qendrim eventually met Luma and joined her refugee soccer team. The Fugees had since become the center of Qendrim's social life. He had grown particularly close with Eldin, the Bosnian goalie, who also happened to live in his same apartment complex. Qendrim and Eldin had their own morning ritual. On weekdays, their parents left their respective apartments not long after dawn for their long commutes to work. Qendrim would get dressed and walk down the driveway of the complex to Eldin's, where they would play video games or watch ESPN with no adults around, until it was time to go outside and wait for the school bus. They were best friends. Qendrim had become close with his other teammates as well: Grace, the midfielder from the Congo, who lived up the street; with Josiah and Jeremiah, the Liberians; with Bienvenue, the Burundian; Shahir, who was from Afghanistan; Robin and Idwar Dikori, the Sudanese brothers. Having friends from all over the world seemed perfectly normal to Qendrim; it was all he had known since arriving in the United States. Qendrim was smaller than most of his teammates, but he had their respect; when he called out directions during games, the others listened. Qendrim had come to feel the other players were more than just teammates.

"It's like they're all from my own country," he said. "They're my brothers."

INDEED, WHILE THE Under 15s were struggling to keep their team together, Qendrim and the Under 13s were beginning to gel. They had started the season with a tie and a loss but had since won their last two, putting them in a position to actually win their division. Their play was improving, they were communicating better and with more confidence, and above all, they were having fun.

During practice, the usual custom was for the players to strike out on their laps at their own pace; Qendrim, Josiah, Jeremiah, Bien, and the Dikoris would take off, while Eldin, Mafoday, and Santino— the recently arrived Sudanese refugee—would follow, each at his own slower pace. On Wednesday, though, as Luma was watching her Under 17 team scrimmage, she looked over to see the 13s running together in a kind of chorus line: the faster players had slowed down for the slower players, who in turn had sped up so as not to hold their teammates back. They ran like this quietly for fifteen minutes or so, at which point the boys began to clap in rhythm with their strides. Eventually the boys initiated a call-and-response chant.

"Who are the kings?" someone would shout to the group, in time.

"The Fugees!" the team would answer.

Luma remained focused on the older boys' scrimmage, but the 13s wouldn't be ignored. They chanted louder with each pass until Luma finally turned around to see what the fuss was all about. When the 13s saw they had their coach's attention, someone else called out: "Who is the queen?"

"Luma!" the boys shouted.

When Luma shook her head to convey her befuddlement, the boys tumbled to the ground in laughter. It was a small, ridiculous moment, but also a sign of more significant developments. Boys from thirteen different countries and a wide array of ethnicities, religions, and languages were creating their own inside jokes. Even Mohammed Mohammed, the Iraqi Kurd whose family had arrived in the United States only a few months before the season and who spoke almost no English at all, was chanting at the top of his lungs and laughing as if someone had just told him the funniest joke he'd ever heard.

AS THE BOYS became more comfortable with each other, Luma was making progress on the sideline as well. She was getting a better feel for her roster and for the ways she could move players around for different effects. She had learned, for example, that Bienvenue was a kind of secret weapon. She would keep him hidden on defense for the first half or so of a game, then switch him to offense as the other team tired, a move akin to holding back a racehorse and then letting him go on the final stretch. By the time the competition realized the threat—usually when Bien fired a perfect cross or else let loose with a perfectly executed bicycle kick—it was often too late to make adjustments. Jeremiah could play both offense and defense equally well, just as he could kick the ball equally well with his left and right feet, making him a threat on corner kicks from either side. Mohammed Mohammed was proving a relentless and tough defender despite his pint size. Luma still had to direct him mostly in Arabic, but it was no coincidence that his limited but rapidly expanding English vocabulary consisted largely of soccer terminology. On offense, the Fugees' strength was at left forward in Josiah, a fast and agile ball handler, whose streaking forays down the sideline had resulted in a half dozen goals so far. Qendrim was an able midfielder, capable of directing his teammates and setting up his talented front line, while Shahir, a quiet and unassuming left midfielder, was getting more confident and reliable with each practice.

There was still a glaring weakness on the Under 13s, though, in goal: Eldin and Mafoday, the heavyset young man from Gambia with the blinding smile. A good goalie was quick, determined, and not a little menacing. Ideally, attacking players would fear a keeper's aggressiveness, especially when they took the ball in to the goalie box. Eldin and Mafoday inspired no such fear. They didn't go to the ball so much as wander to it, and standing in goal with their innocent, slightly goofy smiles, they gave the impression that they were less likely to take out an attacking forward than to hug him and invite him over to play. But Eldin and Mafoday had been with the team since the beginning. They were on time. They did their homework. The boys set a stellar example, so Luma had resolved to coach around their weaknesses in goal.

Such a strategy suited Luma well. As rigid as she could seem about team rules and the like, she favored a flexible, unregimented approach to the game itself. In the spectrum of international soccer styles, Luma favored the Latin American, and particularly Brazilian, style over the more regimented and methodical styles of European soccer. In drills and in games, she assigned her players a particular task but left it up to the players themselves to find their own personal ways of achieving that goal. Where some soccer coaches might have emphasized, say, striking the ball on a particular part of the foot to achieve a specific effect, Luma instead focused on the end result, and graded her players on their ability to find their own personal ways of achieving the end. Creativity was essential in overcoming weaknesses in soccer, and beyond. Before one early game, Luma had mentioned idly that her strength was coaching offense, since she'd never actually played defense herself. So what was her defensive strategy for the game? I asked.

"Score a lot," she said.

Chapter Twenty-three

Showdown at Blue Springs

"**C**oach," Mafoday said in a whisper. "*It's all white people.*"

The Under 13s were walking onto the home field of the Blue Springs Liberty Fire in Loganville, Georgia, an old southern town still beyond the grasp of Atlanta's creeping tendrils, and down the road from other old southern towns with names such as Split Silk and Between. Luma looked around. It was true. Loganville was more than 90 percent white, and there wasn't so much as a suntan on the faces of the Liberty Fire or their parents, assembled on the sideline with an array of lawn furniture, coolers, and picnic blankets. Luma reminded Mafoday that the Fugees rarely faced teams with black players.

"I know," Mafoday said, marvel in his voice. "But they are *all* white."

"Let it go," Luma said.

The Blue Springs Liberty Fire had a 3–2 record, but they had proven themselves capable of scoring a lot of goals. Three weeks previous, they had throttled one team by a score of 10–0. Their home field was a rumpled approximation of a rectangle, with dips and rolls and patches of cinnamon-colored dirt that from a distance looked like a threadbare green towel tossed carelessly on an earthen floor. The field was also small, a disadvantage for the Fugees, who preferred to play on wide-open pitches where they could rely on their conditioning to wear out the competition. The Fugees were at another disadvantage: they were groggy. The game was at nine a.m. Luma had called her players the night before to remind them of the early start. It was chilly out, so she wouldn't have them walking to the library for pickup, as was the custom. Instead, the bus would go from complex to complex to pick the players up. She expected everyone to be waiting and ready. One by one the Fugees had climbed onto the bus, weary and puffy-faced—all except for Jeremiah. He wasn't waiting out front, and there was no sign of life at the Ziatys' apartment. Luma knew that Beatrice had been working a night shift at the box factory. She would be sound asleep and unable to wake Jeremiah. So Luma told Tracy, the team manager and occasional bus driver, to knock on the door. Jeremiah was still slumbering inside. Startled awake, he grabbed his uniform and dashed to the bus. At game time, he was more or less sleepwalking.

Luma had been going over the game plan in her head. She was going to hide Bienvenue on defense—if the need arose, she could switch him to offense later in the game—along with Jeremiah. Qendrim would play in the middle; Josiah in his favored spot at left forward. Luma told Mafoday that she would try to get him on the field on defense, but that she planned to go with Eldin in goal for the entire game. She thought he was stronger. Mohammed Mohammed would play defense—he was tiny but as persistent as a gnat—and she could move the Dikori brothers around as needed. Santino, the meek Sudanese boy who had arrived just before the season began, would sit on the bench, but Luma planned to put him in later in the game, to give more experienced players a rest.

Blue Springs struck first, taking the lead on an unspectacular shot from ten yards out. The Fugees were still not fully awake. They were playing flat and getting knocked around. Grace caught a hand to the face and crumpled over in pain. Qendrim was getting knocked around like a pinball in the middle by the bigger Blue Springs midfielders. He was already getting frustrated.

"You better watch out," Qendrim said at one point to a Blue Springs player who'd gotten away with a push.

"What are you going to do about it?" the boy asked.

Qendrim didn't have a comeback for that one—he was too small to do much harm to anyone, and he knew that if he tried anything rough, Luma would bench him. So he sucked it up. A few minutes later, Qendrim was chasing after a free ball in the Blue Springs goal box when the goalie took him out at the knees. Play was stopped, and Qendrim was taken to the sideline wincing in pain.

With her team trailing 1–0 at halftime, Luma lit into them. They were playing lazy soccer, she said. They were dribbling too much and not looking for the open man. And they were allowing themselves to get pushed around. Luma made just one adjustment, moving Jeremiah from defense up to midfield, where he could potentially set up Josiah. Qendrim's knee was still throbbing, but channeling the toughness he'd learned from his professional-playing grandfather, Qendrim told Luma he was ready to go back in.

"When I'm hurt and, like, we have to win because it's a hard team," he boasted later, "I just take the pain."

Just two minutes into the second half, Josiah made his way through three defenders, dribbling the whole way, before finding himself with a clear shot. Having flouted his coach's instructions to dribble less and pass more, Josiah knew he was on the hook now to score. He wheeled in behind the Blue Springs defenders and blasted a clean shot from fifteen yards out: 1–1. The Fugees were awake.

A few minutes later, Blue Springs was attacking when Mohammed Mohammed went in for a tackle from behind. He missed the ball and took out the Blue Springs forward—a nasty foul. The referee blew the whistle, and Blue Springs quickly set up for a direct kick from nearly twenty-five yards out. The ball sailed over the Fugees' wall, across the face of the goal and just into the top far corner. It was an amazing shot, and Eldin didn't stand a chance. It was 2–1 Blue Springs. Sensing a shift in momentum, the parents of the home team were now more vocal, and Luma began to worry about how the crowd would affect her kids' minds.

Now ahead 2–1 with fifteen minutes to go, Blue Springs slowed the pace. At one point, the ball sailed off the field of play, and the Blue Springs player who went to retrieve it took his time, walking slowly in order to burn as much playing time as possible. Frustrated by the stalling tactic, Qendrim decided to go for the ball himself, but the Blue Springs player artfully blocked his path. Qendrim was getting angrier by the minute.

Luma decided it was time to deploy her secret weapon. Quietly, she signaled to Bien to swap with Jeremiah from defense to center midfielder. The boys stealthily and casually switched positions, and to Luma's relief, the Blue Springs coach didn't seem to notice. Moments later, the Fugees managed a long pass down the field. Bien controlled the ball, and tapped a pass to a streaking Idwar Dikori, who deflected the ball into the net. As he did, the linesman raised his flag: offsides. The goal didn't count.

The Fugees, though, were undeterred. They had a new spark on offense in Bien, and Blue Springs still hadn't marked him. There would be other chances. Minutes later, Qendrim and Bien worked the ball toward the goal. Qendrim controlled a pass at the top of the box, and crossed it to Bien. For a moment, as the Blue Springs defenders converged, Bien looked as though he would pass it back to Qendrim, who was now unmarked. But Bien fired a shot instead, surprising everyone, including the Blue Springs keeper. It was a goal; the game was now tied again, at 2–2.

"Mark number three!" came a voice from the Blue Springs sideline, calling out Bien's number. "She just changed him!"

Shhh! Luma thought.

The next few minutes of the game were frantic. Both teams were playing desperately, and the excitement of a close game had drawn the attention of parents and players of other local teams scheduled for games later in the morning. Together, they added numbers to the already crowded Blue Springs cheering section. Tipped off by that vocal parent, Blue Springs defenders now covered up Bien, who was being set upon each time he touched the ball. But with five minutes left in the game, Bien again found himself on the receiving end of a pass. He looked upfield. With the Blue Springs defense converging around him, there had to be an open player somewhere. Out of the corner of his eye, Bien spotted an orange jersey in open space: it was Idwar Dikori. Bien paused to let defense commit, then flicked a crisp pass to Idwar, who volleyed it into the net. With minutes to go, the Fugees were finally ahead, 3–2.

Blue Springs wasn't finished. They sent a long pass down the field, and a Blue Springs forward managed to slip behind the Fugees defense. The ball was the only thing between him and Eldin in the Fugees' goal. The forward sprinted downfield; he'd have a shot. Out of the corner of her eye, Luma caught a glimpse of a streaking orange jersey: it was her youngest player, Robin Dikori, whose older brother Idwar had just scored. With arms and legs churning, tiny Robin slipped between the Blue Springs player and the ball, and kicked it clear.

Where did he come from? Luma wondered.

Now it was the Fugees' turn to stall and run the clock. When the ball sailed out of bounds, Qendrim found himself side by side with the player who had been stalling earlier for Blue Springs. He volunteered to get the loose ball, and when the boy bit on his ploy by waiting on the field, Qendrim slowed down to a snail's pace. When he finally got back on the field, the boy cursed at him. Qendrim, smaller by a head, handed him the ball and responded with an English idiom he'd only recently picked up from a Justin Timberlake tune.

"What goes around," he said, "comes around."

A moment later, the referee blew the whistle to signal the end of the game. Luma was elated. Her team hadn't given up, had played as a unit, and had come from behind on a hostile field—a sign of mental toughness and resolve. She was happy too with her coaching job; her position changes had worked perfectly. And the victory put the Under 13 Fugees within striking distance of first place, if they could keep winning. The boys were ecstatic too. Spontaneously, they broke into song, and began dancing as a group, to the bewilderment of their hosts.

But even the disappointed fans and parents on the Blue Springs sideline seemed to understand and appreciate the effort the competition had shown. As the Fugees walked off the field toward their bus, a man on the Blue Springs sideline called out to them in praise.

"I'd have paid money to watch that game!" he said.

Chapter Twenty-four

Coming Apart

A day later, on Sunday, it was the Under 15s' turn for a big away
game, against a team from the Roswell Soccer Club called the
Santos in an affluent suburb north of Atlanta. The sky was a satin
azure, dimmed slightly by the haze, the air cool and light with a me-
andering breeze. The Santos, contenders for the division championship, were well-coached, disciplined, and quick. The Under 15 Fugees
were still very much a work in progress. After their big win in their
first game back after Luma's enforced hiatus, the 15s had lost 4–1 to
a middle-of-the-pack team. Luma had hoped to use a two-week break
after that game to build a sense of cohesion among a group of boys
who were still just getting to know each other. But Tito's shooting,
the cancellation of practices that followed, and the change of practice
venues had prevented the new version of Kanue and Mandela's team
from getting into anything like a groove. To complicate matters, in
the intervening two weeks since the shooting, Mandela's mood had
continued to darken. He missed his old Liberian teammates, and his

interest in the Fugees—let alone his commitment—seemed increasingly in doubt. The Santos were an excellent team, and the Fugees needed Mandela, and everyone else, to play well if they hoped to stand a chance.

At the starting whistle, the Santos settled in to a routine of sharp, controlled passes that demonstrated discipline and experience. And yet it was the Fugees who threatened first. Mandela bolted through the Santos defense and made a solitary dash for the goal. The Santos' goalie stepped forward to cut off the angle of his attack. Mandela tapped the ball out to Muamer, the new Bosnian forward. Only Muamer wasn't there to receive the pass, and the ball rolled out of bounds. Mandela barked at Muamer in frustration. His teammates glanced at one another. Mandela, it was clear, was in one of his moods.

A few minutes later, it was Kanue's turn. He was shoved in the back while going for a ball in the Fugees' box, and in the confusing tumult of limbs and falling bodies that followed, the referee pegged Kanue as the offender. It was a foul in the box, and a penalty shot for the Santos.

"Kanue—stop it!" Mandela yelled from midfield.

Roswell converted on the penalty kick to take a 1–0 lead. Minutes afterward, a fox-quick striker for the Santos snuck behind Kanue, Alex, and Hamdu on defense and fired off a blistering shot. Ervin, the 15s' goalie—a Bosnian refugee and another newcomer to the team—dove to the right. The ball sailed past his fingertips and into the net. As the Santos were celebrating, Mandela laid into Ervin.

A few minutes after that score, the same wily forward for Roswell snuck behind the Fugees defense and blasted another shot past Ervin. It was now 3–0. Again, Mandela laid into the new goalie. Ervin shrugged and shook his head: he wasn't getting any help on defense, he said. The Fugees were bickering with one another. They were falling apart. Mandela had all but quit. For the rest of the half, whenever he got the ball, he turned and made a furious and lonely dash for the Santos' goal—dribbling all the way and refusing to pass to his open teammates. Head down as he charged, Mandela seemed intent on ignoring them. The runs were wild, and each failed; Mandela lost control of the ball once, and twice it was stolen by Santos defenders. On the changes of possession, Mandela made no effort to get the ball back. He simply stopped, and eventually, as play moved in the other direction, began to walk upfield at a casual pace. When the referee blew the whistle at halftime, the Fugees trailed 3–0.

"What the fuck?" Mandela said. He muttered the words under his breath, but he was right in front of his coach.

Luma was angry, but she remained calm. She ordered Mandela to sit on the bench and told the rest of her players to follow her to midfield and to take a knee. They were bunching up in the middle on offense, she said. Muamer was dribbling too much and not keeping his head up to look for open teammates. Sampson, a Liberian who sometimes played goalie, she said, would move to center mid—Mandela's position.

"Thank you," several players said, grateful to hear that Mandela wouldn't come back in the game.

Mandela was sitting alone now, out of hearing range. He leaned back on the bench, raising his arms and resting the weight of his legs on the backs of his heels, before dropping his head back and staring into the hazy sky overhead. He grabbed the bib of his sweat-soaked jersey, pulled it up over his face, and stretched it over his head, to block out the sun, the game, everything. When Luma returned to the bench, she didn't acknowledge him. He took his jersey off and heaved it into the dust in a damp clump. A moment later, the referee approached and told Luma that her player needed to put his jersey back on if he intended to come back in the game—those were the rules. It was all right, Luma told the referee. He wasn't going back in the game.

The Fugees played better soccer in the second half, even with one of their most talented players sitting on the bench. They spread the ball around and managed to attack a few times and eventually, late in the game, to score. But the Santos were in better shape and played with the smooth confidence of a group of young men who had been together for years and who trusted one another. They were unrelenting on offense, and added one goal, and another, and another. When Luma gathered her players at the end of the game, the score was 6–1.

"What they got you on was you're way out of shape," she told them, refusing even to acknowledge Mandela's behavior. "You made some sloppy mistakes on defense, and you weren't aggressive enough. So we have a lot of stuff to work on this week. You show up promptly to start at five—not to change, not to complain about how much running you're going to do. You show up at five to start practicing. All right? We've got a lot of work to do."

Luma led her players toward the parking lot and the team bus. She ordered Natnael and Mandela into her Volkswagen. They set off on a long, uncomfortably silent ride back to Clarkston.

"I'VE GOT THIS problem," Luma said eventually to Natnael. "I need your advice. I've got this kid who shows up to practice when he feels like it. He cusses at his teammates. He disrespects his teammates. He won't even talk to his coach at practice. The only time he'll talk to his coach is when he needs something. He'll only do it over the phone."

Mandela squirmed uncomfortably but said nothing.

Luma told Natnael of the things she'd done for this player: When his free lunches at school were cut off because his mother hadn't properly filled out the paperwork, Luma took care of it. When his family was hungry, Luma said, she had taken them food. When they needed help moving, Luma helped them move.

"The problem is, I think I just love his mom and his brother so much that I think I'm willing to let some things go," Luma said. "And I think I shouldn't have let some things go. Because I wouldn't have let it go for anyone else."

Mandela's eyes were fixed straight ahead.

"And so today," Luma continued, "we're walking off the field, and he says, 'What the fuck?' So what am I supposed to do?"

Natnael watched the passing cars through the window. He wasn't sure if Luma really wanted his opinion. He said nothing.

"No, Natnael," Luma pressed. "What *would you do,* if you were the coach?"

Mandela was Natnael's friend. They had played together for two years, and they had worked to make sure the Under 15s could continue, against the odds. Natnael could empathize with the frustration and loneliness of being a young man caught between worlds. He knew Mandela had been separated from the few Liberian friends he had who understood exactly what he was going through. Natnael also knew the ease with which that frustration could morph into simple rage. He dealt with it himself. At the same time, Natnael had found a way to contain his anger and to find a place for himself through the team he, Mandela, and Kanue had worked to preserve. He knew it was possible. He took no pleasure in it, but Natnael knew the answer to Luma's question.

"Let him go," he said.

A FEW MINUTES later, Luma pulled her Volkswagen into the apartment complex off Indian Creek Way, where the Ziatys lived. Luma's first words to Mandela came when they pulled into a parking space in front of his family's front door.

"For a while I expected you to be like Jeremiah," she told him. "Actually, you're a better athlete—but you don't have the discipline or the respect to play. You don't respect me, and you don't respect your team."

Mandela's expression remained blank. He didn't respond.

"Get out," Luma told him. "Don't call me Coach, and don't ever call me again."

Luma wasn't particularly proud of the moment. She was responding out of anger and hurt—much more like a wounded parent than a soccer coach—when she lashed out at him. Indeed her language and tone eerily echoed the complaints of Mandela's mother, Beatrice, to her sons: *You forgot, but I not forgot . . . and after all we passed through.* Natnael understood.

"She knows his family, and she loves him," he said. "That's why she didn't kick him off the team earlier. He said he would do better, and he might have done it for a little bit. He is a good person but he has his moments—sometimes he has a real good attitude and sometimes a real bad attitude. So that's the reason she kept him—because she was close to him."

In one way, at least, Luma's harsh reaction to Mandela had precedent. It was how she had often dealt with violations of the sense of control and order she worked diligently to create around herself. When that control was violated—or perceived to have been violated— Luma's reflex, it seemed, was to banish the violator. At various times in the last year, she had dismissed Christian Jackson, Prince, Fornatee, the entire Under 15 team, and even a young boy on the Under 13s for skipping during practice when he should have been running. But those close to Luma said the episodes had less to do with punishment than with Luma's need to conceal her vulnerability from others, especially the boys who depended on her. "When her boys are in trouble, she tries to be tough and wants to be the tough figure in their lives," said her sister Inam. "She has these emotions, but she doesn't want people to see them."

The episode with Mandela left Luma exhausted and heartbroken. She spent the evening and most of the next day at home in her apartment. She didn't want to talk to anyone. She didn't want to be around the kids for fear that she might say something she might later regret. So she kept to herself.

"It's like a kid you were hoping . . . and a family you're really close to," she said, trying to explain before interrupting herself.

"You don't want to give up," she said.

SUCH MOMENTS OF despair and deep frustration were common among those who worked in refugee resettlement in Clarkston. The work had a Sisyphean quality. Individual refugee families often needed more help than an individual could give, and because new families kept arriving, the need was constantly multiplying. Resources for providing help were limited—there were never enough English classes or decent jobs. Sometimes refugees themselves were distrusting and rejected help. And adding to the frustration was a sense that the world beyond Clarkston seemed not to know or particularly to care about the struggles taking place there. For many who worked in resettlement, the steady accrual of disappointment eventually led to burnout.

Those who stuck out the frustration and remained committed tended not to strike a balance between their private lives and the lives of the refugees so much as to give in to the idea that Clarkston and the refugees were a large part of their lives. They tended also to be searchers who were capable of reframing the terms of transaction between themselves and newcomers in a way that emphasized the benefits of getting involved.

"You have to remember that you're being given a lot more than you're giving," said Jeremy Cole, a youth services coordinator at Refugee Family Services, an aid agency just across the Clarkston town line in Stone Mountain. "Because the refugees give you something in return—an understanding of international cultures, of generosity."

Cole was emblematic of a small but passionate group of volunteers and social workers in Clarkston who powered through the daily frustrations and who as a result had found their lives transformed in surprising ways. Soft-spoken and contemplative, Cole had lived a comfortable life before coming to Clarkston. He now spent much of his day going from one crisis to another—working with families from dozens of countries, including the Ziatys, and educating local police departments about the refugees in their jurisdictions. Persevering through daily disappointments was his stock in trade, because the families who came to Refugee Family Services were frequently among the neediest in Clarkston. They came Cole's way after their three months of assistance from the resettlement agencies had expired, often broke, often depressed or dealing with post-traumatic stress. When I sat down with him for the first time at his cubicle at Refugee Family Services, Cole was working on the case of a troubled thirteen-year-old Sudanese boy whose father had killed himself three months before.

"He has a lot of problems—discipline problems—which of course were made much worse with the suicide," Cole said. The boy had been arrested for carrying a gun at a local mall, he said, and suspended from school for unrelated disciplinary reasons. "So I'm dealing with trying to get him back into school," he said. "And working with his teachers to figure out what's going on while also referring him to a new mental health program here."

As someone who dealt frequently with refugee boys and teenagers like Mandela, Cole understood the difficulties they faced. They were caught between worlds, first as teenagers moving from childhood to adulthood, but also as resettled refugees, transitioning from one culture to another. Social scientists refer to the state of being between worlds as liminality, which the anthropologist Victor Turner described as the state in which a person "becomes ambiguous, neither here nor there, betwixt and between all fixed points of classification; he passes through a symbolic domain that has few or none of the attributes of his past or coming state." The process is hard enough on the average teenager, but compounded for refugees and immigrants, who social scientists say possess "double liminal status." A teenager who'd left Liberia at the age of seven or eight for America—and who now spoke English fluently, had friends from around the world, and had been educated in American culture—was not Liberian exactly, or American. In fact, the hardest moments for kids on the Fugees came when they were expected to be entirely one or the other: when their parents pressured them to dress and speak the way children did in the old country, or when the American kids at school mocked them for their accents, strange mannerisms, and unfamiliarity with American customs.

"We hear a lot of stories about parents with kids, because our kids are the ones who are getting in trouble," Cole said. "The parents see this and know the kids are on the wrong track, and they go into this long story about 'what I went through to get here—I walked carrying you on my back, barefoot, for a hundred miles in the desert, just so we could survive, eating roots and anything I could, and you're acting like this?' It's sort of a guilt trip—it *is* a guilt trip—and it's a hard thing for the kids to deal with."

Understanding this dynamic in abstract terms was useful, but it didn't necessarily help Cole get through to young men or their parents, because of the profound distrust many refugees had built up through the process that led to their flight in the first place.

"They've been betrayed by their country, their government, their soldiers, the police, the refugee camps probably," he said. "How can you trust easily having gone through those circumstances?"

Cole was not necessarily the likeliest person to be advising refugees from Africa or the Middle East on how to live their lives. He came from a solidly upper-middle-class American family of Methodists in Macon, an hour and a half south of Atlanta. His mother was a federal magistrate, his father, a law professor. He attended Oberlin, and after college worked for a while at a homeless shelter in Boston before moving back down south to Atlanta. He took a job at Refugee Family Services mostly because it was available. He began working on an after-school program for refugee kids and supervised a tutoring program for adults, and in the process found his worldview unexpectedly challenged. The refugees Cole worked with came from literally dozens of different countries and ethnic groups, and yet there was something culturally similar about them in Cole's eyes. They tended to value family above all else. Most were pious Christians or Muslims. Many were welcoming and reflexively generous in ways Cole had never experienced in America. Whatever their personal troubles, most seemed blissfully nonmaterialistic and free from the consumerist obsessions that drove the world Cole inhabited when he was not at work. And Cole was taken by something else he saw in many of the refugees he met: an improbable optimism and clearheadedness about what was important.

"To be ripped from their home and forced to another place is enough to make you think that people would give up," Cole said. "Not only do they keep going, but they cling to the vital aspects of their lives as closely as possible—family, friendship, love, kindness, community."

Cole didn't know exactly what to call this worldview—he settled on simply "traditional," and contrasted it with the world he was familiar with and that he saw as driven largely by ego and selfishness. Whatever one called this new worldview, Cole began to crave it.

"The thing I got to thinking about," he said, "is—what are the conditions that lead to larger portions of society being generous, humble, and selfless? While we have the conditions for economic opportunity here—and that is a blessing—do we have the conditions to learn how to self-regulate our own passions for the good of the whole?"

At the same time Cole was contemplating these lofty questions, he began pursuing his master's degree in religion at the University of Georgia. For his studies, and out of his own curiosity, he also wanted to learn Arabic, a language spoken or at least understood by many of the families Cole worked with from Africa and the Middle East. He mentioned his interest in Arabic to one of his clients, a well-educated Kurdish woman who had fled Iraq and persecution under the rule of Saddam Hussein and who now lived with her husband and children in Clarkston. She offered to tutor Cole in Arabic for free. He began making regular visits to the family's apartment, where he was welcomed with tea and traditional Kurdish food. As his Arabic improved, he grew closer with the family, and received invitations to social events, including their daughter's wedding. He began to feel as though he were part of their family.

Cole's time with the family also deepened his interest in Islam, the religion that he most strongly associated with the openness he felt in the refugee community. It was a view of Islam not widely held among Americans, particularly the folks in Macon, Georgia, where Cole had grown up.

Interestingly to Cole, few of his Muslim clients showed more than a passing interest in his curiosity about their faith, a reaction at odds with the aggressive proselytizing that characterized the conservative Christians Cole knew from growing up in Georgia.

"I expected an overwhelming response trying to convert me, calling me every day, asking me how my 'faith decisions' were going," Cole said. "I never got this. I just had clients who were kind, and generous, and fair."

In 2003, Jeremy Cole—an otherwise typically polite, khaki-wearing southerner from Macon—converted to Islam, joining the exceedingly small subset of people who use the phrases "y'all" and "Salaam Alei-chem" with equal ease. He began to pray at the Masjid al-Momineen, the multinational mosque on Indian Creek Drive in Clarkston, and cut pork from his diet—not an easy decision for a man from Macon, a place, he said, with some pretty good barbecue. Cole's family—his parents and his wife, who was raised Catholic, reacted to his deci-sion with confusion, surprise, and "many, many questions," he said. But Cole's marriage was strong, and he was on good terms with his parents. All, he said, have respected, if not entirely supported, his deci-sion. Cole doesn't make a point of declaring his faith to others—he dresses no differently than he did before, in the same khakis and ox-ford button-downs, and he hasn't grown a beard.

COLE'S TRANSFORMATION WAS a striking example of the cul-tural osmosis taking place in and around Clarkston. The refugees were assimilating, to varying degrees, into American culture, and the natives—at least those who dared to interact meaningfully with the newcomers—were changing as well. Of course, few were converting to Islam as Cole had, and in fact many of the most zealous support-ers and volunteers of the resettlement community came from local churches. But his story was a reminder that those who had commit-ted themselves to working in resettlement over the long haul and who had managed to persevere through the inevitable letdowns and frustrations often did so in part also out of a search for meaning in their own lives.

"Working with refugees makes you think that maybe there is something we need to learn from the 'traditional' world," Cole wrote in an e-mail to me one evening. "Maybe our modern, 'civilized' world has lost something that we need as human beings."

Chapter Twenty-five

Hanging On at Home

On the morning of September 6, early in the Fugees' season, a team of federal agents descended upon the small town of Stillmore, Georgia, about three hours south of Atlanta, looking for illegal immigrants. The raid targeted Crider Inc., a local chicken processing plant that employed hundreds of Latino immigrants, some of them illegal, and the trailer parks where Crider's workforce lived. By the end of the day, 120 people—most of them Mexican—were in custody. Hundreds more, including women and children, had fled into nearby woods, fearing arrest or deportation.

Poultry processing plants had become the front lines in the nation's increasingly heated debate over immigration policy. They offered low-paying, dangerous work in revolting conditions and at an unrelenting pace, work Americans seemed less willing to do than immigrants, at least for the wages offered. Plant managers had come to value immigrant laborers. They worked hard, and fearful of getting detained or sent back to their native countries—and often separated from family in the process—they were more compliant than American workers, less likely to file workers' compensation claims or to support union organizing drives. A significant number of those Latino workers were in the United States illegally. The federal government estimated that the total number of illegal immigrants in Georgia had doubled from 220,000 in 2000 to 470,000 in 2005. The state's Republican governor, Sonny Perdue, had pledged a crackdown.

The Crider raid was simply a higher-profile version of raids that had been occurring with increasing frequency at slaughterhouses and processing plants around the South. Stillmore, Georgia, Crider's home, became a kind of ghost town after the raids, as the remaining Latinos left for home or, more likely, for jobs in other American communities. The company raised wages and conducted aggressive recruiting efforts, which included busing in workers from surrounding counties, and yet still couldn't match its pre-raid production levels. Crider bused in workers from a homeless shelter, and even cut a deal with local corrections officials that resulted in a controversial program to compel probationers and convicted felons to work in the plant as part of their restitution for their crimes. Even after all these efforts, the plant was still three hundred workers short of its pre-raid workforce of one thousand. That's when company officials implemented another outreach program: to lure Hmong refugees who had been resettled in Minnesota and Wisconsin to move to Stillmore.

Refugees, if you could find them, were a good substitute for illegal workers. Most important, they were legal, having been granted asylum by the U.S. government. They were often poor and often desperate, and since many didn't speak English, they had few options when it came to employment. Consequently, they worked for low wages and they labored hard to keep the jobs they could get. For the most part refugees, at least in their first few months or years in the United States, were every bit as fearful and compliant as illegal immigrants, if not more so. Latino immigrants to Georgia plugged into a vast and experienced network of other Latinos who had come before them and who knew the ins and outs of the American system. There were more than 600,000 Latinos in Georgia *legally,* in addition to the hundreds of thousands there illegally, and there were whole neighborhoods south of Atlanta where Spanish was the predominant language. By contrast, there were only a few hundred Somali Bantu refugees—or

Burundians, or Meskhetian Turks, or Burmese Karen—in the Atlanta metropolitan area, and most had arrived at around the same time and were learning the ropes together. They were not likely to cause much trouble.

Crider had to recruit Hmong from Wisconsin in part because much of the refugee workforce around Atlanta had been spoken for by chicken processors in the north of the state. Recruiters for the processors kept in touch with the job placement coordinators at the resettlement agencies, and as a result, the first full-time job for many refugees in Clarkston was cleaning and butchering just-killed chickens. Many chicken plants around Atlanta ran twenty-four hours a day, and many refugees—starting out at the bottom of the employee hierarchy—ended up taking jobs on the night shift. Managers didn't care what language workers spoke, so long as they showed up on time. And anyway, it was too loud in a chicken plant to carry on a conversation.

With a newborn baby girl to take care of and no husband around, Generose—the mother of Alex, Bien, Ive, and six-month-old Alyah—needed income, but she couldn't take just any job. She spoke almost no English and couldn't afford day care for Alyah. There was one obvious option: a night shift job at a chicken processing plant.

The plants were in a constant scramble for new workers, so Generose had no problem finding a plant with an opening. She simply asked other refugees she'd gotten to know in Clarkston. They inquired with their bosses on her behalf, and within a couple of days she was piling into a friend's car with other refugees for the hour-long commute to a local plant. Her shift ran from late afternoon to two in the morning; with the commute, she would get home just after three a.m., in time for a few hours of sleep before the boys woke up for school. Wearing a gown, hair covering, and plastic gloves, Generose joined a group of twenty or so line workers charged with butchering dead chickens into cuts. The floor was loud, the smell, acrid and nauseating. And of course, the work was relentless; during the eight-hour shift, chicken carcasses kept coming—pink piles of warm flesh coated in a white smock of skin and fat. It took Generose only a few shifts to develop a revulsion toward chicken. Now on the rare occasions when she'd eat meat, she stuck to beef and fish.

Generose did the work without complaint. She seemed to find the exercise more confounding than anything else. The idea of leaving one's family at home, driving an hour away to work at a factory to get paid by the hour struck Generose as a weird and inefficient quirk of American society. In Burundi, a mother worked within sight of her children. Commuting—an hour in each direction, no less—was an alien concept. Far worse than the actual work was the idea of being so far away from her children. Generose had lost a nine-year-old daughter in the camp in Mozambique in a cooking accident. Now her boys—fifteen, thirteen, and seven—were at home alone with an infant.

Taking care of Alyah in the evenings fell mostly to Alex, the quiet defender for the Under 15 Fugees, who assumed his new responsibility as Mister Mom without complaint. He would hurry home after soccer practice in time for Generose to leave for work. In the early evening, he fed Alyah, warming milk in the microwave and then stirring in powdered baby food to form a gooey white pabulum, which he would then spoon patiently into her mouth as he held her on his lap. When Alyah was fed, Alex would then turn his efforts to making dinner for his brothers—sometimes warming food Generose had made during the day, sometimes making hot dogs or some other simple fare himself, while Bien and Ive watched television or did their homework. After dinner, Alex cleaned the kitchen as well, scrubbing the pans and wiping down the counters and stove top with the same graying cotton rag. He didn't seem to view all the work as a burden in the least, but there was no doubt it was affecting Alex in one important way. He was handling the babysitting, cooking, and cleaning in the time he had previously devoted to doing homework. Of the three brothers, he was the farthest behind with his English and reading.

Alyah was a beautiful child with long, thin fingers, perfectly formed little lips, and for an infant, an improbably serene demeanor. She rarely cried. She could sit for an hour or more in her walker, gazing calmly at her brothers or at guests with her giant brown eyes without so much as a peep. Alyah seemed to understand that she was loved and safe. After all, she had a team taking care of her. Alyah spent much of the day sleeping in a kanga on her mother's back, as Generose made dinner in the kitchen in the afternoons. There she would be rocked into deep slumber from the motion of Generose's stirring a thick clump of foofoo, the starchy paste of pulverized and boiled cassava root, which had to be stretched and stirred and fought with, like taffy. In the evenings, when the boys came home, they would pick up Alyah and carry her around like a rag doll, eventually plopping her into a crease in the sofa cushions, where she would sit quietly, curiously, it seemed, for hours, at least until she got bored and squirmed her way off the edge. The typical American parent, used to coddling infants as though they were made of glass, might have been unnerved by the freedom Alyah was granted to wiggle about, and the rough-and-tumble way her brothers toted her back and forth as they did chores. But Alyah herself seemed content to bop along for the ride, and if she was accidentally dropped onto the carpet, say, by seven-year-old Ive, she was less likely to cry than to look up at him with a quiet but firm expression of disapproval: another little sister in the world convinced her big brother was a klutz.

Each evening, the phone in the apartment would warble at around nine o'clock. It was Generose, calling by cell phone from the chicken plant to make sure everything was all right. In truth, there was little she could do if she found out things weren't. She was an hour away, and relied on a carpool for transportation. If something went wrong, her sons would have to take the initiative to call for help. The boys would put their mother on speakerphone and share a chaotic group conversation before saying good night.

ONE EVENING AFTER practice, Alex came home weary, and set about making dinner. He put some hot dogs in a pan for himself and his brothers and placed it on an orange-hot coil on the electric stove. Then he got to work on Alyah's dinner. He washed a plastic container in the sink, poured in a dollop of milk, and placed the container in the microwave. Alyah was hungry now, and as she sat in her walker in the next room, she had a rare meltdown, crying out for food. Bien was on the sofa doing his homework, while Ive was lost in an episode of *The Simpsons*. Alyah's cry rose to a marrow-curdling shriek as Alex waited impatiently for the microwave to beep. He stirred in the pow-dered formula and tested the steaming mixture with his finger. It was too hot. He stirred some more and blew into the container to cool the food. The hot dogs were sizzling in the skillet. Alex then hurried into the living room to Alyah, who was still crying. Bien had put down his book and was now bouncing his little sister on his knee, but she was in no mood to play. Alex took over. He perched Alyah on his knee and leaned her back into the crook where his arm met his body, and began to feed her, blowing on each spoonful of pabulum until it was cool. Alyah was ravenous and happy. She ate sloppily, with food pouring from her mouth. With the small spoon, Alex patiently scraped the dripping food from Alyah's chin and the corners of her lips. Alyah's eyes lit up with each slurp of her dinner.

The smoke came first as a faraway scent, and then as a quick moving thundercloud rolling from the kitchen into the living room: the hot dogs. Alex put the food down and propped Alyah against the arm of the sofa and ran into the kitchen. The hot dogs had melted into a black goo in the skillet, which was now billowing a foul-smelling smoke. Alex grabbed the wet rag he used to clean the kitchen, took the scalding skillet by the handle, and hurried to the sliding door at the back of the kitchen. He dropped the pan on the small concrete apron that constituted the back porch, overlooking the noisy interstate below. He closed the door to keep the smoke out. By now Bien and Ive had appeared at the kitchen door. Alyah was crying in the other room.

The three boys stood quietly and watched the skillet smoke through the glass.

"What was that?" Ive asked finally.

"Dinner," Bien said.

WHEN MANDELA ZIATY walked into his apartment after getting kicked off the Fugees, he walked past his mother, Beatrice, without saying a word, and went upstairs to his room. Beatrice asked him what was wrong, but he wouldn't answer. He just brooded. It took another few days for Beatrice to learn what happened, which came when Mandela announced he wouldn't be going to practice.

"Why you can't go to practice?" Beatrice asked him.

"Mandela quit from the team," Jeremiah told her.

"Jeremiah, shut up your mouth," Mandela said.

BEATRICE WAS WORRIED for Mandela. Without soccer, he would be free in the afternoons and evenings to roam around Clarkston, to get into trouble. She'd been mugged herself there. Tito had been shot right in front of their apartment complex. Like Generose, Beatrice now worked a night shift, folding cardboard at a packaging factory that made boxes for takeout pizza chains. While she was at work, Mandela, now untethered from the Fugees, would be free to do as he pleased. What was Mandela going to do with himself to avoid this kind of trouble?

"He ain't got nothing to do," Beatrice said.

IN CLARKSTON, BEATRICE had met a Liberian man named David Faryen, a political scientist in their old country, who had come to the United States a decade or so before. They came from rival tribes, he Gio, she Krahn, but they liked each other and had started dating. Their relationship was sometimes contentious. They argued, sometimes about money, sometimes about the boys. Faryen had been in the United States longer than Beatrice, and thought he understood certain things better. He wasn't exactly a father figure to the boys—Beatrice was too strong a presence and felt too possessive of her boys to cede authority over them—but he helped the boys when he could, and he didn't hesitate to express his opinions, especially about the other Liberian kids Mandela hung out with when he wasn't playing soccer. Faryen distrusted them. He thought Liberians who came to America succumbed to bad influences and did bad things, especially to one another. Faryen frequently brought up what had happened to the Jackson family after the apartment fire that had killed four of their children. A local Liberian had volunteered to collect donations for the family, who was also Liberian. The community responded by donating thousands of dollars, but the man promptly disappeared with the funds. That's what we're up against, Faryen would tell the boys.

Faryen's reflexive distrust of others was perhaps excusable, given his personal history. Despite his Gio heritage, he had found a job as a public servant in the mostly Krahn government, a position that made him the target of distrust among other Gios. On a Saturday night in January 1990, a group of rebels showed up at his house with guns. They spoke a dialect he didn't recognize, and said they had orders to take him away. Faryen stalled. He pointed out that he was in his shorts, and that he hadn't showered. The rebels told him he didn't need to shower. There was a discussion among the strangers that he couldn't understand, and then, to his surprise, one of the armed men told him to go inside and to put some clothes on for their journey. It was a journey Faryen had no intention of taking.

"I know that if I get in the car," Faryen said, "I'd be dead."

Faryen went into his house and fled out the back door—running for all he was worth to the bush. When the rebels eventually left the house after discovering their prey's escape, Faryen's neighbors assumed they'd taken him with them. Word of his supposed disappearance spread, and Faryen's abduction and presumed execution was eventually reported by the BBC as an example of the harassment of government officials by rebels. In truth, Faryen spent two nights in the bush. He made his way to Guinea by foot, where he spent three months before going to live in Abidjan in Ivory Coast, for six years. He applied to the UNHCR for resettlement, and eventually was accepted into the United States. He moved to Staten Island—a resettlement location for Liberian refugees—and later, to Atlanta.

As Beatrice's companion, he spent no small amount of energy worrying about the boys. He liked Luma and what she had done for them. When Faryen had suggested that the older boys get a job at McDonald's, Jeremiah said that his soccer coach said that if you got an education, you wouldn't have to work at McDonald's. Faryen appreciated that. He marveled too that a soccer coach could get through to the boys better than he could.

"They have never had this much freedom," he said of the kids. "They kind of overgrow their parents, and they don't know how to deal with that. The way they dress, the way they carry themselves, the kind of hairstyles, the kind of pants—baggy, baggy—and gradually they go off bounds. The parents are not able to control them.

"We, as Africans, have a way of dealing and bringing up our children," he continued. "And when they get used to that, living in America, you got to be strong, you see, and keep on telling them, 'You are here, but you are not *from* here. You got a culture, and you need to respect it.'"

Faryen believed that the problems of many Liberian boys in the neighborhood could be traced back to their parents. The strategy for keeping kids out of trouble, he believed, was simple.

"You need to make sure you perform, and put bread on the table," he said. "Because once they have enough to eat, and they go out there, there will be something else hopefully positive, not negative. If they are hungry, they will follow some bad friends and do what they're not supposed to do. So we encourage them to go to school, to take their academics seriously, and to also have food available in the house that they'll be able to eat."

As Faryen was speaking, Mandela came home from school. His mood was gloomy, and he offered only a nod of the chin as a greeting to his mother, Faryen, and myself. I asked Mandela about the Fugees, but he said simply that he wanted to play basketball now, and walked into the kitchen to get a snack. He didn't want to talk about it.

Once he was out of earshot, though, Beatrice said she had picked up on some subtle signs that Mandela was more conflicted about his dismissal from the team than he was willing to let on. A few days before, she had overheard him talking to his younger brother.

"Jeremiah, I want to talk to Coach," Mandela had said.

"Why you want to talk to Coach?" Jeremiah asked him.

"Why you want to talk to her?" Beatrice asked her son.

"I just want to talk to her," Mandela said. He didn't appreciate all the questioning, Beatrice could tell, so she let up. But in Mandela's room, there was a sign that perhaps he missed the Fugees more than he was saying. His bed was a mattress on the floor. The walls were bare but for one item. On the wall over his pillow, Mandela had carefully hung a light blue pair of shorts and a jersey of the same color: his old Fugees uniform.

Chapter Twenty-six

The Dikoris

After her fallout with Mandela, Luma tried to regroup. Between running her cleaning business, coaching, and helping the families of players and employees, she had had little time for rest or for dealing with the quotidian tasks of her own life. Phone calls and e-mails were going unanswered. A brake light had burned out on her Volkswagen, and Luma had been too busy to replace it. And every time it seemed as though Luma might get a break, another crisis would bubble up. This week, a Somali woman who worked at Luma's cleaning company had become all but incapacitated from back pain. Luma and Tracy, the team manager, scrambled to find a doctor who would see the woman and rearranged their schedules to drive her to the appointment, where she was diagnosed with a severe joint infection in her spine. The doctor surmised that the woman had developed the infection long before her arrival in America. Unsure of how to navigate the health care system or how she would pay for treatment if she managed to figure out how to obtain it, the woman had simply suffered through the pain.

ON THE SOCCER field, though, things were looking up. The move to Milam Park had invigorated the Fugees, and having a proper field allowed Luma to work on her teams' weaknesses. Throw-ins, especially, had been a problem. There were no throw-ins in the informal games kids played in the parking lots around Clarkston, because there was no real out-of-bounds; when the ball drifted away, someone just chased it down and kicked it back into play. But in formal games, the player throwing the ball back onto the pitch had to keep both feet on the ground at all times, to use two hands during the throw, and to launch the ball from behind and over his head. In their previous games, the Fugees, and especially the Under 13s, had managed practically every illegal variation of throw-in form imaginable: picking up a foot, throwing the ball from the side of their head, and even casually heaving it into play with the motion approximating a chest pass in basketball. The result had been a steady flow of pointless turnovers and no small amount of laughter from rival players and parents who couldn't fathom how kids playing organized soccer could be so ignorant of such basic rules.

Luma opted for a simple fix to the problem. She had the Fugees practice throwing the ball flat-footed and from a stop, rather than the more customary method of running to gain momentum and dragging the toes of one's back foot. She figured that throwing from a standstill offered fewer opportunities for a mistake. The Fugees lined up and practiced the maneuver over and over again; anyone who made an error was ordered to run a lap. With this incentive, the boys quickly caught on, and by the end of a single afternoon practice, the problem was solved.

Luma would have liked to practice corner kicks, penalty kicks, and free kicks, specific situations in which the Fugees needed improvement badly, but she was hamstrung by the failure of the YMCA to come through with those soccer goals. She had managed to scrounge up a couple of small folding practice goals more suited for a kiddie team than her own players—they were perhaps four feet across and three feet high—and while better than nothing, the setup deprived the Fugees of the opportunity to develop a critical aspect of the game: its third dimension, the space between the ground and the crossbar of the goal. Scoring, particularly long shots and penalty and corner kicks, required a natural sense of that space—a feel for the angles to the top corners of the net, beyond the goalie's reach. With nothing to shoot at but the empty space between clumps of T-shirts placed on the ground since the beginning of the season, the Fugees hadn't had the chance to practice in 3D, and their shooting record showed it. While Josiah, Jeremiah, Qendrim, and Bien were dangerous when charging downfield one on one, the Fugees were missing long shots and crosses badly, and their conversion rate on corner kicks was poor as well.

This coming weekend, the Under 13s would be put to the test. On Saturday, October 21, they were set to face their toughest competition of the season—the Athens United Gold Valiants, a team that had not lost a game and that had put some teams away by scores that nearly invoked the league's mercy rule. The game was in Athens, a good hour and a half from Clarkston. Despite their weakness in goal and their shooting problems, Luma felt the 13s had a chance. They were communicating better with one another. Luma herself had a better feel for the roster and how to rotate players through positions to create opportunities. And the team had discovered a secret weapon of sorts: the Dikori brothers.

IDWAR AND ROBIN Dikori were playing their first season with the Fugees and were among the team's youngest players. Idwar was twelve, Robin just nine. Robin was small, with tiny cat feet and spaghetti-thin legs that seemed to extend to his armpits. Idwar was taller, with a frame that had filled out only slightly more than his little brother's. With their wiry builds, the boys hardly presented the image of athletic prowess. They were also quiet, shy, and, seemingly, unassertive. But on several occasions over the previous few games, the Dikoris had each displayed eye-popping speed that seemed to make the rest of the players on the field look as though they were running in slow motion. Luma knew they were quick, but her eyes were opened to the boys' potential at that moment in the Blue Springs game when Robin appeared out of nowhere to clear the ball. If she found a way to utilize the boys' quickness against Athens, Luma felt the Fugees had a chance to knock off the best team in the league.

THE DIKORIS WERE from the Nuba Mountains of central Sudan, an area the size of South Carolina, with more than a million inhabitants. The land is divided between bare, bouldered mountain slopes and fertile, rain-fed bottomlands that supported both grazing and abundant agricultural production. The Nuba region traversed a fault line between African and Arab culture, prompting Yusif Kuwa, the late rebel leader of the Nuba, to declare his people "prisoners of geography." In the Nuba region, some fifty different ethnic groups, including Christians, Muslims, and practitioners of traditional African religions, lived in relative peace. Unlike many in the better-known—to outsiders—regions of southern Sudan and Darfur, the collection of ethnic groups of the Nuba region put a premium on being left alone over political independence from Sudan's central government. They were content to be Sudanese.

But the Islamist regime that came to power in a 1989 coup had no intention of leaving the Nuba alone. The government wanted access to the vital soil of the Nuba valleys, a rich source of food in the midst of an otherwise nearly barren land, where control of the food supply was synonymous with power. During a dry season in 1991 and 1992, the Islamic government in Khartoum declared jihad in the Nuba region and launched an offensive to drive indigenous groups from the valleys. The declaration of jihad was complicated by the fact that there were Muslims among the mostly African Nuba. But that problem was solved when a group of radical clerics in Khartoum issued a fatwa in April 1992. "An insurgent who was previously a Muslim is now an apostate," they declared. "And a non-Muslim is a nonbeliever standing as a bulwark against the spread of Islam. Islam has granted the freedom of killing both of them."

The government waged its jihad in the Nuba with the goal of terrorizing civilians until they fled the fertile valleys—land the government began distributing to its cronies, mostly Arab entrepreneurs from the north. The campaign was run with brutal efficiency. Clumsy government Antonov cargo planes had their bays loaded with bombs, which the Sudanese air force dropped on the clusters of round straw huts that constituted villages in the Nuba. Convoys of government troops combed civilian areas, terrorizing locals with random killings and a campaign of systematic rape intended to speed the population's move to so-called peace camps. In a detail revealing of the government's scorched-earth approach, Muslim soldiers destroyed any mosque they came across that had not been registered and sanctioned by Khartoum. A 1998 report by the U.S. Committee for Refugees estimated that approximately 200,000 people, or slightly less than a fifth of the total population of the Nuba region, were killed in what it called the Nuba genocide.

ROBIN AND IDWAR'S parents, Daldoum and Smira Dikori, were relatively well off before this campaign of wanton violence began. They lived in a fertile valley, of the very sort the government in Khartoum craved. Daldoum had the equivalent of a high school education. He had land to farm, and livestock. The Dikoris were members of the Moro tribe, a mostly Christian group numbering close to 100,000, and among the largest ethnic groups in the Nuba. Their eldest son, Shamsoun, a quietly intense young man with ink black skin and piercingly white eyes, said that the many ethnic groups in the area got along well when the family lived there, and he remembers how the diversity of the region was explained to him as a child.

"We say that there are ninety-nine different mountains in Nuba and each has its own tribe," he said.

Robin and Idwar were too young to remember the violence that came raining down on the family's village in the form of fire and metal. But Shamsoun, now seventeen and a member of the Under 17 Fugees, remembers the first time he saw the planes.

"We were playing outside and we thought it was birds," he said. "Then the bombs started to fall and everyone started running."

WHEN THE BOMBINGS came, villagers fled for the mountains, as the government had hoped. The men, Shamsoun said, first escorted their children and wives into the hills—journeys that took days—and then returned to their villages to salvage what possessions they could before the government convoys arrived. Daldoum was lucky.

He managed to round up a few goats, cows, and a donkey, to help him carry goods and farm the land. The family built a hut in a small makeshift village with other Moro, avoiding the "peace camps" and farming the surrounding hillsides to produce enough food to survive, but not much more. After five months of barely subsisting in the mountains, the family gave up and moved to stay with relatives who had moved to Khartoum, where at least they had food.

"They had open markets where you could buy stuff," Shamsoun remembered. "It was pretty hot. It was not like the Nuba Mountains. They were green. There was a lot of dirt in the streets and lots of people. I didn't feel safe."

THE ISLAMIST GOVERNMENT in Khartoum didn't make life easy for the displaced Christians who descended upon the capital looking for work, food, and housing. The government sought to mandate military service for the men—and to send them, in effect, back into the south or into the Nuba Mountains to continue the campaign of terror that had led these very people to arrive destitute in Khartoum to begin with. Government-backed henchmen demanded that Christians convert to Islam and change their Christian names to Muslim ones. There were haphazard detentions, and a steady campaign of harassment. Eventually, the Dikori family decided to leave and to join the tens of thousands of Sudanese refugees streaming into Egypt in search of, if not economic opportunity, at least a respite from the overt and relentless persecution of Africans and Christians in the Sudan. Daldoum put together enough money to transport his family from Khartoum to Egypt, a two-day journey on a packed and run-down train. Eventually, the Dikoris made it to Cairo, where they connected with friends.

Cairo, while a reprieve from the constant threat of violence, was no paradise. After a failed assassination attempt in Addis Ababa that he blamed on the Sudanese government, the Egyptian president Hosni Mubarak had rescinded a treaty between Sudan and Egypt that allowed unfettered passage between the two countries; entering Egypt for most Sudanese now meant entering illegally. Refugees were not allowed to work either; they had to scrape by in the underground economy, and they were not eligible for the subsidized housing offered to Egyptian citizens. Africans in Egypt also faced racial discrimination—they were disparaged as "chocolata" or "honga bonga" by some hostile Egyptians, who were growing weary of their uninvited guests. An incident in July 2000 in Cairo, where the Dikoris were living in a cramped apartment with four different families, underscored the accumulating ill will. A public bus struck a Sudanese man in front of a church with a mostly Sudanese congregation. A group of Sudanese men gathered to insist that the injured man be taken to a hospital. Tempers flared in the 110-degree heat, and soon a mob of angry Egyptians had formed as well, on a false rumor that Sudanese men had taken the bus driver hostage inside the church. The two mobs threw objects at each other and the Egyptians set fire to a pastor's car before riot police were called in. A week later, the pro-government weekly *Rose El Youssef* published a front-page piece with the headline "Refugees: Guests or Criminals?"

"Many African immigrants are engaging in illicit activities such as drug dealing," the story read. "They get drunk in the streets and harass women, throw wild parties, and in general act like hooligans. Is this a way for guests in our country to behave?"

Daldoum had no intention of keeping his family—his wife, Smira; daughters Sara, Gimba, and Banga; and sons Shamsoun, Idwar, and Robin—in such conditions for very long. He went to the teeming and overburdened United Nations refugee office in Cairo and applied for resettlement. Odds were long—the office was rejecting more than 70 percent of applicants at the time—but the Dikoris were among the lucky minority. In 2000, the family received word that they had been accepted for relocation to the United States and a place called Georgia.

The Dikoris arrived in May 2000. Idwar was just six and Robin four, but Shamsoun, the eldest, was eleven, and remembers well his reaction to the alien scenery that unfolded before him when he stepped off the plane. He was particularly afraid, he said, of the escalators in the Atlanta airport, which looked like the churning teeth of some giant trash compactor. His father nudged him along, and young Shamsoun held on for dear life as the moving stairway carried him toward the unknown.

The family did their best to settle in. They were taken first to Jubilee, a camp of sorts in northern Georgia run by Christian volunteers, who help refugee families adjust to their first few weeks in America. The Dikoris took English lessons and learned about American culture. But the most puzzling aspects of American culture would reveal themselves later, when the Dikoris moved outside of Clarkston to Stone Mountain. The strangest part of life in the United States, Shamsoun said, was the diffidence of Americans toward refugees and immigrants. Americans seemed to look through him, and no one seemed the least bit curious about how this stranger wound up in their midst.

"In my country," Shamsoun said, "if someone comes from out of the country, people want to talk to them and get to know them. Here, it's almost like they're afraid of you."

The kids enrolled in school. Their English improved. Daldoum got a job at a construction supply company, and saved enough for a car, a Mazda minivan that could accommodate his big, tight-knit family. And on November 27, 2002, Daldoum and Smira decided to take their children to visit a family of fellow Sudanese refugees who'd also made it safely to the United States and who had been resettled in Tennessee. The trip was also a chance to explore the family's new, unfamiliar sense of personal liberty. In their new home, they were free to travel as they liked, without fear of getting stopped, harassed, or detained by authorities who were hostile toward their ethnicity or religion. The timing of the trip was particularly poignant: the Wednesday before the family's second Thanksgiving in America. They piled into the Mazda van, all eight of them. Like many refugees who'd arrived recently in Clarkston, Daldoum didn't have a lifetime of driving experience. The route he chose followed Interstate 24, a winding, scenic, and sometimes treacherous road that wends through the southern foothills of the Blue Ridge Mountains near Chattanooga. Daldoum took the wheel proudly, and the family set off for Tennessee in the late afternoon.

The family made it to Tennessee, about two hours north of Atlanta, and was driving through the hills just north of the Georgia and Alabama state lines, and just east of Chattanooga. It was a dark and cool night, but the roads were dry. Daldoum was traveling in the left lane of the westbound side of Interstate 24 between mile marker 164 and 165, a gradual left-hand curve. A trucker named Thomas Combs was traveling ahead of the van, and looked in his side-view mirror just in time to see the vehicle drift to the left and onto the shoulder between the west- and eastbound arteries of the roadway. Daldoum jerked the wheel to the right. Combs saw the van swerve onto the Interstate and begin to tip onto its left side. The van then rolled violently, flipping numerous times across both westbound lanes before coming to a stop, upside down, on the grassy shoulder. Combs hit the brakes, pulled off the road, and ran back to help.

A crash report by Tennessee state troopers offers a chilling rendering of the scene before Combs. The diagram shows the car veering off the left-hand side, then tumbling down I-24 in a trajectory that took it back across both lanes of westbound traffic. On the diagram there are three marks on the open roadway, in the direction the vehicle was traveling, and another alongside the van's final resting place on the grass, numbered one through four. Beneath the diagram there is a key:

Body One:	Gimba	5 yrs old
Body Two:	Banga	2 yrs old
Body Three:	Sara	10 yrs old
Body Four:	Smira	30 yrs old (mother)

The trooper who filed the report added a note at the bottom. "The father knew the names of the children, but did not know their dates of birth," he wrote. "The family are refugees and have no medical records."

SHAMSOUN DIKORI CAME to lying prone on the ground beside the wreck. There was a woman looking down at him, trying to wake him up—he remembers her as a nurse who had stopped to help out. His father appeared a moment later, looking down at him, asking if Shamsoun was all right.

"I could see from his face that something was really wrong," Shamsoun said. Robin, Idwar, and Shamsoun were taken to two separate hospitals. The younger boys had only cuts and bruises, but Shamsoun had a head injury that required surgery and a week-long hospital stay. Soon the two boys were back in Stone Mountain, a world away from where they'd grown up and now without their mother and three sisters.

The next months were trying. Robin began to act out at school, while Idwar retreated into silence. Daldoum continued to work, but his demeanor offered little solace to his children.

"Our father doesn't show a lot of affection—that's how it is with African parents," Shamsoun said. "Robin started messing up in school—not paying attention, getting mad quicker. Idwar keeps most things to himself and didn't talk to anyone else about problems he was having.

"It's hard to live without your mom," he said.

As the oldest brother, Shamsoun did his best to step in and support his younger brothers. But he was a teenager himself, grieving and lost in a strange world. He took his own solace from the occasional pickup games of soccer that he played on weekends and after school. But the games were for older boys and men; Idwar and Robin were too young to join in. During one of those neighborhood games at Indian Creek Elementary, Shamsoun looked at the other end of the field and saw a group of young refugees gathering to try out for the Fugees. He asked a friend for an introduction to the coach, and joined in, bringing his younger brothers later on. They were young—Robin especially, who was four years behind most of the players on Luma's youngest team. But she brought Idwar and Robin on board, assuming they'd find roles on the team in future seasons, as they got older. That was before she recognized how fast they were.

Robin calmed down at school and became outgoing with his teammates. Idwar, still quiet and shy, transformed on the field into a confident young man. Soccer, Shamsoun said, kept the boys sane.

"It kept our minds from thinking about what happened," he said. "We made friends—kids from different cultures. It broadened our minds, and we weren't the only ones going through hard times. That's why the team is so close. It became our family."

Chapter Twenty-seven

"What Are You Doing Here?"

Every coach the Fugees played wanted to win, but for David Anderson, the head coach of the Athens Gold Valiants, his team's current undefeated season represented a triumph over a much more personal struggle. A clean-cut and energetic thirty-two-year-old from Marietta, a suburb north of Atlanta, Anderson had battled a lifetime of chronically low self-esteem and a nagging feeling that there was something about himself that wasn't quite right. His lack of self-confidence had derailed what might have been a promising high school soccer career as a goalie. Anderson had tried out for the team his freshman year, and didn't make the cut for the junior varsity team. Instead, the coaches assigned him to play on a scrub team they'd put together for players who hadn't made the varsity or JV rosters. He played a season with the team, but when the next season approached, he didn't even bother to try out. Anderson had decided he was done with soccer.

He struggled in college, failing out of one and then another before getting fed up. He made an appointment with learning disabilities experts at the University of Georgia and underwent a day-long barrage of tests. (Twelve years later, he remembers the day as one long, harrowing session of trying to arrange colored blocks into particular shapes.) When it was over, Anderson, then twenty, received a diagnosis of attention deficit hyperactivity disorder, or ADHD.

"It was a huge relief," he said. "I'd spent so much of my time thinking I was just dumb. It was like finding a missing piece to a puzzle I'd been searching for my whole life."

ON SOME LEVEL, Anderson saw coaching as a way to exorcise the regrets he felt over having quit his high school soccer team. A friend recruited him to help coach at a local soccer club in Athens, and Anderson loved it. He took over as head coach for the Valiants in 2003, and drew on his own life experience, emphasizing confidence building and discipline, a style that resonated with both players and parents.

Early on, he'd insisted the team learn to play a controlled version of the game that emphasized precise passing as opposed to long, clumsy down-the-field passes that many youth soccer teams relied on to create scoring opportunities. While his kids had struggled early on with the demands of his game plan, the parents understood Anderson had their sons' long-term interests at heart, and they supported him despite early losses. It began to pay off.

The Valiants' star player was a diminutive and rabbit-quick forward from Austria named Jonathan Scherzer. Scherzer—Joni (YANni) to his teammates—was easily recognizable on the field for his floppy flaxen hair and his Beckham-esque ball-handling skills. He had grown up in the town of Speetal and had only recently arrived with his family in Athens, where his father, Jacob, a veterinarian, had come to study at the University of Georgia. From the time he was three or four, Joni Scherzer had been enthralled with soccer. He would contentedly kick a ball around for hours in the backyard in Austria, by himself, and developed his soccer skills along with self-confidence. But Joni had found the transition to life in the United States difficult. He spoke no English when he arrived and found the culture alienating. He was bullied at school because of his size and accent. He had few friends. So he retreated into soccer, practicing by himself in the backyard in Georgia as he had in Austria, often for as long as two hours a day, only now with more zeal. His parents began to get concerned.

"He was suffering for the first year," his father said. "And he put a lot of effort at that time into his practice, taking it very seriously—sometimes too seriously. Football was an escape for Jonathan."

JONI DIDN'T HAVE a team to play for, so on a summer evening his father took him to a casual "kick-around" David Anderson had organized at the Athens United soccer complex. After only a few minutes of watching Joni play, Anderson walked over to a group of his regular players' parents with a question: "Who here speaks German?" A parent raised his hand.

"Could you go over there and ask them if he wants to be on our team?" Anderson said.

Scherzer joined up, adding a final touch to an already competitive team. He brought a passion for the game, speed, and a rifle-accurate shooting foot that earned him a nickname from Anderson: the Austrian Assassin. With Scherzer on board, Anderson's team was fulfilling its promise this season. The Valiants were undefeated and leading their division, and Anderson couldn't help but see the team's success as a reflection of the progress he'd made in his own life. The team opened up Joni Scherzer's world as well. His English improved. He made friends. And he experienced the self-esteem boost that can come from receiving the admiration of one's peers. In the process, coach and player bonded; for both, the Valiants had become a kind of transformational experience.

ON THE MORNING of October 21, the Under 13 Fugees piled onto the white YMCA bus in the parking lot of the Clarkston Public Library and set out for Athens to take on Anderson, Joni Scherzer, and the Valiants. It was a one-and-a-half-hour drive, so the boys settled in, some gazing out the windows at the unfamiliar scenery, others napping with bundles of clothes tucked between their ears and shoulders for pillows. The short wheel base of the YMCA bus made for bumpy rides, so sleep was fitful. Tracy drove the bus while Luma led the way in her yellow Volkswagen. The drive took them out of the bustle of Atlanta and through a collection of small towns in the Georgia countryside. The air was cool, and some of the treetops in the rolling forests along the way were hued with orange and red—the first hints of a late-arriving autumn. Luma cued up her iPod, which was plugged into her car stereo, and turned up the music. The drive offered a brief window of personal time and a welcome respite from the last hectic weeks, and Luma was enjoying it, much as she had those long drives around Atlanta when she had just moved to town. For the first time in a long while, Luma was able to daydream.

Near Monroe, Georgia, about an hour east of Atlanta, Luma was cruising in the right-hand lane when she felt a strange presence over her left shoulder. She looked out the driver's-side window to a Georgia state police car riding alongside her. The car didn't pass, but neither did it slow down. Luma looked at her speedometer. She wasn't speeding. A moment later, the trooper eased his cruiser behind Luma's Volkswagen and turned on his flashing lights.

The brake light, Luma thought.

The light had been on a long list of personal errands Luma had put off to deal with her team and her players' families. She should've known better, she thought, if only because of the ticket-happy police in Clarkston. She eased onto the shoulder and began to slow, with the trooper behind her. The bus carrying the team continued on. Luma looked at her watch; if this didn't take too long, she could still get to Athens in time for a full warm-up.

The officer approached and asked for Luma's license, then disappeared for a moment into his car. By now, the kids on the bus were getting agitated. Some of the boys had seen Luma get pulled over through the rear window of the bus. They asked Tracy what was happening. She wasn't certain, but reassured them that Luma would be on her way shortly. Meanwhile, the officer approached Luma's car again. Her license had been suspended, he informed her, and ordered her out of the car.

Luma was puzzled. There was no reason her license should have been suspended. She'd been ticketed only once in recent memory: for an expired registration, one morning while driving Jeremiah to school, and for which she had paid the fine on time. The trooper had no way of looking into that on a weekend. He only knew what the computer told him. Under Georgia law, he said, he had to arrest her. The trooper ordered Luma to turn around and to put her hands behind her back. She did, and a moment later felt the cold steel of the officer's handcuffs on her wrists.

By now, Tracy had turned the bus around and was pulling onto the shoulder behind the cop's cruiser. Standing against the squad car, Luma explained the presence of the busload of kids. She didn't get into the details—that they were on their way to the biggest game so far of their soccer season against an undefeated team from Athens. She suggested the trooper just let her leave her car on the highway and get on the bus with her players. The officer said he couldn't do that; he had to take her in. He suggested Luma tell the kids that her car had broken down.

"I'm not going to lie to them," she said. "They're not stupid."

Luma asked that she be allowed to give the team's player cards to the bus driver so the team could go ahead to the game without her, and pleaded with the officer to remove the handcuffs while they were in front of the kids.

"If you promise not to hit me," he said—a joke.

Luma didn't laugh.

The officer obliged. Luma took the player cards to Tracy in the bus—the referee would need them to verify the identities and ages of the players. Then she stood to address her players. She told them she wouldn't be able to make their game. She told them they knew what to do. She expected them to win without her. Luma had hoped to reassure the Fugees, but her voice was shaking.

The Fugees sat uneasily on the bus. They saw the strange events unfolding through the windshield in a menacing light. Several had seen or heard of family members getting carted off by authorities— or worse—for the pettiest of offenses. Santino Jerke's uncle had been shot and killed before him by uniformed Sudanese government sol- diers for the mighty offense of stealing a chicken. Shahir Anwar's family had been hounded by Taliban soldiers because his mother ran a school for girls. The boys were also for the most part unaware of the particulars of the American judicial system, or that posting bail could get someone out of jail rather quickly for minor offenses. They simply knew that their coach and guide through the unfamiliar world where their families had settled was getting hauled off by the police. Some of the boys began to cry. As the YMCA bus pulled back onto the highway, Josiah Saydee, the Liberian forward and team leader, was sitting in the back row. He turned around and looked through a rear window of the bus to see the trooper order Luma into the backseat of his cruiser. In hushed tones, Josiah told his teammates at the back of the bus what he had seen: Coach Luma was in a police car. She was going to jail.

THE FUGEES UNLOADED from the team bus in the parking lot of the Athens United Soccer Club a little more than half an hour later. But as they disembarked and began walking toward the field, Anderson saw their faces and got excited. The Valiants had been beating their competition so badly that Anderson was switching his offensive players to defense and vice versa midway through games out of sympathy for the competition. As satisfying as the victories were, Anderson preferred a challenge. Anderson knew next to nothing about the Fugees when they showed up, but at a glance, he assumed they were a notch above the typical local team.

"You see certain nationalities," said Anderson, "and you say, 'These kids can play.' "

Joni Scherzer noticed there was something unusual about the Fugees as soon as they'd pulled up in the parking lot as well. Most rival teams showed up piecemeal, in their parents' cars. These guys had come in a bus. He didn't know what to make of that detail. He was warming up when the Fugees made their way to the field. It was the first time he'd seen a team with so many black players. He watched the Fugees warm up with interest, and quickly concluded they played a higher level of soccer than the Valiants had faced so far this season.

"They played different from American soccer," Scherzer said he realized. "It was more European—not kickball."

Anderson prided himself on his ability to scout rival teams during their pregame warm-ups. He looked them over for any kids who seemed particularly physical or fast, and he made a mental note of the

jersey numbers of anyone he saw who could shoot or pass with both feet, information he'd relay to his players before game time. But as he was watching the Fugees, he noticed a conspicuous absence.

Where's their coach? he wondered.

THE WALTON COUNTY jail was a dull modern structure that stood out from the surrounding neighborhood because of the tangle of razor wire that ran along a chain-link fence and glistened menacingly in the sunlight. Inside, the trooper who had arrested Luma was handing her over to the custody of the Walton County Sheriff's Department. A clerk asked her to state her name.

"Luma," she said.

"How do you spell that?" the clerk asked.

"Don't bother," the trooper said, sliding her driver's license to the clerk.

The clerk noticed Luma's middle initial—H—and asked what it stood for.

"Hassan," Luma said.

The clerk cast a knowing glance at the arresting officer.

"Hassan?" she said. "Where's that from?"

"Jordan," said Luma.

"It's Arab?" the clerk asked. "What are you doing here?"

Luma started to explain that she was on the way to a soccer game when she had been pulled over, but she was cut off.

"What are you doing *here*—in the United States?" she was asked.

Luma didn't respond. It was time to get fingerprinted. When she had registered with the Immigration and Naturalization Service upon filing her green card application, Luma had been fingerprinted; her fingers were placed on an ink pad and carefully rolled over the card beneath. The woman at the Walton County jail had a different approach; she grabbed Luma's hand, inked her fingertips, and then slammed her hand down on the counter. For the first time, Luma began to feel afraid. Her wallet and sweatshirt were taken from her—the bailiff told Luma she couldn't wear the garment in the jail because it might be contaminated with lice. Bail was set at $759.50, and Luma was escorted into a windowless holding cell with a group of women who looked no happier to be there than she was.

BY NOW, DAVE Anderson had learned that the Fugees' coach had been waylaid en route to the game, and he was curious to see how the competition would fare without help from the sideline. Tracy Ediger did her best to encourage the boys, but she was their tutor and an all-purpose aide to refugee families, not a soccer coach. The boys would have to do this on their own. They divvied up their positions and took the field. No one had had a chance even to give a thought to the competition. Robin and Idwar Dikori, whose speed could be useful in trying to neutralize the blond dynamo playing forward for the Valiants, were unaware of the challenge that awaited them.

It took the Valiants less than three minutes to score their first goal. Two minutes later, they scored again. Anderson could tell something was amiss; he knew from what he'd seen in warm-ups that the Fugees could play, and yet on the field they looked lost. They were arguing with one another and giving Eldin, the goalie, a hard time. A few minutes later, the Valiants scored their third goal. The first half was not yet halfway over. Anderson scanned the Fugees' half of the field. Their heads had begun to drop. It was a sign he'd come to know well from the Valiants' opponents.

Aw, man, Anderson thought. *They're done.*

The Valiants scored again. And again. At the half, they led 5–0.

When Joni and his teammates came to the bench, Anderson told them he would be switching them up in the second half. Joni and the other forwards would move to defense. The defenders would play offense. They understood his reasoning—the game was getting out of hand—but they were disappointed and puzzled, unable to understand how a group of kids who seemed so talented in warm-ups could play so badly.

The Fugees spent halftime bickering over who would play where. Tiny Qendrim volunteered to replace Eldin at keeper, a move his teammates roundly rejected, even as they agreed a change was needed in the net. Half the team wanted Bien on defense, where he could clear the ball with his powerful kick; a more vocal group wanted him at forward. Jeremiah would anchor the middle. Mafoday, usually the weaker of the two keepers, would take Eldin's place in the net.

As the second half began, Anderson watched with curiosity to see how the Fugees would respond. A few minutes in, he noticed something: their chins were up. They were going after the ball. The Valiants managed to blast a shot low and to the left. Heavyset Mafoday, whose vertical jump was perhaps three inches, dove and made the stop. A moment later, Jeremiah chased down a free ball and, attempting to clear it, blasted it into Joni Scherzer's midsection with unexpected force. Joni collapsed on the ground in pain and had to come out. The Fugees hadn't caved. Midway through the second half, the score was still 5–0 when the Fugees were called for a foul in the box for slide tackling from behind. The Valiants would have a penalty shot.

Mafoday Jawneh took his place in goal. With his stubby legs and broad waistline supporting a big barrel chest, Mafoday appeared more like a fixture in goal than a potentially mobile obstacle. Against the empty vastness of the net, he looked vulnerable and almost lonely. Mafoday shook out his arms, put his hands on his knees, and looked into the narrowing eyes of the Valiants sharpshooter before him in shiny black and gold. The Valiants parents cheered the shooter on, while the Fugees players encouraged Mafoday with less confidence: there wasn't much difference, after all, between a five- and a six-goal lead.

Anderson had walked toward the midfield line to get a better view. As a onetime goalie himself, he knew firsthand what Mafoday was going through: the "sheer terror," as Anderson put it, of the penalty kick. Penalty kicks, especially in youth soccer, were almost always converted, so Anderson had taken to teaching his goalies to relax by reminding themselves that the onus was entirely on the player taking the kick: he was supposed to score, and no one—least of all the keeper's teammates—expected a stop. On the sideline, Anderson felt a pang of camaraderie with the opposing goalie.

Come on, kid, Anderson said to himself.

The Valiants shooter surveyed the open net in front of him. He cocked his chin into his sternum, stepped toward the ball, flung his leg forward, and connected, firing a low, sharp shot to the goalie's right. Mafoday Jawneh had made his decision. As the Valiants player made contact with the ball, Mafoday tipped to his right and began to fall like a felled tree. He extended his arms over his head and landed on the ground, stretched out and parallel with the crossbar. There was a thud, then a moment's pause as Mafoday and his teammates realized the ball had stopped in his gray padded goalie gloves—and stayed there, just in front of the end line: a save. The Fugees erupted in cheers and surrounded Mafoday. On the Valiants sideline, Dave Anderson was cheering as loudly as anyone.

Huge, he thought to himself. *Unbelievably huge.*

A few minutes later, the referee blew the whistle three times: the final score was 5–0 Valiants. The Fugees hadn't given up a goal in the second half. They weren't playing against the Valiants' toughest offensive setting, but they'd fought and held their own, and in the process had earned a new fan nearly two hours from home.

SITTING IN THE Walton County jail, Luma had lost all track of time. There were no clocks and no windows to help her orient herself within the passage of the day. She thought about her team, and even started counting bricks in the walls to occupy her mind. Eventually, her thoughts turned to Amman, her family, and especially her late grandmother, who had always told her as a child that things happened for a reason. What was the reason in this? Luma wondered. Was it a warning that she should change her middle name in America so she wasn't harassed? That she should pay more attention to her own life by making sure she took care of things like burned-out brake lights? Luma couldn't make sense of it. She thought about what she would tell her players. Luma had always told them they had to shake off bad calls. In all her years of coaching, she liked to say, she'd never seen a referee change his mind about a call because of the arguments of players or coaches. Bad calls were part of the game; you had to play on.

Luma heard her name called. She stepped into a room with an angled view of the clerk's counter, where she saw Tracy's hands signing papers and sliding them back to the clerk, then handing over cash for bail—$759.50 in exact change. A moment later, a door opened and Luma was free to go. She walked out of the building and directly onto the team bus, parked just in front of the Walton County jail.

Luma asked about the score and got the bad news: the Fugees had lost 5–0.

"This was my fault, and I had no excuse for not being there," she told her players. "I should have been there and I wasn't, and the way it happened probably messed you guys up."

"Mafoday stopped a penalty kick!" someone said.

"It was a really hard team, Coach," said Idwar Dikori.

"Were they better than you?" Luma asked.

"No!" the Fugees shouted in response.

"Come on, guys—were they?"

"No, Coach," said Robin, Idwar's little brother. "If you were there, we were going to beat them."

BACK IN CLARKSTON that night, Luma got a call from the nine-year-old little brother of Grace Balegamire, a midfielder for the Under 13s. The boy's mother had gone to the hospital with his older brother and little sister, to visit a friend who had just had a baby. The boy was at home with his twin brother and Grace, but he was unhappy.

"I'm sad," he told Luma.

"Why are you sad?" she asked.

"I'm scared to be alone," he said.

"Oh, quit it," Luma said.

Luma hung up the phone and decided she had an errand to run. She drove to the grocery store, picked up some sweet rolls, then headed over to the boy's apartment. When she arrived, he was in his bedroom with the door closed. Luma knocked, but the boy wouldn't answer. She coaxed him out eventually with the sweet rolls. The two sat and talked.

"I just had a bad day," he said.

Luma smiled. "Do you want to hear about a bad day?" she said.

"Yeah."

Luma told him everything. The cops, the jail, how she missed Grace's soccer game. He didn't buy any of it.

"Coach, don't lie," he said. "You would never go to jail."

"No, I went—ask Grace."

"If you were in jail, you wouldn't be here," he said.

"No—Tracy paid to get me out," Luma said.

"How much?"

"Enough for five hundred ice creams."

"If you pay five hundred ice creams you can come out of jail?" he asked.

Luma started to explain how the process of bail worked, but then she caught herself, finally grasping the boy's confusion. The Balegamires' father was still locked up in Makala, the notorious central prison in Kinshasa. The government of the Democratic Republic of Congo had issued no word on when—or if—he would be released.

Chapter Twenty-eight

Halloween

On October 27, less than a week after Luma's arrest on the way to Athens, Reuters, the BBC, and *The New York Times* each published short notices about a prison riot in Kinshasa, the capital city of the Democratic Republic of Congo. Details of the incident were murky, but taken together, the dispatches sketched a scene of violence and bloodshed. A riot had occurred at the ominously named Penitentiary and Re-education Center in Kinshasa—the prison once known as Makala. The government reported that five inmates had been killed and that fourteen had escaped. The dead and the escaped, the government said, had been involved in the assassination of the former president Laurent-Désiré Kabila, a meaningless detail, perhaps, since the government of Joseph Kabila, Laurent's son who now ran the country, applied this charge to many of its political opponents.

To most of the world, perhaps, a minor prison riot in Congo—five dead, fourteen escaped—was a mundane event, especially against the backdrop of the five-million-plus lives lost in the country's most recent civil war. But just outside of Clarkston, at the apartment of Paula Balegamire—the mother of the Under 13 Fugees' midfielder Grace and the young boy who had puzzled over Luma's explanation of bail—news of a riot at Makala was cause for extraordinary worry. Joseph Balegamire, Paula's husband and the father of her children, was an inmate there. If the riot had involved the so-called Kabila assassins, as the Congolese government claimed, it had likely occurred in Pavilion One, the wing of Makala where political prisoners, Joseph Balegamire included, were held. News coverage of the event was spare: Kabila's security forces had detained two journalists who had shown up at the prison after locals reported hearing gunfire within. Paula called friends but could gather no additional information on her husband. So for now, she waited, hoping for a phone call to tell her of Joseph's fate—whether he was still an inmate, among the dead, or if, God willing, he had escaped.

HALLOWEEN WAS NOT exactly a big holiday in Clarkston, Georgia. Many of the refugees had never heard of it, or if they had, they were certainly not in the habit of knocking on strangers' doors in the apartment complexes around town. But after the arrest in Athens and the news at the Balegamires', Luma decided that the Fugees needed a break and an introduction to America's most sugar-saturated holiday. Trick-or-treating safely meant leaving Clarkston, where gunfire around the apartment complexes on Halloween was common, so Luma arranged to use the YMCA's bus for the evening and called the parents of the Under 13 players to let them know that their sons would be home a bit later than usual. She stopped by a local CVS and bought costumes—a set of matching Ninja outfits that were more or less black plastic sheets with hoods. She held a casual practice in which she scrimmaged and laughed with the kids, and then afterward surprised them all with the news that they were going trick-or-treating.

The neighborhood Luma had in mind for the outing was not one any of the Fugees had seen before. It was an affluent subdivision near Decatur with a series of cul-de-sacs and rolling narrow lanes that closed to traffic on Halloween each year to become a trick-or-treater's paradise. Nearly every house participated, and residents went all out: the adults wore costumes themselves and decorated their homes with elaborate spooky displays—witches and spiderwebs, ghosts and skeletons with flashing red lights for eyes, and dungeon soundtracks blaring from upstairs windows. Behind each door there were staggering supplies of candy: giant boxes of Mars Bars, Hershey's Kisses, Snickers, Reese's Peanut Butter Cups, Jolly Ranchers, and huge, squirming nests of Gummi Worms. It was enough sugar to support the practice of every dentist in east Atlanta.

As they bounced in the bus toward Decatur, Luma passed out the costumes, and the boys began to disappear beneath their black plastic sheets. The exception was Mafoday. On top of his Ninja robe, which stretched at the seams on his round frame, he wore a large pink feather boa and a rubber Elvis mask, odds and ends from the costume bin at the local pharmacy. It was easily the most outlandishly absurd getup anyone in Decatur would encounter this evening.

Luma handed out simple plastic shopping bags for the candy they would collect. It was the first Halloween for most of the Fugees, and they seemed unsure of what they were supposed to do, so Luma gave them instructions: ring doorbells, say "Trick or treat?," take a few pieces of candy, and say "Thank you."

The Fugees were conspicuous as they disembarked. They were the only trick-or-treaters to arrive in the neighborhood by bus, and they were among the only children in the neighborhood who weren't white. But the boys were too taken with the scene before them to note the attention they drew to themselves. One by one they stepped off the bus and gazed at the shimmering suburban wonderland around them. It looked nothing like Clarkston. The houses were in the colonial style, with red brick facades, black clapboard shutters. Gleaming sconces and pendant lights over the front doors were ablaze. Children in elaborate costumes roamed the streets by the hundreds, while parents socialized in packs in the front yards. The cool evening air was filled with playful screams and laughter, punctuated by the occasional cries of toddlers too young to fully appreciate the good nature of the holiday beneath its spooky facade. There were no police to be seen, and no menacing older boys standing around scouting for trouble. There was a strange sense of ease and safety, reinforced by Luma, who told the boys that she and Tracy would stay behind to watch the bus. They were free to roam as they pleased. Halloween, to the Fugees, seemed almost too good to be true.

The boys resolved to give trick-or-treating a try. Grace, Josiah, and Bien led the way to the first house, up a lighted walkway and a flight of brick steps. With trepidation, Josiah rang the doorbell. A moment later, the door opened.

"My word!" a woman said, startled by the sight before her: a pack of small, dark-skinned faces and white eyes peering out from behind black plastic sheeting. The boys were scared silent by the reaction. Finally someone up front mustered the magical phrase: "Trick or treat!"

The woman recovered from the unexpected sight before her and extended a box full of candy through the doorway. One by one the Fugees dipped their hands in to retrieve their bounty. The boys were judicious, taking just one or two pieces and depositing them in the small plastic grocery sacks they carried with them. One by one they said thank you and moved aside for their teammates. The last in line was Mafoday, in his boa and Elvis mask, who waited patiently for his turn. When the other boys finally moved out of the way, he could scarcely believe his eyes: an entire box of candy for the taking. He plunged his two hands deep into the pile of shiny wrappers and shoveled out a good pound of loot into his bag.

"Young man!" said the woman.

"Thank you!" Mafoday said, flashing his giant klieg light smile. He ran after his friends, his pink feather boa streaming behind him in the breeze.

Familiar now with the magical transaction of trick-or-treating, the boys went through the neighborhood methodically, venturing deep into cul-de-sacs and up shadowed sidewalks to houses that many other kids avoided. If there was candy to be had, the Fugees were going to find it. The boys stuck together, and for the most part kept to themselves. Their only real interaction with American kids involved, perhaps not surprisingly, soccer and came about as a result of a misunderstanding. A group of American girls of fourteen or fifteen had dressed up as much younger girls—with pigtails and teddy bears, wearing pajamas and kiddie clothes. One was wearing a soccer uniform, shirt neatly tucked in, socks pulled up to her knees, in the fashion of a peewee soccer player who had been fastidiously dressed by her mother. Grace Balegamire didn't understand that the get-up was a costume and assumed instead that the girl had come straight from practice, as the Fugees had.

"What position do you play?" he asked her earnestly when they passed each other on the street.

"What position do you think I play?" the girl said sassily, in character.

"You look like you play defense."

"Defense?" the girl said, now sounding every bit her age. "I think he just insulted me!"

With that, both the Fugees and the girls laughed, though no one seemed quite sure why, and went their separate ways.

A SHORT WHILE later, the Fugees headed back to the bus. Their plastic grocery sacks were bursting at the seams, leaving a trail of foil wrappers that reflected the light from the houses like gemstones. A quiet fell over the boys. They were weary now from all the walking, and crashing from their sugar highs. When they reached the bus, the boys sat down together on a prickly slope of wheat-colored zoysia. They picked through their stashes of candy and one by one paused to look up and take in the scene before them: the glimmering, gabled homes, the throngs of kids laughing and running freely around a neighborhood, the incredible costumes they'd clearly spent hours perfecting. A comfortable American can afford to take a jaundiced view of suburban life. But this tableau was what many of the refugees who arrived here had imagined—and hoped—America might be like: a land of plenty, where each family had a home and a car, where parents could let their kids play in the streets without worrying about their safety. And the basic transaction of trick-or-treating—knocking on a stranger's door and getting a sweet reward—was thrillingly unfamiliar. Grace was asked what he thought of his first Halloween and if it compared to anything he'd experienced before arriving here.

"Well," he said after careful consideration, "when you knock on somebody's door in Africa—they don't give you candy."

"Yep," Bien concurred, a bit wearily. "You'd be lucky if you got an egg."

———

LATER THAT EVENING, after the bus had dropped the boys off at their apartments around Clarkston, Grace Balegamire lay in bed, sleeping off the day's excitement, when he was startled awake: gunshots—fired just below the second-story window of his bedroom. Grace knew better than to look outside, and instead stayed low in his bedroom. He was afraid. A little while later, the police arrived. The sharp sound of their radios echoed in the parking lot and in the darkened stairwells of the apartment complex, and the blue lights atop the police cruisers flashed menacingly through the windows of the Balegamires' home. A little while later, the cops pulled away. They'd made no arrests. Quiet returned. Grace closed his eyes and tried once again to sleep.

Chapter Twenty-nine

The Fifteens' Final Game

"How come you never told me your father was dead?" Natnael asked Joseph.

The two boys were friends—Natnael, the leader of the Under 15s, and Joseph, a veteran of the Under 17 Fugees—and were riding together in the backseat of a car on the way to the 15s' final game of the season. Joseph was coming along to give the younger team support. Kids on other teams rode to games alone with their parents. The Fugees rode together on the bus or, when the bus was full, in the cars of volunteers, and the trips were a kind of sacred time for talk about life outside of soccer. "We don't talk about the game for very long on the bus," Joseph explained once. "We talk about some crazy stuff."

"I don't really tell anybody," Joseph said, answering Natnael's question about his father. "Because I don't want them asking all sorts of questions about it."

Natnael's curiosity was piqued now. He seemed startled that he didn't know such an important detail of his friend's life.

"Did you cry?" he asked Joseph.

"No," Joseph said. "I didn't cry."

Natnael considered the response.

"How can you not cry?" he asked finally.

"Well, if you don't know somebody—" Joseph cut himself off, and tried to think of an example.

"You got an uncle, right, in your old country?" he asked.

"No."

Joseph thought for another moment. He wanted to explain.

"Well, you got your mom, right?"

"Yeah," said Natnael.

"Well, if your mom died, you'd cry, right?"

"Yeah."

"But if you never knew your mom, then you wouldn't cry," Joseph said.

Natnael nodded. That was why his friend didn't cry at his father's death. He understood now.

A FEW MINUTES later Natnael and the Under 15 Fugees took the field to warm up for their final game of the year. Joseph sat on the bench to cheer them on. It hadn't been the season Luma or the boys on the 15s had hoped. Their goal at the beginning of the fall had been to make the State Cup—a tournament for the area's best teams. Instead, they were fighting for their pride and against the threat of getting demoted to a lower division for next season. Despite all the off-the-field trouble, they had had their moments: the big win after their hiatus, and a 1–1 tie against the best team in their division. Luma had made sure not to point out that team's ranking to her players before the game, because she hadn't wanted them to get intimidated. The ploy had worked. When the Under 15s found out that they had nearly beaten the number one team in their division—they'd held a 1–0 lead until the final moments—they'd seemed stunned.

But with their early loss, the forfeits during the hiatus, the losses since, and a total of eight penalty points against the team for red cards at various points along the way, the Under 15 Fugees faced the prospect of finishing dead last in the league, unless they could manage a big win on this day. In the scheme of things, second to last isn't much to fight for. The Fugees' demeanor reflected the unpleasant reality of where their season had gone. They were in a lackadaisical mood, laughing and joking with each other, trying, it seemed, not to think too much about soccer. Two and a half months of stress had worn them out. Luma urged them to focus.

"You've got your last game of the season today—this is it," she told them beforehand. "The way you play today is going to tell me how you guys are going to play next year. Okay? So let's work it."

The Fugees were playing the Cobb YMCA Strikers, a middle-of-the-pack team that, while ranked higher in the standings than the Fugees, didn't enjoy a particular advantage in talent. The Fugees had managed a win earlier in the season against a team that had beaten the Strikers soundly. Today they stood a chance.

Despite Luma's efforts to wake them up, the Fugees played the early minutes in a daze. They were flat and easily frustrated, and aside from Kanue—playing all-out as usual—the players were walking and showing little intensity. The Strikers countered with calm, methodical passes and controlled the ball. They scored ten minutes into the half, and then again before the half, to lead 2–0. Luma was enraged: it was one thing to lose, and another thing not to try. *After all that we've been through.*

"So, what's wrong?" she asked her players. "Is the ref cheating?"

"No," the boys said.

"Are they faster than you?"

"No."

"Are they better than you?"

"No," the boys said.

"So the score's two to nothing for what reason?"

Silence.

"I'll tell you why," Luma said, her voice rising. "Because you are all a bunch of idiots. You do not know how to play soccer. You know how to play street ball. So everything that everyone has said about this team—that you don't deserve to play, that you don't know how to play as a team, because you don't have the discipline or the respect to play—it's true. Because you don't know how to play.

"If you want to play on the streets, let me know," Luma said finally. "Because this is a waste of my time."

Luma walked away from her players and the boys sat quietly for a moment, heads bowed. They were dejected by their play, wounded by their coach's comments, unsure of what to do next.

"That's what I hate about her, man," one player said. "When she stops coaching us, then we're gonna lose *everything.*"

"She's supposed to be mad, man," said Sebajden, a midfielder from Kosovo. "We're playing like little kids."

"Nobody get mad," said another boy.

"Let's make our coach happy, man," Sebajden said.

"We can do this. Come on."

The boys put their hands together a final time, chanted, "One, two, three—Go Fugees!," and jogged back onto the field to try to salvage the afternoon.

They played harder, Kanue leading the way. Natnael scored on a long free kick, a gorgeous shot that floated just beyond the goalie's fingertips. The Fugees attacked, and chased down free balls. But again the U15s made mistakes. They turned the ball over with sloppy throw-ins, and were called for offsides seemingly every time they managed to gain some momentum. Hamdu Muganga got called for a foul in the box, and the Strikers put away the penalty shot. The Fugees began to get frustrated, and to foul. When Kanue fought his way through two defenders in the box late in the game and prepared to shoot, the referee stopped play and called Kanue for using his elbows against the Strikers' defender. Kanue shouted in frustration. Luma quickly pulled him from the game. When the referee blew his whistle, the score was 3–1, and the Under 15s' season was over.

The boys walked quietly toward Luma after the game and sat down around her. Her tone had shifted. She was no longer angry, or yelling, but she was every bit as emphatic as she had been at half-time.

"You knew better than I did, is why you lost," Luma told the boys afterward. "It's an embarrassment to sit on the sideline and see you do throw-ins with your feet up, and throw-ins with your feet stepping over the line. And it is an embarrassment to sit here as a coach and watch you miss open shots at goal. And it's even more of an embarrassment to see you use your elbows and push players away and lose your cool. That is not the team I coach.

"If you plan to continue with this team," Luma added, "it's my rules, my drills, my way."

Kanue and Natnael sat quietly before her, their heads bowed. They had worked hard to keep their team together, and the season had fallen apart anyway. They'd have to find a way to win next year.

Chapter Thirty

My Rules, My Way

Things were much different for the Under 13 Fugees. Though she was reluctant to admit it, Luma's bond with the 13s was deeper than that with the older boys. She had been coaching some of them since her first season, when they were younger than ten years old. The 13s had more faithfully adhered to her system—my rules, my drills, my way—and their record, Luma felt, showed the results. After the Athens game, the 13s had tied two games and lost one, but they had never folded, and in each of the contests, they had fought until the very end. The 13s had clearly improved. They had learned their own strengths—how to attack quickly using Josiah on the left wing, and how to attack more methodically, with quick passes from Qendrim, Bien, Jeremiah, and Shahir. The defense had improved perhaps the most. With the Dikori brothers—bottle rockets in cleats—they were able to chase down attacking forwards, and Mohammed Mohammed, a newcomer who hardly spoke a word of English at the beginning of the season, was now calling out instructions to his teammates from the back line. Despite his diminutive size, he had also proved improbably tough and hardheaded as a defender, willing to take on much bigger boys without flinching. A better defense took the heat off Mafoday and Eldin in goal, but even they had stepped up in the clinch, especially Mafoday after his penalty shot stop against Athens. They kept their cool; the Under 13s had received no red cards during the season. The boys had chemistry, and perhaps most important, they looked out for one another. When Josiah heard that Santino, the quiet Sudanese boy who had arrived in the United States just before the season, had no winter clothes, he dug around in a closet and found his old winter coat, which he gave to his teammate. No member of the Fugees, Josiah reasoned, should go cold.

Something else occurred toward the end of the season that lifted the 13s' spirits, a miracle of sorts, in the form of the arrival of two long, heavy cardboard boxes: a set of portable but regulation-size goals from the YMCA. With help from the boys, Luma and Tracy unloaded the boxes from Tracy's small pickup truck, carried them down to Armistead Field, and dumped their contents in the grass. The goals, in their unassembled form, were a collection of long metal tubes with fluorescent orange nylon nets. When put together, they were not the sturdiest contraptions—a line drive to the top crossbar caused the goals to shudder violently as though they might collapse. But in the last weeks of the season, the goals allowed Luma's team to practice set plays like corner and free kicks, and to get a feel for the game's third dimension, between the ground and the top of the goal, where points were scored.

THE UNDER 13S played their final regular-season game beneath the lights on a dark, misty November afternoon in Lawrenceville, Georgia, against the Georgia Futbol Club. Both teams had a lot riding on the game. The undefeated Athens United Valiants, who had beaten the Fugees following Luma's arrest, were a shoo-in to win the division, but the Fugees and Lawrenceville were both among a cluster of teams with similar records and point totals that were vying for the remaining slots at the top of the rankings. If they hoped to finish

well, the Fugees needed to win, and as important, to avoid getting
any red cards, which brought mandatory point deductions. They had
to keep their cool. It wouldn't be easy. The team from Lawrenceville
had managed some big wins earlier in the fall, defeating one club
10–0 and another 6–0, and to a player, they were bigger and taller
than the Fugees. They would win a physical game, and perhaps, if
they managed to goad the Fugees into retaliating, they could provoke
a red card as well.

Luma had a plan. The Fugees were to keep the ball on the ground
to negate the competition's height advantage, and whenever possible,
to send the ball away from the middle and toward the wings, where
Josiah and Idwar could use their speed and where the Fugees were less
apt to get knocked around. If they got bumped or manhandled, she
told them, they were not to retaliate. Take the fouls, she told them,
and above all, keep your cool.

"Let them push you down," Luma said. "I don't want anyone out
there who's scared."

BEFORE THE GAME, the Fugees found themselves with some time
to kill. A game between two older girls' teams was winding up on an
adjacent field. The boys splayed on the sideline to watch and were
quickly drawn into the action—cheering together at each shot and
steal, laughing and trading high-fives when one of the girls dribbled
artfully around a defender, leaving her competitor in the dust.

A few minutes later, the Fugees took the field and ran through their
warm-ups. They performed a familiar ritual with the referee during
the pregame lineup; after mangling a few of the boys' names, the referee shook his head and gave up, handing the roster over to Luma and
asking her to call the boys' names out herself. The boys laughed, first
at the referee, and then when Luma became tongue-tied herself. Soon
it was time to take their positions on the field. But first Grace had an
idea. He thought the Fugees should pray together. The idea presented
a quandary; there were both Christians and Muslims on the team.
How could they accommodate everyone? With no help from Luma
or any other adult, the boys quickly worked out a solution. Grace
would offer a Christian prayer, Eldin, a Muslim one. There was no
lengthy discussion of the matter, no self-congratulatory commen-

tary on togetherness or the need to respect each other's views—just a simple, practical ordering of business so that everyone felt included. The boys formed a circle at midfield, draped their arms around each other, and bowed their heads. Both Grace and Eldin felt more comfortable praying the way they'd been taught—in their native languages. No one objected as Grace prayed aloud in Swahili and Eldin in Bosnian, first for the health and safety of their teammates, and if God saw fit, a victory. The sentiment was understood even if the words were not.

"Amen," Grace said.

"Amen," the boys responded.

"Amin," said Eldin.

"Amin," said the boys.

MOMENTS LATER THE game was under way. The Fugees attacked. Midway through the first half, Bien snuck through the Lawrenceville defense and dished a pass to Jeremiah, who quickly sent the ball across the field to Josiah. Without hesitating, Josiah took a shot from twenty yards out: goal. The Fugees went ahead 1–0 and carried that lead into the half.

"One to nothing is not enough," Luma told the boys. "Keep calm. Keep your game. Start smiling. Let's start having a good time and let's kick some butt."

The Fugees started the half by attacking down the touchlines, as Luma had instructed them. Eventually, Jeremiah controlled a pass at the top right corner of the box, rolled around into the open space near the corner, and fired a shot clear across the middle that slipped between the goalie's fingers and the inside of the far post. The Fugees were up 2–0. A late foul in the box gave Lawrenceville a penalty shot to pull within a goal, but the Fugees held off the opposition's final, desperate charges to win the game 2–1.

The victory gave the Fugees enough points to overtake a handful of teams to finish third in their division, behind Athens and the Dacula Danger, a team the Fugees had tied 2–2 earlier in the season. As a reward for their hard work and their successful season, Luma had registered the Fugees for the Tornado Cup, a tournament that would feature some of the best teams from around the state. The Under 13s had a week to prepare. In the meantime, Luma didn't want a 2–1 win over Lawrenceville to go to their heads.

"You got really lucky," she told them after the game. "You play like this next weekend, you're going home in last place. It's going to be some tough practices this week."

Chapter Thirty-one

Tornado Cup

Luma knew that if the Under 13 Fugees hoped to compete against the teams in the Tornado Cup, they needed to make some quick improvements, and for that, they had to have an intense and focused week of practice. The Fugees were still shooting poorly, which Luma blamed in part on the lack of goals for much of the season. Luma planned to put the Under 13s through three days of intense drills on crosses, corners, and free kicks, followed by a scrimmage on Thursday with the 15s. But even this schedule—four practices instead of the usual two—wouldn't leave the Fugees much time to improve. Daylight savings time had ended—the clocks had been set back an hour—and darkness fell on Armistead Field not long after six o'clock each afternoon. Practices started at five o'clock. There were some old lights mounted on telephone poles around the field, but they didn't work—or at least, the city refused to turn them on. There was no point in moving practice earlier either. Most of the Fugees depended on school buses to get them back to Clarkston from the various schools in the county where they were enrolled, and some players had to take two separate buses on journeys that could take as long as an hour and a half each way. Luma told the boys to come straight to practice when they got home and to arrive ready to play.

In the end, it was the weather—not darkness or bus schedules—that interfered with Luma's plan. Heavy thunderstorms rolled into Atlanta early in the week and hovered overhead, soaking the field into a tepid mush, like a cotton mop dunked in a bucket. The rain trailed off on Wednesday night. The scrimmage was on. So on Thursday afternoon, the 13s and 15s gathered at Milam Park beneath a canopy of steel-colored clouds. The air was cool and damp, and long puddles of runoff from the field's crown collected around its perimeter, rippled by breeze. On the field itself, the wet grass clung to the ball like glue.

"You play this game like it's a real game," Luma told the 13s. "No clowning around. No joking around. No switching up your positions when you feel like it."

Luma left the Under 15s to coach themselves. Kanue, Natnael, and Muamer took charge. They understood that their pride was on the line. They hadn't had a successful season, but they had no intention of losing to—or even getting challenged by—the younger team. The 13s had something to prove themselves. Some of the boys, such as Bien and Eldin, had older brothers on the 15s. But even the younger boys who didn't have blood relatives on the older team had come to see players such as Kanue and Natnael as brothers of sorts. They wanted to earn the older boys' respect.

Luma blew the whistle, and the game began. From the outset, the 13s showed they had come to play. They fought the older boys for loose balls, made crisp passes, and managed one run after another against the 15s' goal. And yet, they kept missing their shots. Josiah missed an open shot high, and another wide. Jeremiah missed with a wild shot that soared twenty feet over the crossbar. By the end of the first half, the 13s had taken eight shots on goal and missed all of them. The 15s, badly outplayed by the younger boys, held the lead, 1–0.

Luma summoned the Under 13s over to a corner of the field. She had diagnosed the problem: the younger boys were trying to show off. She told the boys to forget the dramatic blasts from outside. She wanted them to calm down and to aim their shots. She wanted her defense to move up the field and to stay even with each other, in order to draw the offsides calls on the faster competition. And she wanted the 13s to keep the pressure on.

The 15s, meanwhile, were angry. Even though they led by a goal, they knew they were being embarrassed by a younger team that included a ten-year-old on defense. They'd lost their last game of the season, and the idea of losing to the 13s was more than they could bear. So when Luma blew the whistle to start the second half, the U15s came out attacking. Muamer, Kanue, and Natnael worked the ball down the center of the field, away from the standing water near the sidelines that threatened to slow them down. But the 13s held fast. Robin cut off one attack and Prince Tarlue, a speedy Liberian, clogged up another run by the 15s. Eventually, the 15s began to wear down the younger boys and to find the seams in the 13s' defense. Muamer scored on a touch shot from just in front of the goal. And though the 13s managed to move the ball down the pitch, they continued to miss—a disturbing sign on the eve of their year-end tournament. In the end, the 15s won the scrimmage 3–1, but not before the 13s managed a final blow to the older boys' pride. It came near the end of the game, as Muamer was chasing down a ball near the touchline, alongside a trough of gray-green water that ran the length of the field just beyond the boundary. Muamer controlled the ball and attempted to make a move down the sideline, as the 13s' defenders converged. Prince went in for the tackle. The ball froze, but Muamer tumbled out of bounds, face-first in the murky puddle. Muamer looked helplessly at Luma, hoping she'd call a foul. But she waved it off; the tackle was clean, and to the delight of the 13s, now bent over in hysterics, Muamer decidedly wasn't.

"If the Under 13s win this weekend, they have you to thank," Luma told the 15s after the game. "You taught them to be a bit more aggressive, and that was something they hadn't been doing all season."

She turned now to the 13s.

"The way you guys fought for the ball today, the way when one of them gets the ball four of you charged him, that's what you need to do on Saturday," she said. "And none of you quit the entire game. I didn't see any of you walking.

"It was an okay scrimmage," she told the boys before sending them home. The Fugees understood it as high praise.

IF A CASUAL youth soccer game in the American suburbs has the feel of an outdoor concert, tournaments are the Woodstocks. The events draw crowds of players, coaches, parents, siblings, friends, and onlookers, and take place over acres of green space so vast that tournament organizers, like music promoters, often need golf carts to get around. If there is one thing that every youth soccer tournament has in common it is that there is never enough parking. Parents are forced to park their minivans, station wagons, and SUVs on grass byways, on inclines, alongside ditches, or in the woods, precarious terrain for which family vehicles are not designed. (In the course of a weekend, typically at least one family's car requires extraction by tow truck.) American families don't stop by soccer tournaments so much as temporarily move to them. In terms of outfitting, the quantity of gear and provisions required for a single soccer game versus a weekend-long tournament is akin to that difference needed for a day hike and an attempt on K2. Consequently, there is an iconic image familiar to anyone who has ever attended such events: mothers and fathers, loaded like pack mules with folding chairs, blankets, coolers or picnic baskets, trekking from wherever they've managed to park to the far-off fields where their children's games will take place. Expert tournament-goers will conduct this exercise while also carrying a cup of coffee, which sloshes onto their wrists and forearms, while other hapless souls will do so while also chasing toddlers. As these beleaguered adults approach, the uniformed sons and daughters whose pursuit of soccer has inspired their expeditions are nowhere to be seen. They've usually run ahead on the pretense of making warm-ups or an important pregame meeting. There are few things more embarrassing to an American teenager, after all, than a parent loaded down with stuff.

Such was the scene at the Gwinnett YMCA on Saturday morning when the Fugees arrived in their usual configuration: a white bus trailing a beat-up yellow Volkswagen Beetle. The Fugees arrived early, so after a few laps around the parking area, Tracy, at the helm of the bus, and Luma, driving her Beetle, managed to find parking nearby. The boys unloaded and made their way toward the playing fields. They were confident to the point of cockiness, and on their way to their assigned field made fun of the competition—decked out with matching gear bags, embroidered with their jersey numbers, and all those silly-looking parents bivouacked on the sidelines. Today, they were sure, would be their day.

In their first of two games on Saturday, the Fugees would face a familiar opponent: Blue Springs Liberty Fire, the team the Fugees had beaten in a 3–2 comeback earlier in the season. Luma viewed that victory as the turning point of the Under 13s' season, the game in which they found confidence and a sense of team identity. The game had also helped nudge the Fugees into third place in the league's final rankings, one point ahead of none other than the Blue Springs Liberty Fire themselves. The Fire wanted revenge.

Luma was confident, if anxious. Her team was playing better now than at any point in the season, but she was worried about their inaccurate shooting and their inability to finish runs with goals. Before the game, Luma had the Fugees line up and take simple shots from directly in front of the net. She wanted them to get a feel for scoring, to absorb a sense of place on the field relative to the crossbar and a feeling for the angles. And yet even this simple task proved difficult, as balls sailed high over the bar and clunked against the posts. The referee blew his whistle. Practice was over. It was time to play.

"I want to have a hard time picking out MVPs today," Luma told the boys. "I want to see your best game, and I know what your best game looks like, each and every single one of you. I want to kick some major butt today. I want to have some fun. I've been excited about this all week."

"Me too," the boys responded, nearly in unison.

"Let's go," said Luma.

The Fugees controlled the game from the outset and played the first ten minutes on the Fire's side of the field. Early on, Josiah fired a shot from the top left of the box, which sailed high. Moments later Jeremiah booted a corner kick across the face of the goal, but there was no one in the middle to finish. The early minutes of the game felt eerily similar to the scrimmage days before against the Under 15s; the Fugees were outplaying the competition but unable to score.

"Time to get physical!" one of the Blue Springs dads shouted from the sideline.

The Blue Springs players, particularly the midfielders and forwards, towered over the Fugees, especially little Qendrim, Mohammed, and Prince. Qendrim, though, wasn't intimidated. He was confidently directing his team from center midfield, ordering his defense to move up the field in an effort to set up the offsides trap. The timing was perfect: a Blue Springs midfielder booted the ball over the Fugees defense, and to an apparently offsides forward. But the linesman didn't raise his flag. The Blue Springs player, alone now and unchallenged, dribbled toward Mafoday, who stood impassively in goal, waiting for the inevitable shot. When it came—high and toward the middle of the goal—Mafoday raised his arms over his head and tried to jump. The ball sailed just over his fingertips. Blue Springs was up 1–0.

The Fugees' earlier confidence seemed instantly drained. Several players lowered their heads. They began to play flat, as if convinced that no matter how hard they tried, they would not be able to score. Just before the half, they stumbled into an opportunity, when Grace controlled a ball on the right wing. He lobbed a beautiful cross toward the center, but again, there was no one in the middle to finish. At the half, the Fugees trailed 1–0, and Luma was livid.

"You guys are a pathetic excuse for a soccer team," she told the boys, her voice breaking with anger. "They're beating you to the ball, they're outhustling you, and they're taking more shots. I want to know why that cross that Grace just sent over had nobody to finish it off. Josiah? What the hell was that? All you guys did was talk, talk, talk on the bus. Talk, talk, talk before the game. Making fun of every kid on the field. And look at the way *you're* playing. Stupid! If I had some eight-year-olds out here they'd be laughing at you. You got one player doing his job out there, and that is Qendrim—and that is it! He's the only one telling you to push up, turn around, hustle, and you're not even listening to him! And the thing is, you beat this team already! So you think you're better than them. And you're playing like you think you're better than them. But the fact is, they're better than you. Because they don't want to go home today losing. And it looks to me like I've got players who know how to talk and don't know how to play. You are down one to nothing, and you will not finish this game off unless every single one of you plays his position, fights for that ball, and takes some shots!

"I've been waiting to see you guys play your best and I haven't seen it," Luma said. "It had better happen in this half."

THE FUGEES TOOK the field in silence, and traded guilty looks as they waited for the referee. When play began, they seemed more focused, more communicative. Qendrim doled out passes to Josiah and Jeremiah on the wings. The Fugees attacked once, then again. Ten minutes into the second half, Josiah tapped the ball past his defender on the left wing and then sprinted after it, leaving the Blue Springs player frozen behind him. Alone now, he dribbled toward the goal. On Thursday, Josiah had had just such an opportunity against the older Fugees and had blown it by blasting a long shot over the top of the goal. Today, he was patient, dribbling all the way toward the Blue Springs keeper before tapping the ball to his left: a gentle shot that rolled into the net. The game was now tied, 1–1. A few minutes later, Bien had a go. The Blue Springs goalie came out to meet him, and Bien took the shot, which rolled all the way across the face of the goal, wide. The Fugees kept fighting, firing a series of quick shots from around the perimeter of the box. Midway through the half, the Fugees had taken seven shots and Blue Springs none, and yet the score was still tied. Qendrim ordered his defense to move farther up the field; he wanted to keep the pressure on.

"Come on, guys," he said. "We gotta win. We gotta get one more."

The Fugees now had a corner kick. Bien floated the ball toward the center of the field, but a Blue Springs player volleyed it back toward him and out of bounds. Quickly, Bien heaved the ball back into play. Jeremiah controlled the throw-in and tapped it back to Bien, who crossed the ball back into the middle and right at Idwar Dikori, who was unmarked. Idwar extended his leg and the ball ricocheted off his instep and into the back of the net. The Fugees were now ahead 2–1.

A few minutes later, Jeremiah added another with a canon shot from fifteen yards out. His teammates responded by getting on the ground and kissing his shooting foot. When the final whistle blew, the Fugees had won 3–1.

"You played a first half that sucked so bad, I just wanted to make you run laps all season," Luma told them afterward. "To come back and play a second half like that . . . I can't handle it, okay? I almost had a heart attack."

The boys responded with applause. The Fugees had played their best half of soccer yet. The comeback, though, had come at a cost. Qendrim had twisted his ankle and was now limping badly. Shahir, the left midfielder who frequently set up Josiah for attacks down the left sideline, had lost the nails of both of his big toes because his cleats had been too tight. He was growing quickly and hadn't been able to afford new shoes. And after a frantic and relentless second half, the Fugees were tired. Luma moved the team to the shade, handed out bananas and snack bars, and encouraged them to drink water. They wouldn't have much time to recover. Their next game at the Tornado Cup started in less than an hour.

IN THEIR SECOND game of the day, it took the Fugees' opponents just forty-eight seconds to score—on a long pass down the left side and a quick shot that surprised Mafoday and slipped through his hands. A short while later the opponents, a team from Warner Robbins, Georgia, called the Strikers, scored again, this time on Eldin. The Fugees were getting manhandled. Shahir, already limping, caught an elbow to the face and came out with a bloody lip. Later, Grace was elbowed in the midsection and crumpled over. The Fugees didn't give up. Josiah scored early in the second half, dancing around the keeper, who had come out of the goal to challenge him. But as time wound down, the Fugees still trailed 2–1. In the final moments, Jeremiah fired a shot from ten yards out. The Strikers' keeper bobbled the ball and seemed to stumble back into the goal. But the linesman ruled that the ball had not completely crossed the end line. The Fugees were spent. They failed to mount another attack. Less than three hours after their best soccer of the season, they were beaten 2–1.

THE FUGEES WERE scheduled to play a morning game on Sunday, and there was an outside chance—if other teams lost—that the morning match might count as more than a consolation round. But Luma didn't have high hopes. A single loss, she assumed, would knock the Fugees out of contention for the cup. To be sure, she'd have to wait for results from the other afternoon games. For now, Luma had other things to worry about. She had arranged for a Saturday-night team sleepover at the YMCA, and she had to get her team fed and rested.

The boys brought blankets and sleeping bags and arranged themselves on yoga mats around a TV in an upstairs room at the Y. Luma put on a video of old World Cup highlights and the movie *Goal!* Despite the excitement of a rare spend-the-night gathering, the boys dropped off to sleep one by one, exhausted from the day's soccer. Luma meanwhile logged on to the Tornado Cup website to check the standings. The Fugees, she learned, were still in it. If they won their next game against the Concorde Fire, they were going to the finals.

THE CONCORDE FIRE were, in almost every way, the antithesis of the Fugees. The team came from one of the Atlanta area's most prestigious—and expensive—soccer academies, the Concorde Football Club, in the upscale suburb of Alpharetta. Registration fees for the club cost upwards of $1,200, but with equipment, tournament fees, and the like, Nancy Daffner, a team mother and volunteer for the Fire, estimated that she and her husband spent more than $5,000 a year on soccer.

Daffner, a chipper part-time substitute teacher whose son Jamie played on the Fire, was the perfect embodiment of a suburban soccer mom—which was not lost on Daffner herself. Standing before a large bulletin board bearing the Tornado Cup tournament bracket, she wore a custom-made gray sweatshirt with the words SOCCER MOM on the back.

Most of the boys on the Fire had been playing together for years. Their coach, Jeff Franks, a former high school and college player, had led the team for five years, since the boys were eight or nine years old. He had spent that time developing basic skills patiently, in a way he knew wouldn't necessarily lead to victories early on but that he believed would pay off over time. The Fire practiced twice a week from six-thirty p.m. to eight p.m.—their practice facility was lighted so evening practices were not a problem—and the team met on additional nights for speed and agility training. The Fire kept sharp during the off-season by attending at least half a dozen tournaments. In the wintertime, they practiced at an indoor facility, and in the summer, the boys attended soccer camps, including a popular program hosted each summer by Clemson University in South Carolina.

With so much soccer and travel, the parents of the Fire players had become especially close. Daffner, who estimated she spent fifteen hours a week working on behalf of the team, said that the Fire had become a central part of the parents' social lives. The moms went out together for margaritas while the fathers watched their sons practice, and the adults spent time together on those trips and camp outings.

"Instead of just dropping and running, you socialize," she said. "Yesterday all of us went out to Fuddruckers in between games. Parents sat at a group of tables. Kids sat at one big table, and played arcade games. We have an end-of-the-season party each season. We take lots of pictures."

Soccer was not the only extracurricular activity for the kids on the Fire. One player on the team was a cellist with the Atlanta Symphony Orchestra's youth program. Daffner's son was a sportscaster at his school's own radio station, a gig that required him to get to the campus an hour early each day. Many of the boys on the Fire were so-called TAG children—a school system designation that meant "talented and gifted."

"Most of our boys are overachievers," Daffner said.

While the boys on the Fire were dedicated to their team, their other activities cut into the amount of time they could devote to soccer.

"We live in neighborhoods where they come out, and they play football," Daffner said. "They play baseball. They jump on a trampoline. They ride their bikes. They're all organized activities. So if it's not organized soccer, they're not playing soccer."

There was one exception to this rule: a young Colombian immigrant on the Fire named Jorge Pinzon—Nini to friends and teammates. Pinzon lived far from Alpharetta, in the Atlanta suburb of Lawrenceville, a rapidly growing town with a large Latino population. His parents were separated; his mother, Pilar, spoke little English and cleaned houses for a living, and his father lived in Colombia. Pinzon's interaction with his father was limited to occasional and usually short phone calls. The boy felt his father's absence, especially on game days.

"It would be different if my dad was here to support me," Pinzon said. "He loves soccer."

Unlike the other kids, Pinzon didn't pay to play on the Fire. Instead, parents of the other boys pitched in to cover his expenses and went out of their way to support his participation on the team. When his mother couldn't get him to games because of her work schedule, parents of the other players would drive across town to pick him up. Few were familiar with Lawrenceville, so they usually arranged to meet Pinzon at easy-to-find landmarks—the parking lots of local gas stations or convenience stores.

Nini Pinzon was passionate about soccer. On nights when he didn't practice with the Fire, he could often be found on fields at Bethesda Park, near his house, playing with older boys and grown men. That was the way to get better, he believed. Pinzon was easily the best player on the Fire. Daffner joked that he had probably had a soccer ball in his crib.

Pinzon had connected with the Fire through an uncle who was familiar with the soccer scene in Atlanta. The Concorde program was too expensive for Pinzon, so he was given a "scholarship": his fees were waived, and expenses for gear and travel were covered by the team. This arrangement benefited everyone; the Fire got a ringer, and Pinzon got to play organized soccer on a traveling team for free. In the process, he made friends with his teammates, and he appreciated the concern the other parents showed for him and his family.

"They're very supportive of me," he said.

Pinzon had heard about the Fugees from other kids in town. He knew they were from parts of the world where kids played street soccer—with quick passes and nimble footwork. The Fugees were supposed to be fast—and good. As he watched the opposition warm up before the game, Pinzon said he felt he had something in common with them. He could tell from their mismatched socks and from the array of faces that they probably didn't live as comfortably as his teammates did. He thought he knew how the Fugees might feel, showing up to play a group of mostly white kids with all the latest gear.

"My teammates are, like, much better off than me," he said. "They got a lot of stuff. So I just feel different. It's all Caucasian people; I'm the only Latino. It can be intimidating."

Pinzon let the thought drop. There was a game to play. He intended to win.

The Fire was too far behind in the standings to advance to the finals with a win over the Fugees, but they were in a position to play

the role of spoiler. The Fugees needed an outright win to advance; a
tie or a loss would send them home. Luma gathered the Fugees before
warm-ups to make sure they understood.

"Play to the whistle," she told them. "If the ref makes a bad call, you
keep playing. Okay? You focus on the game and how you're going to
win it. Because if you don't, we're going to lose your last game of the
season, and you're going home early. And you're going home to your
parents, and you're going to tell them you lost. You'll go home to your
brothers and sisters, and you're going to tell them you lost."

Luma narrowed her eyes.

"I'm not going home telling anyone I lost," she said.

Luma ran through the game plan. From watching the Fire warm
up, she had already determined that their biggest threat was number
26—Jorge Pinzon. She wanted Grace to mark him and stay with him
the whole game. The Fugees defense would play upfield, to try to pull
the Fire offsides. Qendrim would dole out passes to Jeremiah and
Josiah, and she expected them to shoot—a lot.

Just before the whistle, some of the Fugees looked toward the sideline and saw a strange sight. A teacher from Josiah's school had come
to see him play. Some older refugee kids from the complexes in Clarkston had managed rides to the game, an hour away from Clarkston,
and several volunteers from resettlement agencies showed up as well.
For the first time all year, the Fugees had fans.

The Fugees came out shooting. Shahir, the Fugees midfielder,
blasted a shot that hit the left post and went wide. Josiah missed another, high. The Fugees had other opportunities—two free kicks and
a handful of corner kicks—but time and again the plays were broken
up by a ubiquitous presence for the Fire: Jorge. Pinzon was fast and
amazingly determined. He fought for every ball, and didn't hesitate
to put his body at risk if he thought he could gain an advantage. He
and Grace leaped in the air to control a high ball, and their skulls collided with a gruesome thud. Grace collapsed to the ground. But Jorge
shook off the pain and kept playing.

The Fugees, though, kept attacking. Their passes were sharp and
controlled. With eight minutes left in the half and the score still tied
at zero, Jeremiah Ziaty carved his way through the Fire defense at the
top of the box. He pivoted and turned, and with his left and weaker

foot, kicked a line drive that curved down just under the Fire goalie's hands. It was a goal score. At the half, the Fugees led 1–0.

Luma hurried her players into a huddle and began to tick through the adjustments she wanted. Bien was dribbling too much. Josiah needed to shoot more, and to keep the ball on the ground: the Fire defenders were taller than the Fugees, she said, and there was no point trying to fight with them for headers. Shahir had taken his first shot of the season—she wanted him to shoot more. She wanted her defense to play farther up the field, particularly on goal kicks; the Fire's keeper had a weak leg, she said. She told Jeremiah that he needed to concentrate on placing his corner kicks better. She reminded the boys that a one-goal lead was not enough. They needed two more, she said, and reminded them of the stakes.

"You got thirty more minutes—thirty more minutes to decide if this is your last game or not," she told them. "I can't do it."

And there was one more adjustment. She wanted Robin Dikori, the Sudanese speedster, to take over Grace's role in marking Jorge Pinzon.

"Robin, number twenty-six is yours," she said. "I don't want him touching that ball."

In the second half, the Fugees let loose with another fusillade of shots—and misses. Jeremiah kicked one high. Bien missed one left. Josiah hit the crossbar. Grace set up Jeremiah on a perfect cross, but Jeremiah rushed the shot and missed again, this time wide right. It was as if there were some sort of force field in front of the Fire's goal, deflecting the Fugees' shots. Midway through the half, a Fire forward got behind the Fugees defense and began to charge the Fugees' goal. Eldin, alone now at keeper, seemed unsure of what to do. He didn't move out to cut off the attacker's angle, but instead stood beneath the crossbar, waiting for the shot. When it finally came, Eldin froze, and the ball sailed past him, clean: goal. There was a roar from the sideline. The Fire parents had been joined by the players and parents of the team that stood to advance to the finals should the Fugees tie or lose. This newly formed coalition quickly drowned out the voices of the small group that had come out to support the Fugees.

The Fugees, though, weren't finished. They immediately charged down the field with a quick sequence of crisp passes through the heart of the Fire's defense. Jeremiah again found himself with a clear shot, this time with his right foot. The ball sailed just high. The Fugees had now missed four shots in the second half alone. The Fire responded with an attack of their own. Again, the left forward for the Fire snuck in behind the Fugees defense and began to charge toward the goal. This time, Eldin came out to challenge. Hurried, the Fire player booted the shot but the ball flew wildly off course. Then, with fifteen minutes to go in the game, Josiah controlled a loose ball on the left side of the Fire's goal. He tapped a pass to Jeremiah at the top of the box, and Jeremiah charged the goal at a full sprint. He took five steps and fired a shot just over the goalie's head. The Fugees led again, 2–1.

The final minutes of the game were desperate and thrilling. By now, the other morning games had finished, and as word of the stakes in the Fugees-Fire matchup spread around the complex, the parents and players of other teams had gathered on the slight rise alongside the field to watch and cheer. The boys in gold—the team from Warner Robbins, Georgia, who would advance if the Fugees lost their lead—pleaded with the Fire to score one more. But there were others who'd wandered up to the game and who, like TV viewers who stumble upon the final minutes of an otherwise meaningless game and nevertheless make a snap decision to pull for one team over another, drifted toward the set of bleachers where the Fugees' fans had gathered. With help from the older boys who'd come to watch the 13s play, they quickly learned a few of the Fugees' names, and so as the Fugees fought to keep their season alive, they experienced the odd sensation of hearing their names called out by strangers.

"Let's go, Josiah!"

"Nice pass, Bien!"

"Shoot, Jeremiah, shoot!"

As the final minutes of the game oozed by, the Fire scrambled to get some kind of shot, but they couldn't find an opening. Prince cleared one ball, Shahir another. Robin was doing his job on defense in shutting down Jorge. During a lull when the ball rolled out of bounds, Qendrim summoned the defense for a quick conference in front of the Fugees' goal. Eldin, Prince, Robin, and Mohammed put their heads together with him, talking urgently but quietly, hands and arms wagging for emphasis, discussing how they were going to keep the Fire from scoring. It was the sort of scene that happens at countless youth soccer games, and surely looked routine to the new fans the Fugees had recruited in the waning minutes of the game. But of course the reality was more complicated and, perhaps, beautiful. The boys were from Kosovo, Bosnia, Liberia, Sudan, and Iraq. Three months before, Mohammed Mohammed spoke almost no English. Now he and Qendrim were discussing soccer strategy with casual ease.

The final minutes of the game were chaotic. Spectators were shouting now, and the boys on both the Fire and the Fugees were calling out desperate instructions to one another. As the clock ticked toward zero, the teams traded assaults, but neither could find enough time or open space to take a clean shot. Then, Jorge Pinzon of the Fire got free from Robin, about twenty-five yards from the Fugees' goal. Mohammed, Prince, and Qendrim converged, and Robin sprinted to catch up. Pinzon must have sensed that he had little time. He squared his shoulders and leaned his body into the shot, which arced beautifully over the players' heads. Eldin leaped into the air. The ball brushed his hands and deflected just under the bar to tie the game 2–2.

When the final whistle blew a few moments later, the team on the sideline erupted in cheers. They were advancing to the finals. The Fugees' season was over.

"You had 'em," Luma told the boys after the game. "You had 'em at two to one, and you wouldn't finish it.

"You deserved to lose," she continued. "You didn't play your best."

The Fugees gathered their gear lethargically. Mafoday Jawneh gazed out at the empty field.

"We lost, I mean, we tied our game," he said. "It was so—" Mafoday interrupted himself and his eyes dropped to the ground.

"I don't know what it was," he said.

THE HOLIDAYS WERE a festive time in Clarkston. The boys got a break from school, and since few had anywhere to go, they passed the time shuttling between one another's apartments, playing video games and hanging out. Luma and Tracy baked cookies and dropped them off for Mayor Swaney at City Hall with a card bearing a photo of the Fugees—a gesture of thanks for his support in their quest to use Armistead Field. A few days before Christmas, Santa Claus came by helicopter to Clarkston City Hall. Mayor Swaney was there to greet him, and in the crowd of kids who'd gathered, some of the Fugees milled about and took in the odd sight of a man with a white beard and red suit who traveled by chopper.

The Fugees also had work to do. Luma had told them that she would enter the Under 13s and Under 15s in a big tournament to be held in Savannah in January, on the condition that the boys raised the one thousand dollars necessary for travel and lodging. She helped them organize car washes in the parking lot of the YMCA, but the boys had come up $130 short of their goal. Luma held fast. If they didn't have the money, she said, they weren't going. When someone suggested they ask their parents for the money, Luma told the boys that any player who asked a parent for tournament money would be kicked off the Fugees.

"You need to ask yourselves what you need to do for your team," she told them.

"YOU NEED TO ask yourself what you need to do for your team," Jeremiah said. He was on the phone with Prince, spreading the word about a team project. The boys were going to rake leaves to make that extra $130. The boys figured they could knock on doors in town and offer their services. There was no need to tell Coach about their plan, unless they raised enough cash. Some of the older boys had agreed to help out. It was time to get to work.

In the evening, Luma's cell phone rang. It was Eldin. He wanted to know if she could pick up Grace and take him home. They'd been raking leaves all day, and he was too tired to walk the two miles up the road to his apartment complex. And oh yeah, Eldin said, he wanted to give her the money.

"What money?" Luma asked.

"You said we needed a hundred and thirty dollars," he told her. "So we've got a hundred and thirty dollars."

LUMA RELISHED A few days of rest during the holidays. She spent Christmas visiting her players' families and delivering boxes of food.

The day after Christmas, Luma received a fax on the Town of Clarkston's letterhead. The letter, dated December 26, was addressed to the "Fugees Soccer Team."

> *Dear Coaching Staff (Luma Mufleh and Tracy Ediger):*
> *This letter is to serve immediate notice that the activity/ball fields located at Milam Park and Armistead fields will no longer be available due to the cities [sic] reactivation of its youth recreation program that will be administered through a local organization. We sincerely hope that the time allotted for the teams [sic] practice was useful and productive for the coaching staff and the players alike.*

Luma was stunned. The city council had voted unanimously to grant the Fugees six months' use of the field in October—just over three months ago. Luma called Mayor Swaney at City Hall, but he wouldn't take or return her call.

It didn't take much in the way of probing to discover that the letter—signed by a city official named M. W. Shipman but authorized, as the mayor would later admit, by Mayor Lee Swaney himself—was as full of holes as the mayor's earlier attempts to keep soccer out of the town park. For one thing, the mayor had no authority to single-handedly contravene the city council's vote to let the Fugees use the field for six months—a vote, after all, he himself had insisted on when others had wondered if a less formal arrangement might have sufficed. His letter, one council member asserted, was simply illegal. But further, no one on the city council seemed to know anything at all about the "reactivation" of the Clarkston youth sports program. The City hadn't voted to authorize or fund such a plan, and when pressed, the mayor wasn't willing to get into specifics. He refused, for example, to cite the "local organization" that was going to take over, or to explain why no one on the council had heard about the program that only they could authorize. Later, the mayor would change his story entirely. It wasn't the reactivation of the youth sports program that had caused him to kick the Fugees off the field, he would say. Rather, he explained, he had seen some adult refugees playing soccer in the park and had assumed they were affiliated with the Fugees. He had kicked the Fugees out of the park, the story now went, for violating the terms of its agreement with the city. But that argument didn't hold up either. The Fugees had no affiliation with any adult soccer players, as the mayor well knew. Luma had provided City Hall with a roster of her teams, along with their ages. Any confusion over the issue, of course, could have been cleared up with a simple phone call, but the only communication Luma had from Mayor Swaney or the town government of Clarkston came in the form of that fax the day after Christmas. For reasons only he knew, Lee Swaney just didn't want refugees playing soccer in Milam Park.

These details and inconsistencies would take a while to reveal themselves. In the meantime, Luma had a tournament to prepare for, and she needed a place to practice. That evening, she logged on to Google Earth once again and scanned satellite images of Clarkston. There it was: a small southern town, cut through by railroad tracks and abutting the river of concrete that was I-285. You could easily make out Thriftown and City Hall and all those apartment complexes—shadowed squares and rectangles around half-empty ponds of asphalt. There were a few green patches visible from the sky. Luma knew those well: the fields at the community center and in Milam Park. Those were off-limits, of course. The field behind Indian Creek Elementary leaped off the screen—a glowing white bowl of chalk that from above looked like some sort of quarry. And that was about it. Amid the gas stations, strip malls, fast food joints, and the tangle of roads and highways, open space in Clarkston was hard to find. Pull back the view and the familiar landmarks of Clarkston grow indistinct. Atlanta encroaches, and seems to swallow the little town. There was plenty of open space in the city's big parks and in the suburbs, outside of Clarkston—and out of reach for the Fugees. That was frustrating. Pull back farther, and you get a sense of where Clarkston sits on the great expanse of America—tucked in a verdant corner of the country beneath the rippling gray ridges of the Blue Ridge Mountains. Pull back again, and the blue oceans come into view, then other continents and countries—Congo, Sudan, Afghanistan, and Iraq—all looking deceptively serene. Pull back farther still and the curved horizons of the planet reveal themselves—a beautiful ball of green, white, blue, slate, and brown, ringed by a hazy corona. Someday, somewhere down there, the Fugees would find a home.

Epilogue

On a fall afternoon not quite two years later, Hassan al-Mufleh sat at the dining room table of Luma's house just outside the Clarkston city limits. His daughter was out back reading on a rare quiet Sunday after a morning game. Inside, Hassan was trying to stifle tears.

I'd asked him if he had any regrets over how things had gone between himself and his daughter when she told him she'd be staying in the United States.

"I hate to remember how she felt being alone in the States," he said, his voice breaking. "It was difficult for me, but it was more difficult for her. She was twenty-one years old—"

Hassan became overwhelmed.

"I should have left her alone," he said finally.

Luma's grandmother Munawar had always urged her to be patient with her parents. She believed that in time they would come to forgive her for deciding not to return to Jordan, and as with so many things, Munawar was right in her quiet wisdom. There were phone conversations, and eventually Hassan and Sawsan, Luma's mother, visited the United States to see their daughter and the new home she had created for herself. On one of those visits, Hassan had offered to buy Luma new clothes, but she declined. *If you want to spend your money,* she told her father, *come with me.* They got in Luma's yellow Beetle and went to Target, the department store, with a list of school supplies for the Fugees. Luma put together bags of pens and notebooks and binders, and happily stuck her father with the bill. Hassan began to understand.

There was still hurt. The hardest thing, he said, was living so far from his daughter.

"We've had some very bad days when Luma was away from us," Hassan said of himself and his wife. "But you have to let go. Now it's easy for me to say. I'm older, I'm more experienced. We have a saying. Everything in the world starts small and then becomes bigger— except bad things. They start big, and then get smaller."

IN THE MONTHS following the Fugees' 2006 season, a number of big things grew smaller, more manageable. Paula Balegamire, Grace's mother, learned in a cell phone call from Kinshasa that her husband, Joseph, had not been injured in the riot at Makala after all. Some months later, Joseph was free. He promptly left Congo—which recently descended once again into civil war—and hopes to reunite with his family, either in the U.S. or Europe.

Mandela and Luma made up. The rapprochement took place gradually, rather than at any sort of intense heart-to-heart meeting. Jeremiah, Mandela's younger brother, began to call Luma after the U15 games to ask about the scores. Jeremiah had never shown much interest in the outcomes of the older boys' games, so Luma rightly deduced that Mandela was putting his younger brother up to the calls. Mandela wanted to know how his former team and his old teammates were doing. As tough as Luma could be, as absolute as she was in enforcing her own rules, she didn't hold grudges. That wasn't her way. She started talking to Mandela again, advising him. She told him she thought it would be a good idea to get away from Clarkston and from Prince and some of his other friends who were dropping out of school. She suggested he apply for Job Corps, a U.S. government program that provides vocational training to people between the ages of sixteen and twenty-four, and that offered the chance to earn a high school degree. There was a Job Corps program in Kentucky, she said, far away from the bad crowd in Clarkston. Luma dropped off an application at the Ziatys' apartment and told Mandela that if he wanted to go, he'd have to fill out the application himself. A few weeks passed before Mandela called. He'd filled out the paperwork. He wanted to go. Mandela was accepted, and shipped out soon to Kentucky. He studied construction as his vocation and in November 2008 graduated with his high school diploma.

There were other academic success stories among the 2006 Fugees. Shamsoun, Natnael, and Yousph were all accepted at Pfeiffer University, a liberal arts college in North Carolina. Shamsoun received a scholarship to play soccer at Pfeiffer and since enrolling has been working with a pastor from his village in the Nuba Mountains to someday start a school for Moro children. Through family and friends in the Sudanese community, Shamsoun raised more than $2,000 in order to attend the inauguration of President Barack Obama with a student group.

Shahir Anwar, of the Under 13 Fugees, was accepted at Paideia School, a private school in an affluent Atlanta neighborhood, on scholarship. Many of the Fugees have seen their grades improve as they have become more familiar with English, and have taken advantage of the program's tutoring sessions. Luma's hunch that soccer could serve as a carrot to goad young refugee children into the hard work necessary to succeed in a new country has in many cases proven correct. But there are still enormous challenges. Kids fall away or get dropped from the program if they don't meet academic expectations. And the local public schools continue to fail the refugee population— and American students as well. The angriest I think I ever saw Luma was when one of her young players proudly showed her his report card, which revealed an A in English. From tutoring sessions, Luma knew the boy was almost completely illiterate.

THERE HAVE BEEN departures—from the program and from Clarkston. For many refugee families, Clarkston is just a first stop in America, a place to get a foothold before moving on to secondary migration centers in the United States. Liberians, for example, often moved to

Iowa, Somalis to Minneapolis or Lewiston, Maine, and Sudanese to Omaha, Nebraska, to seek out the support of communities comprised of family, friends, and countrymen. In the summer of 2007, Beatrice Ziaty decided to leave Clarkston for Iowa, taking young Jeremiah with her while Mandela was in Job Corps in Kentucky. Generose decided to move her three boys, Alex, Bienvenue, and Ive, and her little girl, Alyah, to Fort Wayne, Indiana, a place, she had heard, where life was quieter and safer than Atlanta. Kanue Biah decided to try out for the Silverbacks, the elite Atlanta soccer club, and made the team, while Qendrim left the Fugees because he could no longer get rides to and from Clarkston from his family's apartment outside of town.

At first, these sorts of departures wounded Luma. She had poured so much energy into her program and into bettering the lives of her players and their families that a parent's decision to move or a player's decision to give up soccer or to join another team felt like a profound rejection. Sometimes Luma was angered by what she believed was the naïveté behind such moves, as when Generose decided to give up the safety net Luma had helped create for her boys in order to move to Indiana, a place with limited employment opportunities for a Burundian refugee who spoke no English and where Generose knew just one person—a woman she'd met in a refugee camp. Luma tried to cope with the departures, as best she could. She understood that the refugees were doing the best they could, and that it was difficult to second-guess a mother's instinct to seek a better environment. Clarkston, after all, was neither the safest nor the most comfortable place to raise a family. And moving by choice—as opposed to simply fleeing—could be an act of self-determination.

In their new homes, the families Luma worked with are settling in, once again, to new lives. The moves can be jarring for everyone, but especially so for children who are just getting used to life in Atlanta, though in the case of eight-year-old Ive, his family's move to Indiana wasn't as difficult as he had feared it might be.

"Hey, guess what?" Ive said excitedly by phone soon after his family had arrived in Fort Wayne.

"I don't know—what?" I said.

"Indiana," Ive declared, "is *in America*."

"I know—it's in the Midwest."

"Well I thought we were moving to a *totally different country*!" he said.

For weeks after Generose told her boys that they were moving to Indiana, Ive had believed that he would have to learn a new language and new customs when he got there, as he had when he moved to America in the first place. But in Indiana, people spoke English. They ate pizza. You could watch *The Simpsons* on TV. Ive was relieved.

Generose works as a cleaning attendant at a hospital in Fort Wayne. The boys are doing well in school, and of course playing soccer. Bien broke his middle school scoring record his first year in Indiana, with nineteen goals. Like many of the boys who've come and gone through the Fugees, they stay in touch with their old coach, and even took a Greyhound bus to Georgia one summer to spend a week at Luma's house.

To cope with the difficulty of these separations, Luma has learned to turn her attention to other kids in need in Clarkston. A steady flow of refugees into town—most recently, Burundians and Karen, a persecuted ethnic group from Burma—has meant that there has been no shortage of boys who want to try out for the Fugees.

"The minute some kid leaves our team you have five more kids who want to take his place," Luma said. "And they're all just as beautiful and innocent or messed up as the kid before them. So you can't stop."

AS FOR CLARKSTON, the town has continued to change and, haltingly, to adapt. From time to time incidents occur that underscore the challenges the town continues to face. In March 2007, for example, a National Guardsman named Craig Perkins, just back from a tour of duty in Iraq, got into an argument with two Middle Eastern men in the parking lot of the Kristopher Woods apartment complex, where Perkins had gone to visit his girlfriend. Perkins said the men insulted him for serving in the military. But the men, Tareq Ali Bualsafared, a twenty-six-year-old immigrant from the United Arab Emirates, and Saleh Ali, a seventeen-year-old refugee from Iraq, claimed to police that Perkins had accosted them because they were Arab. Whatever the cause of the argument, it escalated, and ended when Perkins pulled

out a .45 caliber automatic and shot Bualsafared in the leg. Bualsafared survived and denied to the *Atlanta Journal-Constitution* that he
or his friend had insulted Perkins for his military service—pointing
out that neither man knew Perkins was a soldier since he wasn't in
uniform. And for his part, Perkins denied that he shot the men because they were Arab. He wasn't prejudiced, he said: his girlfriend was
white and though he appeared African American, he had white and
Native American ancestors.

In Clarkston, even your basic parking-lot fight was super-diverse.

In November 2008, there was another ugly incident in town, one
that confirmed Luma's suspicions about the crowd of young men who
hung out around the basketball court next to the Fugees' old practice
field at Indian Creek Elementary. Angry over a foul committed during a pickup game there, a group of mostly American players vented
their rage on the perceived offender, a twenty-three-year-old Somali
refugee named Yusuf Heri. They attacked Heri on the court and literally beat him to death. As of this writing, five suspects, all of them
locals, had been arrested in connection with the killing. Police were
searching for at least two others.

And there was still more tragedy in the fall of 2008. A few days
before Thanksgiving, one of Luma's former players, a Liberian tenth
grader, was playing with a gun in a bedroom of his family's apartment
in Clarkston when the weapon discharged. The bullet struck and
killed a seventeen-year-old Burundian refugee named Gerali Kagwa,
one of his best friends. Police, who arrested the former player and
charged him with murder, said that photographs on the walls of his
bedroom suggested membership in a gang. There's no way of knowing how the young man's fate—or Gerali's life—might have turned
out differently if the alleged shooter had stayed with the Fugees, but
the incident was a painful reminder of what was at stake in Clarkston
each day.

IN JANUARY 2007, *The New York Times* ran a front-page story I'd
written about the Fugees, one of three articles about Clarkston that
I wrote for the paper while working on this book. The article, which
detailed Mayor Swaney's soccer ban in the town park, prompted an
unexpected and somewhat overwhelming response. Mayor Swaney

was deluged with angry phone calls and e-mails from *Times* readers who were appalled that he had kicked the Fugees out of the town park after Christmas. The mayor protested his treatment in the article, claiming he had banned soccer in the park only for adults, not kids, and that I had confused the town baseball field—on which no soccer was allowed—with the town's general-use field. A taped interview with the mayor contradicted the first claim. As for confusing fields: there was only one field in question—the one on which both the Fugees and the Lost Boys soccer team had played and from which both teams had been ejected. The mayor also gave shifting explanations for that holiday fax he'd sent notifying the Fugees that they were no longer welcome. He was making way for a youth sports program, he'd said at first—a falsehood—before arguing that the real reason for the move was that he'd seen refugee men playing soccer on the field and had assumed they were affiliated with the Fugees. Never mind of course that as the mayor knew, there were no grown men on the Fugees.

As the mayor scrambled to explain and re-explain himself in the wake of public outcry, the City Council of Clarkston took up the matter once again, and reaffirmed the Fugees' right to use the field through the spring.

The *Times* article about the Fugees changed things for the team in other ways. The newspaper's readers donated to the Fugees in amounts large and small, and a deal was made for film rights to the Fugees' story. The donations—which included a bus—allowed Luma to end her relationship with the YMCA. Nike stepped in to provide equipment and uniforms. Since then Luma has been free to run her program the way she sees fit, and to fund-raise toward her real ambition: building a tutoring center and soccer facility within walking distance of Clarkston.

Already, Luma hired two teachers to work with her players. Twelve members of the team now attend classes full-time at the Fugees Academy.

The media attention had other implications. At the tournament in Savannah that the Fugees had raked leaves to attend, for example, locals who'd read about the team came to watch them play and to cheer them on. To his surprise and utter delight, Qendrim was asked to give his first autograph—to a young boy who'd turned out to see the

Fugees play. Volunteers have reached out to the program; the Fugees currently have seven interns who help with logistics. The extra help has freed Luma to focus her energies on her real love, coaching.

Relations between the City of Clarkston and the Fugees, for the most part, have improved. There was some resentment about the media attention the Fugees received and over the reports of the movie money; during a discussion of a police department budget shortfall at one city council meeting Luma attended, for example, someone in the gallery proposed that the Fugees pick up the tab. But the city council stuck by the team. Periodically, Luma has had to go back to ask to extend the team's use of the field in Milam Park, and so far, the council has always agreed. Luma has even become friendly with Emanuel Ransom, the town curmudgeon, bonding over their shared admiration of Hillary Clinton. As for Mayor Swaney, his term ends in 2009. He recently announced he would not seek reelection.

LUMA INSISTS THAT she hasn't changed since the 2006 season, but to an observer she seems calmer, more relaxed. Running the program herself, she says, has eliminated the frustration that can come from relying on others, and volunteers have eased some pressure. She still gives fiery halftime speeches, and admits she had a hard time controlling herself when one of her teams recently blew a 5–1 second-half lead. In the months after the *Times* story about the Fugees, Luma frequently found herself approached by teachers, parents, coaches, and volunteers who wanted her advice on how to handle various situations involving difficult children or kids who were struggling with their circumstances. Luma was reluctant to give advice. She doesn't believe in any single method for dealing with struggling kids, and freely admits that the Fugees hasn't worked for everyone. Failure and mistakes, she believes, are unavoidable.

"You're not going to be able to do everything for all the kids," she said. "There's not a perfect system. There's nothing wrong with another way of doing it."

Like some of those who reached out to Luma for advice, I would sometimes press her to explain her philosophy, to attach words and maxims to the deeds in order to provide a framework for others who hoped to replicate the kind of program she'd created. Luma always resisted, perhaps because there was no great secret to what made the Fugees work, just as there was no great secret to the success of those other clusters of hope and connection within Clarkston. They were powered by simple but enduring ideas: a sense of fairness, love, forgiveness, and, most of all, a willingness to work—to engage in the process of turning these simple notions into actions that could affect others.

I once asked Tracy Ediger, the Fugees' team manager and all-around helper to the players and their families, what she thought people most misunderstood about Luma and the Fugees program. She didn't hesitate with her response: it was the tendency of people to ascribe mystery or some saintly qualities to the simple work they did.

"Putting Luma on a pedestal is counterproductive," she wrote me once in an e-mail. "Luma is really a normal person doing what she can for the people around her. If people can look at her and see that, that she's human, not a saint or a super-hero, and that she doesn't—can't—do everything or effect miracles, then maybe they can say to themselves, 'I need to look around myself and see my neighborhood, and what is going on here and five streets over, and what I can do in terms of investing myself and my time, to be present for the people around me, and to do something positive for change in my community.'

"No one person can do everything," she said. "But we can all do something."

THE FUGEES ARE going strong. In the fall of 2008, Luma coached four teams, from ages twelve to nineteen. On a warm Saturday afternoon in early November, the Under 14 Fugees took the field to play the second best team in their division, from the Rockdale Youth Soccer Association in Conyers, Georgia. The best team in the league was none other than the Fugees themselves, who were undefeated in five games and who had delivered a 9–0 drubbing to one of their hapless rivals a few weeks before. The Fugees had a cheering section. Some of the older players, including Josiah, Mafoday, and Idwar, had come out to see the younger team play, and especially to root on Robin and Santino, their much younger former teammates who were now playing in their proper age division. Luma's father, Hassan, was on the sideline, in the middle of a long visit from Jordan, most of which he'd spent either watching soccer or cooking traditional Jordanian meals, which he served heaped on steaming platters to Luma and her players. Tracy too was on the sideline, taking photographs, and volunteers who worked with the Fugees came and went and added to the voices of support.

On the field, Robin, once quiet and shy, was now running the defense with confidence and authority—calling out to his teammates in unaccented English, urging them to move up the field and to mark their men. The stars of the Under 14 offense were a small, agile Eritrean refugee named Ashora, who had been referred to Luma after repeatedly acting out at school, and a tall, muscular center forward from Liberia named Luckie, who had a habit of commenting on the games from the field, in real time, in the manner of an excited television play-by-play announcer. Since joining the Fugees, Ashora had become practically docile at school—Luma had run him into submission—and Luckie had emerged as a good student and a team leader who oversaw calisthenics at practices and held the respect of his teammates the way Kanue once did.

It took the Fugees only a couple of minutes to score their first goal, on a quick attack by Luckie, who, perhaps out of modesty, declined to offer the play-by-play for his own score and instead quietly jogged upfield as his teammates celebrated around him.

The Fugees kept the heat on the Rockdale defense, scoring one, then another, then another. Late in the game, tiny Ashora carved his way through the Rockdale defenders at a downhill pace, arms whirling as he dribbled cleanly past one player then another. Once in the clear, he took a shot. The ball sailed upward, well out of the reach of the Rockdale keeper and into the top of the net: score. The older boys on the sideline shouted in delight, and Ashora's teammates swarmed him on the field. On the Fugees' bench, Luma was impassive, as usual, pausing only to look at her watch to check the remaining time. The Fugees were ahead 5–1, their unbeaten streak alive. The boys jogged toward their side of the halfway line to get set for the final minutes of play. In the peaceful lull that followed, Luckie leaned his head back and offered his commentary on Ashora's goal into the blue sky overhead.

"Beautiful!" he called out, his voice echoing across the complex's terraced array of green fields. "Beautiful! Beautiful! Beautiful!"

Author's Note

This book could not have been reported, much less written, without the support, wisdom, and patience of many people.

I am especially grateful to Coach Luma Mufleh and team manager Tracy Ediger, both of whom agreed to let a stranger into the fragile and complex world of the Fugees, and who, for this act of openness and generosity, were rewarded with a hovering presence and a seemingly never-ending torrent of annoying questions. Even so, both served as generous liaisons to the players' families and sources of invaluable perspective on their community, as well as inspirations, in their tireless advocacy of refugee families.

I am thankful to Spencer Hall, who, after reading my first book and my work for the *Times*, rightly surmised I'd be interested in the story of Clarkston and the Fugees and made a point of saying so. He initially put me in touch with Luma and kept me company when I more or less moved to Atlanta, and has since become a close and valued friend.

I benefited from the support of many editors and staff members at *The New York Times*, who granted me the months necessary for the sort of immersive reporting I needed to do in order to grasp the outlines of the Fugees story, first for three lengthy features for the paper, and then for this book. Glenn Kramon, my editor, added insight and genuine zeal, and also indulged my quirks as a writer, which include a pathological inability to let go of copy. Trip Gabriel, my editor at the Sunday Styles section, granted me the freedom to embark on this reporting, despite the considerable headache it caused for him and his deputies. Susan Edgerley worked behind the scenes to get institutional backing for this project, which was enthusiastically offered by Bill Keller, Jill Abramson, and Bill Schmidt. I am very grateful for their support.

Through the *Times*, I was also very fortunate to get to work with the gifted photographer Nicole Bengiveno and the videographer Kassie Bracken, whose beautiful and sometimes haunting images, as selected by photo editor Meaghan Looram, illuminated life in Clarkston for *Times* readers around the world. Marty Gottlieb added nuance on deadline, and copy editors Mona Houck, Jack Kadden, and Kyle Massey saved *Times* readers from having to wade through countless mangled phrases. Kyle, a noted headline wizard, also gets thanks for offering the title of this book, which appeared first as a headline in the paper. *Times* bylines usually carry only one or two names, a convention that hardly does justice to the true tally of people who contribute to each story. I'm very lucky to have been able to work with those mentioned above.

I owe a special debt of gratitude to Lindsay Crouse, my researcher, who proofread, transcribed, and fact-checked with gusto, and whose eye for detail is reflected on nearly every page of this book.

When I arrived in Clarkston, I thought I knew the South, and even Atlanta, pretty well, having grown up in Birmingham and having made the two-and-a-half-hour trip to Atlanta more times than I could remember. But Clarkston, I quickly learned, was not like Atlanta, or perhaps any other place. Many people offered their time to show me around and to try to educate me about the complexities of the town and the process of resettlement that had transformed it. I'm thankful to Susan and Kevin Gordon; Barbara Thompson and Sister Patty Caraher of the International Community School; Ellen Beattie of the International Rescue Committee; Paedia Mixon of RRISA; Dennis Harkins, the Provost of Georgia Perimeter College; Rev. Phil Kitchin of the International Bible Church; Salahadin Wazir at the Al-Momineen mosque; Bill Mehlinger and Hong Diep Vo from Thriftown; Rev. William B. G. K. Harris; David Faryen; Chris Holliday; Jeremy Cole of Refugee Family Services; Ardell Saleem of Indian Creek Elementary; Clarkston Police Chief Tony J. Scipio; Emanuel Ransom; Mayor Lee Swaney; restaurant owners Phuong Thu Chu and Fesseha Sebhatu; and Nathaniel Nyok, the founder of the Lost Boys Soccer Team.

Thanks also to Rick Skirvin at the Georgia State Soccer Association; to David Anderson of the Athens United Gold Valiants; to Nancy Daffner of the Concorde Fire; to Jorge Pinzon, the Fire's young star; and to numerous parents who were happy to share insights about youth soccer from the sidelines as their sons played the game.

I'm also grateful to Hassan, Sawsan, and Inam al-Mufleh for speaking with me about their family.

At Spiegel & Grau and Random House, I've been lucky to get to work once again with Christopher Jackson, a thoughtful, curious, and enthusiastic editor and friend who instantly understood my interest in the Fugees and who provided much-needed encouragement and wisdom along the way. I'm grateful for the support and hard work of Cindy Spiegel and Julie Grau, Gretchen Koss, Meghan Walker, Todd Doughty, Anne Waters, and Mya Spalter, a publishing dream team; Elyse Cheney and Nicole Steen at Cheney Literary; Howard Sanders; Julian Alexander, Nicki Kennedy, and Sam Edenborough in London; and Nicholas Pearson at Fourth Estate.

Many friends and family members provided support and comments on my rough pages, including Robert Fox, David Fox, Rufus Griscom, Jane Welna, Natalie Robbins, Susanna Davis, and Chris Knutsen. Irma St. John, Mary Claire St. John Butler, Scott Davis, and Edward Butler provided moral support, as did my late father, initially no soccer fan, who called regularly for updates on Fugees' scores during my reporting and who, as much as anyone, would have wanted to know how things turned out in the epilogue.

I am also deeply grateful for the backing and encouragement—as well as the plainspoken editorial advice—of my wife, Nicole, to whom this book is dedicated.

Reporters, it might be said, scour for facts in the hope of uncovering truths, and while the former may make the page, the latter take root in the mind and heart. Through the Fugees and their families, I've learned some truths—about generosity, kindness, and perseverance—that will remain with me well beyond the experience of writing or talking about this book. For that I am grateful, especially to Beatrice Ziaty and her sons Mandela, Jeremiah, and Darlington; Shamsoun Dikori and his bothers Robin and Idwar; Kanue Biah; Generose Ntaconayigize and her sons Alex, Bien, and Ive and daughter Alyah; Paula Balegamire and sons Grace and Josue; Xhalal Bushi and his son Qendrim; Ziagul and Mohammad Hassan; as well as Eldin, Ervin, Sampson, Safi, Sebejden, Zaccadine, Hamdu and Jeylani, Prince, Mohammed, Santino, Josiah, Shahir, Tareg, Mafoday, Fornatee, Natnael, Muamer, and others who played on Luma's oldest team or who passed through her program.

The Fugees and their families opened their homes and their lives—and often, their cupboards—to a stranger in an act of faith that this person would relay their stories to a broader audience with empathy and accuracy. I hope I've lived up to the task.

Warren St. John
New York City

A Note on Sources

While much of this book was reported in the apartments of refugee families in Clarkston and on the sidelines of soccer fields throughout the state of Georgia, I am fortunate and grateful to have been able to draw on the work of many other journalists and authors for valuable insights and background into the accidental cultural experiment that led to the formation of the Fugees.

I am especially grateful to the reporters of the *Atlanta Journal-Constitution*, particularly Mark Bixler, whose sustained attention to the ongoing story of refugee resettlement in and around Atlanta has yielded an invaluable record of the struggles of newcomers and locals alike to create a sense of safety and community amid social and economic turbulence.

For background and context on the refugee experience and on the cultural diversity brought on by immigration and resettlement, I benefited from reading *The Middle of Everywhere* by Mary Pipher; *Reconstructing Lives, Recapturing Meaning: Refugee Identity, Gender, and Culture Change* by Linda A. Camino and Ruth M. Krulfeld—particularly Ms. Camino's chapter, "Refugee Adolescents and Their Changing Identities," and Patricia A. Omidian's chapter "Life Out of Context: Recording Afghan Refugees' Stories"—and *Case Studies in Diversity: Refugees in America in the 1990s,* edited by David W. Haines.

Steven Vertovec's paper "New Complexities of Cohesion in Britain: Super-Diversity, Transnationalism and Civil-Integration" was invaluable in providing a lens through which to view and comprehend the sorts of changes taking place in Clarkston and beyond, as was Garrett Johnson's Oxford University master's thesis on Clarkston: "Refugees and Sports: Re-evaluating the Game."

I am also grateful to Dr. Art Hansen of Clark Atlanta University, who opened his papers on Clarkston, and who provided advice and guidance during my reporting.

For history and background on the various conflicts behind the flight of the refugees who arrived in Clarkston, I relied on Bill Berkeley's *The Graves Are Not Yet Full: Race, Tribe and Power in the Heart of Africa*; Howard W. French's *A Continent for the Taking: The Tragedy and Hope of Africa*; *The Mask of Anarchy: The Destruction of Liberia and the Religious Dimension of an African Civil War* by Stephen Ellis; *The Root Causes of Sudan's Civil Wars* by Douglas H. Johnson; *The Fate of Africa: A History of Fifty Years of Independence* by Martin Meredith; *Africa: A Biography of the Continent* by John Reader; *Burundi: Ethnic Conflict and Genocide* by René Lemarchand; *They Poured Fire on Us from the Sky: The True Story of Three Lost Boys from Sudan* by Benson Deng, Alephonsion Deng, and Benjamin Ajak; and the white paper "The Somali Bantu: Their History and Culture" by Dan Van Lehman and Omar Eno, which was published by the Center for Applied Linguistics in Washington, D.C.

I also relied on accounts of the conflicts from *The New York Times, The Washington Post* (particularly for an account of the assault on Kacanik), *The Wall Street Journal,* and *BBC,* as well as reports from the Office of the United Nations High Commissioner for Refugees and Amnesty International (especially the group's reports on the nineteen men detained in Brazzaville and returned to Kinshasa).

Several books provided helpful context on soccer culture in the United States, including Jim Haner's *Soccerhead,* about youth soccer in the U.S.; *A Home on the Field: How One Championship Soccer Team Inspires Hope for the Revival of Small Town America* by Paul Cuadros, about a Latino team in North Carolina; *Offside: Soccer and American Exceptionalism* by Andrei S. Markovits and Steven L. Hellerman; and *National Pastime: How Americans Play Baseball and the Rest of the World Plays Soccer* by Stefan Szymanski and Andrew Zimbalist.

For More Information

To learn more about the Fugees, and for ideas on ways to help or get involved, please visit www.FugeesFamily.org.

Or write to: Fugees Family, P.O. Box 388, Scottdale, GA 30079-0388

For more about the book, including guides for book clubs and educators, visit www.OutcastsUnited.com.

And visit the author at www.WarrenStJohn.com.

OUTCASTS UNITED

WARREN ST. JOHN

A Reader's Guide

A Conversation with Warren St. John

Random House Reader's Circle: What is *Outcasts United* about?

Warren St. John: In the most literal sense, it's the story of a soccer team for young refugees, of the remarkable woman who founded that team, and of the town where these people came together. But more broadly I think the book is about dealing with change—large-scale social change—as well as the problem of creating a sense of community in an environment in which people, at least on the surface, don't seem to have a lot in common. I think the changes that occurred in Clarkston are a hyperspeed version of the sorts of changes that are happening all around the world. So I went to Clarkston to see what lessons there were to be learned.

RHRC: Can you explain?

WSJ: Well, Clarkston, Georgia, where the Fugees are based, was once a simple southern town. And now between a third and a half of the town are foreign-born, and the high school has students from over fifty countries. Even the Fugees comprise kids from over a dozen countries, and the coach is from Jordan. And then of course there are people who've spent their entire lives in Clarkston. So the question then is, how do you make all this work? It seems like a fairly pressing question because this sort of change is happening all over the United States and Europe as well, though perhaps a bit more slowly than in Clarkston. That's what attracted me to this story.

RHRC: How did you hear about the Fugees?

WSJ: I was in Atlanta giving a talk about my first book at a conference of educators, and a reader of the book invited me to join him and his wife for dinner. He worked in refugee resettlement, so over a hamburger, I suppose my reporter's instinct kicked in and I started grilling him, asking, "Refugees from where? How did they get here? Where do they live and how do they build new lives here? Who helps them?" That sort of thing. He very patiently answered my questions and then casually mentioned that there was a soccer team of young refugees on the eastern side of town, and he encouraged me to check them out. So I called the coach and went to a game. It was a surprisingly powerful experience. Luma was this mysterious, intense presence. The kids themselves were quiet and focused, and they played beautifully. And there was one player in particular who had survived an apartment fire a few months before that had killed a number of his family members. Luma was tough with him—he didn't get a break at all. And without giving too much away, his response was remarkable. I came away from that afternoon truly moved, and I knew that day that I'd found my next book.

In the meantime, I learned more about Clarkston, and I realized that so much of the tension over refugee resettlement was just coming to a head. There had recently been a case of police brutality against a Nigerian immigrant. That summer the mayor had banned soccer from the town park. So it wasn't only a story about a team—there was this momentous kind of reckoning going on in the community as well. And that's what made it clear to me that I needed to get there quickly and to start reporting.

RHRC: Did being from the South influence your interest in the story or how you saw Clarkston in general?

WSJ: Absolutely. I grew up in Birmingham, just two and a half hours from Atlanta. My mother is from Savannah, and I went to Atlanta countless times when I was younger, so I was familiar with the city. But mainly I think I knew enough about the southern psyche, and life in a small town—my father was from a town in northern Alabama called Cullman, where I spent a lot of time as a kid—to know that the influx of a large number of refugees, including many from Africa and the Middle East, a decent number of them Muslim, was going to produce some interesting fallout.

RHRC: You did a series of articles about Clarkston and the Fugees for *The New York Times*—did the book come out of that work?

WSJ: It was actually the other way around—the book gave rise to the articles. I knew from the outset that this was a subject I wanted to immerse myself in, and that the scope of it could easily support a book-length treatment, demanded it even. I talked to my editor at Random House, told him what I planned to do, and he was enthusiastic. So I was on my way. When I went to ask for a leave from the *Times*, my editors there asked what I was writing about, and when I told them, they asked if I'd write pieces along the way, during the process of reporting and writing the book. It seemed like a great way to test and formulate my thoughts about the material. But by then I was already flying down to see games in Atlanta on weekends and getting absorbed completely by the story. So I was working on the book a full six months before the first feature ran in the *Times*.

RHRC: How were you received by the refugee families in Clarkston?

WSJ: There is very understandable reticence among many of the refugee families I met. Their experiences make it difficult for them to trust strangers, particularly anyone seen as part of an apparatus—the government, the army, the media, even the relief bureaucracy. Refugees have often faced a great deal of betrayal. That said, I had an introduction in most cases from Luma, someone the families knew and trusted, and that was invaluable. And among the refugees, there is also a natural curiosity about locals—they want to meet Americans and get to know them. They live in apartment complexes full of other refugees, many from other countries—people whose language they may not speak. So refugees in Clarkston don't actually have many opportunities to just sit down and talk to an American. And when they do, they have lots of questions. They want things explained.

RHRC: Can you give an example?

WSJ: When I was reporting, I'd frequently show up—to soccer practice or games, to people's apartments—in a rental car. One afternoon one of players on the Fugees said, "You must be a very wealthy man." I asked, "Why do you say that?" And he said, "Because you have so many cars—you're always showing up in a new one." So that became an occasion to explain the mundane but not entirely obvious practice of rental cars, and why one week you might have a minivan and the next week a PT Cruiser. Most refugees are coming from places where owning a car is exceptionally rare, so the notion that you could essentially borrow one for a few days was almost unfathomable.

RHRC: Tell me about Coach Luma.

WSJ: Luma is a force of nature. She's a doer. She offers an example of stability in an otherwise fairly chaotic environment. And perhaps more than anything, she does what she says she's going to do. If Luma tells her players to show up at 8 A.M. to meet the team bus, she's there by 7:55 A.M. Likewise, when she says the bus is leaving at 8:10, the bus leaves at 8:10. So, yes, by spending time with the Fugees—at practice, at games, at tutoring—that's less time for boys to get into trouble or to get drawn in by the wrong crowd. But there's also a powerful learning component to the entire program. The boys learn what it means to be consistent and to follow through, to take responsibility. And while some may find Luma's rules rigid, they also come to appreciate their predictability.

RHRC: Like a lot of people in the book, Luma is searching for a home in a way as well, isn't she?

WSJ: I think that gets back to what the book is really about. So many of the people I met in Clarkston—refugees, Luma, even the long-term residents, and especially a lot of the people who work in refugee resettlement—are looking for something: stability and safety, a sense of belonging to a larger community. And in a way that becomes the one thing that many people—even from very different backgrounds—have in common. The trick is opening enough of a conversation that strangers learn that about each other. And in Clarkston, there are these pockets where that conversation happens—among the Fugees players, at the International Bible Church, at Thriftown, the local grocery store. But it's hard to realize that you and a neighbor may actually have the same interests if you don't ever speak to one another.

RHRC: And what about the distance between the Fugees and the teams they are playing? Do they ever have an opportunity to connect?

WSJ: Yes and no. Fundamentally, when the Fugees take the field against a rival team, both teams want to win. It's a competition, not an afternoon of group singing and camaraderie. That said, there are many members of the Fugees who have never been outside of Clarkston except to go to away games. Their parents don't have cars. They take the bus to school each morning. So the simple act of traveling to a game—riding on the interstate past downtown Atlanta or past some of those big beautiful houses in the suburbs with swimming pools and lush green lawns—becomes an act of exploration into another world. And even the competitive banter and ribbing that goes on between kids—while not always entirely polite—is a form of communication and connecting.

RHRC: There's a scene early in the book in which the father of a rival player is watching his son select the proper cleats for his soccer shoes and he says something like, "I paid $200 for those shoes, so you better pick the right ones." What did you learn from watching the economic disparity between the Fugees and their competitors?

WSJ: I think the example of the Fugees might come as a relief to overspent soccer parents everywhere—you don't have to have $200 cleats or matching team duffel bags with your jersey number embroidered on them to play the game well or to enjoy it. A passion for the game

318 • A Reader's Guide

will trump having the best gear every time. I think that's a shortcoming of the American approach to the game—we tend to emphasize gear and the consumer stuff, and to restrict play to a formal setting like practice and games, whereas most of the world plays the game all the time, more the way Americans play basketball. Watching the Fugees play definitely taught me about the value of cultivating that approach to the game and making room for it and encouraging it in a child's life.

RHRC: You seem to avoid making judgments about the people you write about.

WSJ: I generally go into most situations assuming that people are doing the best they can, and I challenge myself to try to understand the motivations behind actions that I disagree with or that strike me as wrong or wrongheaded. In the case of Clarkston, I think it's important not to get caught up in the game of issuing simplistic moral judgments—saying this person is "good" or "bad"—but to acknowledge the complexity of a place and of the people there, and to acknowledge the incredible challenge that resettlement has posed. So that's what I've tried to do in my book. There are no simple answers in Clarkston, which is what makes it so interesting.

Questions and Topics for Discussion

1. When played beautifully, as Coach Luma might say, soccer is one of the world's most fluid and graceful games. How does the nature of soccer reflect and influence the ways in which the refugee children respond to the challenges of life in Clarkston? Is there something about the game that might make it particularly compelling for children who have endured war, violence, and displacement?

2. Coach Luma is also a Clarkston "outsider" in terms of her nationality. In what ways does her experience as an immigrant compare with those of her players? How does her "outsider" status affect the bond between the coach and her team?

3. Chapter 3 describes a study led by Harvard political scientist Robert Putnam that states that inhabitants of hyperdiverse communities tend to withdraw from collective life and distrust their neighbors. Are you surprised by Putnam's findings? Why or why not? How can communities best overcome this unfortunate tendency?

4. How has the history of migration altered the cultural landscape in your community?

5. The Under 13s managed to develop a warm, familial connection with little regard to their cultural and religious differences, while the Under 15s were less successful in creating such an environment. Why were the younger Fugees able to bond in a way that their older counterparts were unable to achieve? How did that bond, or lack thereof, affect their performance both on and off the field?

6. The refugee community in Clarkston is composed of a conglomerate of religions, ethnicities, and languages. How do the contrasting experiences of the Under 13 and Under 15 players relate to the complexities that face the refugee community as a whole?

7. With the arrival of the Somali Bantu in Clarkston, longtime Clarkston residents became alarmed about changes in their community even though refugees had been resettling in Clarkston since the 1980s. Why was the local response suddenly more intense at this point in Clarkston's history of refugee resettlement?

8. How does Mandela Ziaty's struggle with issues of identity differ from that of many American-born teenagers? Are there more similarities than differences? How does his dual identity as a defacto American and a displaced Liberian complicate this struggle?

9. In chapter 24, Jeremy Cole, a case manager at one of the refugee agencies in Clarkston, challenged his traditional beliefs by converting to Islam. How were he and other Americans working with the refugee communities provoked to reexamine their own identities based upon their interactions with different cultures?

10. Discuss the problems involved in the Fugees' search for a home field. Did the Clarkston government violate their human rights? What about the situation of the Lost Boys and the use of the soccer field?

WARREN ST. JOHN has written for the New York *Observer*, *The New Yorker*, *Wired*, and Slate, in addition to his work as a reporter for *The New York Times*. His first book, *Rammer Jammer Yellow Hammer: A Journey into the Heart of Fan Mania* (2004), was named one of *Sports Illustrated*'s best books of the year and ranked number one on the *Chronicle of Higher Education*'s list of the best books ever written about collegiate athletics. He was born in Birmingham, Alabama, and attended Columbia College in New York City, where he now lives with his wife, Nicole, and daughter Serena.